CW00542442

(i.v 1)

New Testament Theology

AN INTRODUCTION

The Library of Biblical Theology

Leo Perdue
General Editor and Old Testament Editor

James D. G. Dunn
New Testament Editor

Michael Welker
Systematic Theology Editor

LIBRARY OF BIBLICAL THEOLOGY

NEW TESTAMENT THEOLOGY

AN INTRODUCTION

JAMES D. G. DUNN

Abingdon Press
Nashville

NEW TESTAMENT THEOLOGY: AN INTRODUCTION

This book is printed on acid-free paper.

Library of Congress Cataloging-in-Publication Data

Dunn, James D. G., 1939-
    New Testament theology : an introduction / James D.G. Dunn.
      p.   cm. — (Library of biblical theology ; 3)
    Includes bibliographical references and index.
    ISBN 978-0-687-34120-7 (pbk. : alk. paper)
    1. Bible. N.T.—Theology. 1. Title.

BS2397.D835 2009
230'.0415—dc22

                                                                                    2009003083

09 10 11 12 13 14 15 16 17 18—10 9 8 7 6 5 4 3 2 1

MANUFACTURED IN THE UNITED STATES OF AMERICA

CONTENTS

V. The Church of God

VI. The Ethical Outworkings

Conclusion

INTRODUCTION

How should a theology of the New Testament be written? The question begs a number of issues that will have to be addressed before we can begin the task itself. Does the title refer to the theology espoused by the *writers* of the NT documents, or the theology of the *documents* themselves? And so, should we speak of *theologies* (plural) rather than theology (singular), or does the title (NT theology) suggest a search for the shared theology of (all?) the NT writers, assuming that they had such a (singular) theology? Or is a theology of the NT always just that—*a* theology, rather than *the* theology? That is to say, is a/the theology of the NT always in part at least a matter of the present-day writer's *interpretation* of the NT documents? Some indeed might want to speak rather of a theology that emerges from the encounter between the present-day reader and the first-century text—even of a theology *created* by the encounter.

The fact that this NT theology is written as part of a Library of Biblical Theology adds a further dimension. What is meant by *biblical*? What *Bible*? If the prospect of a New Testament theology raises the questions outlined above, these questions are compounded when it is a NT theology *within the context of biblical theology* which is in view. What is a biblical theology of the New Testament—or a New Testament biblical theology?

Such issues will demand immediate attention in chapter 1. But once we have achieved some clarification there, how then should we proceed? I suggest the desirability of exploring the factors which initially determined NT theology—a chapter (chapter 2) that is rarely included in volumes with "New Testament Theology" as their title. The absence of such a chapter seems strange to me, since the motivating and inspirational factors which came to expression in ways of talking about God and concomitant beliefs, and in the practical outworking of these beliefs, would seem to me to be fundamental to a proper appreciation of these beliefs and their outworking.

What then of the substance of NT theology itself? Various methods and procedures have been practiced in the past. Some have proceeded by reviewing previous studies on or related to the subject.[1] And certainly no attempt to write a NT theology can proceed very far without considering or at least taking into account the issues raised by such major contributors to the subject as Gabler, Wrede, and Bultmann.[2] However, there is some danger in such an approach that the discussion is then "tramlined" into the language and proposals of these earlier treatments and never escapes from these tramlines. I prefer to try to let the material being examined (the NT texts) themselves suggest the principal themes and issues to be discussed and limit the interaction with other protagonists to the footnotes. Even so, the interaction has had to be illustrative more than comprehensive, and focuses mostly on recent bibliography, since the possibilities of debating disputed issues and points of exegesis with others is almost endless.

Some proceed systematically through the NT documents, laying out the theology of each writer, or indeed of each document, in turn. This has proved the most popular way of doing a NT theology today, and reflects the extent to which the task has come to be seen as historical and descriptive.[3] Such a procedure is not realistic in a volume of the present length and scope, or else would likely result in a very superficial survey and summary. The intention in this case is rather more to provide an introductory volume to a series, a series whose subsequent volumes should have more scope for detailed discussion. This volume cannot and does not pretend to be a full scale theology of the New Testament to join the recent spate of two—(and more)—volume sets on the subject.

A third procedure has been to adopt a thematic approach, with material gathered under headings like "Creation," "Christology," "Salvation."[4] This approach reflects more of the older dogmatic approach, using categories provided by systematic theology. In contemporary jargon, the second approach is more diachronic, the third more synchronic.[5] The second procedure can run the risk of setting to one side the fact that the NT writings are documents of faith and have functioned for nearly two millennia as Christian scriptures. But the third too easily loses sight of the historical particularity of individual writings and the awkward distinctiveness of each document in the situation that it envisaged or confronted.

My own desire and preference is to get *inside* the process by which the theology of the NT came about, to see and treat the theology of the NT writings as a living, moving thing, a grappling with issues for faith and life which came to expression in these writings and was both the reason for their being written in the first place and also for their being retained as vital resources for ongoing faith and life, and hence to become regarded as scripture. I describe and characterize this process as *theologizing* and suggest that to see NT theology as NT theologizing should help to appreciate both the historical production of the NT writings and their continuing impact on subsequent thinking about and enacting Christian faith.

As is appropriate for a Library of Biblical Theology, the subject matter is determined not by the NT alone, but rather by the themes common to OT and NT, the continuities and discontinuities between the two Testaments of Old and New. For the purposes of the series, the subject matter has been divided into four segments, which should be sufficient to give overall coverage—God, Salvation, Israel/Church, and Ethics.[6] In this introduction I attempt a preliminary review of the (most important of the) material which each subsequent volume will have to consider, and I sketch out the issues which will have to be discussed, focusing particularly on the tensions which the developments of earliest Christianity provoked within the scriptural traditions of Second Temple Judaism. If I manage to whet the appetite for the subsequent volumes I will consider my job well done.

WHAT IS NEW TESTAMENT THEOLOGY?

1. INTRODUCTION

Biblical theology as a distinct discipline is usually traced back to the essay of J. P. Gabler published in 1787.[1] The Bible, of course, had been a source and resource for the crafting of theology from the earliest centuries of Christianity. Indeed, Irenaeus can be regarded as a credible candidate for the title, "the first biblical theologian."[2] But prior to Gabler it was more a matter of the Bible in the service of systematic or dogmatic theology than of a biblical theology as now understood. It was Gabler who initiated the distinction and separation of *biblical* theology from *dogmatic* theology[3] and promoted the understanding of biblical theology as a *historical* exercise to determine what were the theologies (not just theology) of the biblical writers.[4] Since then the discipline of biblical theology has had an up and down history, but interest in it has recently re-emerged in some strength, which makes the present series timely.[5]

The role of NT theology within or as part of or in relation to biblical theology has also re-emerged as an important aspect of the larger discussion—as indicated by the sequence of volumes in the 1990s on the theology of the NT[6] that revived the nineteenth century title "Biblical Theology in the New Testament."[7] Robert Morgan can even say that "a theological NTT [NT Theology] is defensible only as part of a biblical theology."[8]

So the principle and task of writing a New Testament theology within the framework of biblical theology is easy to state. But when we begin to unpack what is involved, questions and problems quickly emerge and soon multiply. When, for example, R. H. Fuller wrote his piece on New Testament Theology for the Society of Biblical Literature 1980 Centennial volume on the New Testament, the influence of Rudolf Bultmann still loomed large, and it was the questions that the latter's *Theology* continued to pose that were important for Fuller: "(1) the place and role of the historical Jesus in a NT theology; (2) the adequacy of the anthropological interpretation of Paul and of 'deworldification' as a hermeneutical key for John; (3) the problem of variety and unity in the NT; (4) whether the NT contains a stratum to be designated 'early Catholicism,' and if this is admitted, how that stratum is to be assessed."[9] It will be apparent from the first two chapters of this volume both that some of these issues are still alive, and that the debate has moved on during the past quarter of a century.

In what follows I will attempt to give a fresh perspective on some of these problems by moving away from traditional formulations and expressing the problems in my own terms.[10]

2. WHICH "BIBLE"? WHOSE BIBLE?

The initial problem is posed by the very title, "Biblical Theology of the New Testament." The problem lies with the term *biblical* itself. (1) The title assumes a Christian perspective, in which there is already an entity called the *New* Testament, and, explicitly or implicitly, another entity called the Old Testament. From this perspective the *Bible* is the Christian Bible made up of these two testaments. (2) At the same time, a *biblical* theology of the NT is inevitably an attempt to expound the NT writings from *within* the NT, using as a major explanatory key the NT writers' use of the OT.[11] But since for the NT writers there was as yet no *New Testament* as such, *Bible* here, that is, from the perspective of the NT writers, can denote only the (Jewish) scriptures.[12]

Thus the very concept of biblical theology immediately presses upon us the recognition that the biblical writings referred to are described as Bible/scripture because they function as *Bible/scripture* for *two different reli-*

gious communities—the Jewish and the Christian. The point would have been difficult to avoid anyway, since the interdependence of a text, particularly a religious text, with its interpretative community, the community for which it is scripture, is more or less self-evident (*scripture* for whom?) and has rightly been an emphasis in recent broader hermeneutical discussion.[13] It is this fact, however, that causes tension between the two usages of *biblical theology*. For, on the one hand, Christianity is unique among world religions in the fact that it has absorbed the scriptures of what is universally understood to be a quite distinct religion and has claimed them as its own. But is the Old Testament only Bible as *Old Testament*, that is, as interpreted by and in the light of the *New Testament*? If on the other hand, the Jewish scriptures are Bible independently of the Christian writings, should they not be allowed(!) to have their own voice independently of the NT? Is a Jewish theological interpretation of their own scriptures not equally biblical theology? One of the strengths of Brevard Childs's *Biblical Theology* is that he sees the issue and poses it a number of times,[14] but clearly understands biblical theology as a Christian enterprise through and through.[15] My point, however, is that biblical theology (however defined) cannot be carried forward without close regard for the fundamental issues of self-identity and mutual recognition at the heart of Jewish/Christian dialogue.

This problem cannot be ignored. It is in fact constitutive of biblical theology properly so called. Of course Christians could ignore the fact that their OT is also the Jewish Bible and affirm that their biblical theology is concerned only with their Bible. But that would immediately run counter to *central concerns of the NT writers themselves, for whom the Jewish scriptures were the only Bible*. Consequently such a New Testament biblical theology could be regarded as an oxymoron since it runs counter to the historical character of biblical theology, as formulating the subject matter in the terms and from the perspective of the NT writers themselves. As we shall note further in chapter 2, it was crucial to earliest Christian self-understanding and to NT apologetic generally that the gospel they were proclaiming was in direct continuity with and validated by those writings that were already recognized as scripture by Jews generally and not just by Christians.[16] Not only so, but if the *Bible* in *biblical theology* is concerned with the Jewish scriptures only as Old Testament, Jews in turn, insofar as they might be interested in a subject called *biblical theology*,[17] could all the more readily ignore the writings added to their scriptures by the Christians and confine their interests to their Bible

3

alone. But that would too easily sideline the question whether Jesus ought to be counted as one of their own prophets (or rabbis, or messiah?). And once Jesus the prophet from Nazareth is brought into play, dialogue with Christians becomes virtually unavoidable and cannot easily be excluded from the proper concerns of a Jewish biblical theology. Here the issues of continuity/discontinuity are at the heart of any biblical theology of the NT.[18] As I noted elsewhere, "At the heart of biblical theology is the interface between a Jewish biblical theology and a Christian biblical theology—the interface that is the New Testament itself."[19]

In short, the dynamic of biblical theology is that its subject matter is determined and defined by texts that are Israel's scripture (the Torah or Tanakh as a whole) and not *merely* the *Old* Testament, but are also Christian scripture (the scriptures for the NT writers) and therefore have some sort of defining role for the texts that were to become the *New* Testament. What is the relation of New Testament to Old Testament? Does "New" indicate movement on to a different plane of revelation, with "Old" subordinated to a merely background role? Or is "New" a new form of the "Old," with each vital to a proper reception and understanding of the other? Or do they have to be regarded as in the end two distinct and even discontinuous bodies of sacred writings?[20] This is the fundamental problem of biblical theology, and its impact on the task of NT theology is obvious.

3. THE QUESTION OF THE CANON

A second and unavoidable issue is the canon, for canon defines the content and scope of the Bible, and is particularly pressing for those who, like Childs, want to deal with a *canonical* biblical theology. The difficulty in this case is that for the crucial period when the NT was being written, but was not yet "the New Testament," the boundaries of the canon were fuzzy. What counted as the law (Torah) and the Prophets had been more or less agreed from the second century B.C.E.[21] But the number of the Writings was far from clear, including the status of a major Second Temple Jewish writing like ben Sira. And are we talking about the Hebrew Bible or the Greek Bible (LXX), the latter with several Hebrew Bible texts elaborated and extended, and ben Sira and other apocryphal works included?[22] Although the Protestant canon sided with the Hebrew Bible, it cannot be without significance that, as is clear from OT quotations in the NT, the LXX was the principal text for the NT writers.[23] That fact in itself complicates quite seriously the issue of continuity/ discontinuity between the Jewish Bible and the Christian Bible.

With the NT writings the problem is still more serious. For in the first century, there was, properly speaking, no NT canon. We can certainly speak of traditions of Jesus that were prized and functioned authoritatively, and of letters of Paul that were soon circulated and began to acquire a kind of proto-canonical status for a steadily widening circle of churches. But of little more than that. Nor should we forget that canonical status has never really meant a parity of status across the board for the NT writings. Those whose apostolic authority was doubted well into the fourth century are probably better designated as deutero-canonical.[24] And questions about the status of secondary items have never been finally or satisfactorily dealt with.[25]

The real problem with tying a NT theology to the canon of the NT is that it takes not so much the NT documents as the norm for NT theology, but rather the fourth-century evaluation of the NT and authorization of the NT canon. The voices of the NT writers are valued not so much for their individuality but for their agreement, or, perhaps more worryingly, for their assent to a creed or rule ("the rule of faith") that has been partly drawn from some of the writings but has also in effect been imposed on the others and reflects more the priorities of the subsequent centuries than those of the NT writers themselves. But what if conformity to such a rule is an imposition on much more diverse patterns of speech, belief, and praxis? In which case, is that properly *New Testament* theology, or the theology of the fourth-century church? The fact, for example, that the heirs of the first-generation Jerusalem church (within the canonical documents almost certainly best reflected in the letter of James) are arguably to be found more completely in the so-called heretical Jewish-Christian sects of these later centuries raises a troubling question as to whether the Christianity that James reflects was fully accepted by those who authorized the canon of the NT.[26]

This issue underlines the importance of biblical theology as a *historical* discipline: the importance of *hearing the texts in their historical context*, as they were heard when first or finally written down in their enduring form; the importance of reading them diachronically, taking into account the influences that shaped them, and not simply synchronically where complementarity to other canonical texts becomes the primary hermeneutical principle.

The issue of canon also raises the question of non-canonical texts and their relevance to the task of elucidating the theology of the NT. Here of particular relevance are the so-called intertestamental Jewish writings, or, more satisfactorily, the post-biblical Jewish writings of Second Temple Judaism.[27] They are relevant for the simple reason that, as we shall see, *many NT passages cannot be understood historically except in some degree of interaction with several of these texts.* No respectable NT theology can confine its inquiry to the canonical writings, since many of the writings included in the NT canon cannot properly be grasped without appreciating the interaction with issues and themes attested in extra-canonical writings that was part of their *raison d'être.*

More sensitive are the so-called NT apocrypha, including such texts as the Gospel of Thomas.[28] A strong argument has been pressed in recent years for some of these texts, the Gospel of Thomas being the test case, to be regarded as comparable to the canonical Gospels, as bearing witness both to a stream of tradition equally ancient and to a different version of Christianity with equal claims to stem from Jesus.[29] And certainly for biblical theology as a historical exercise it is important to be aware how fluid and open to diverse interpretation so much of the Jesus tradition (the Q material in particular) proved to be. However, the difficulty with making the case for regarding Thomas as a source of equal value with the Synoptic Gospels is that it is precisely the overlap with the Synoptic tradition that gives the Thomas tradition its credibility as a source that leads us back to the fountainhead (Jesus) himself.[30] The more plausible explanation, therefore, is that Thomas constitutes clear evidence of how the Q tradition in particular was developed and interpreted by one or more strands emerging from first-century embryonic Christianity. Like Q itself, however, it reveals a source and development that was discounted and set aside within the mainstream that became Christianity. It therefore constitutes data of importance for any consideration of what constitutes a Gospel. The main body of second-century Christians came to the conclusion that only those accounts of Jesus and his teaching that climaxed in the passion narrative of Jesus' crucifixion and resurrection were gospel and disowned collections only of his teaching. The process by which this conclusion was reached takes off from the fact that what were to become recognized as the canonical Gospels followed Mark in writing Gospels as passion narratives with lengthy introductions. A NT biblical theology should find in this whole issue a question to be grappled with as an intriguing historical question and in the process a model for how the question might or should be pursued.

The important point for a biblical theology, which I shall develop in chapter 2, is that canonization should not be seen simply as the endpoint in the formation of the NT and of NT theology. Rather the canonical process is itself an expression of NT theology. So the NT biblical theologian is bound to the NT canon, at least to its main components, simply because the canon demonstrates the power inherent in the documents concerned, the theological authority they themselves exercised as was acknowledged when the canonical status of just these documents was affirmed, or better, confirmed.[31]

4. THEOLOGY OR THEOLOGIES?

If the relation of the NT to the Bible is a problem for a biblical theology of the NT, so too is the New Testament itself. The very manner of talking about "the New Testament" and "NT theology," as though each was a single, unified entity, poses several issues.

One is signaled by the fact that as a first-century term *bible* (*biblion*) never refers to what today would be called the Bible, or even to the Hebrew Bible or LXX as a whole. When used in reference to sacred writings, it always refers to a particular writing: one of the Torah scrolls;[32] or the scroll of one of the prophets (Luke 4:17, 20); or an apocalyptic scroll;[33] it is used also of John's Gospel (John 20:30). So by talking about the Bible do we not impose a unitary perspective that is quite unknown to the NT writers?

Similarly, in talking about "the New Testament" there is a danger of implying that there is *the* NT view of any issue, the NT belief about Jesus, the NT attitude to women's ministry, and the like. On the contrary, one of the primary concerns of a NT biblical theology should be to allow each of the NT writers to speak with *his own* voice. Given that most of the NT writers wrote only one book,[34] should we speak of a theological assertion by only one of them as what "the NT teaches"? The question is even asked whether we can speak of the theology of Paul, to whom is attributed thirteen different letters. It is not simply that several of these letters are widely regarded as written by someone other than Paul;[35] in which case, on which letters do we draw to compile his theology? It is also that his letters are for the most part episodic, written to particular

7

congregations and dealing with particular issues. Can one, then, easily extrapolate to a theology that Paul retained in his mind, independent of these letters, to a kind of cistern on which we envisage him drawing in order to write particular letters?[36] Or do we have to limit ourselves to the theology of the individual letters?[37]

And what is true for the one who wrote a number of documents now part of our NT applies even more forcefully to the NT writers as a whole and as individuals. Do they in fact speak with a single voice, or even with complementary voices that can be blended into a single NT teaching?[38] Or can we only ever expect to write the theologies (plural) of the NT, that is, of the various NT documents?[39]

Consequently, it must be a major responsibility of the NT biblical theologian to make clear the *diversity* of the NT, a responsibility that (s)he may not shirk. The alternative would be to reduce a NT biblical theology to the highest common denominator of what they all agreed,[40] or to assume uncritically that what one said explicitly, all the rest affirmed too—so *NT* theology, and not simply the theology of Matthew or James or the theology of Paul or Luke-Acts, or the theology of John or Hebrews. In contrast, it is important that the biblical theologian makes clear the divergent or discordant views of Matthew and Mark, or of Paul and James, precisely because such discordance is part of the NT testimony, part of NT theology. *The diversity of early Christian theological reflection on Jesus is as much constitutive of NT theology as that which unifies the different documents.*[41] The unity of the NT can be conceived and grasped only as a unity in diversity, that is, a unity that is like the unity of the body, a single identity composed of and made possible by the integration and interaction of the diverse parts.[42]

The corollary issue can be posed as *the question of or search for a center or unifying principle,* or alternatively, for "a canon within the canon."[43] It is noticeable that the quest for such a single formulation in regard to the Jewish scriptures has never been satisfactorily resolved.[44] The revelation of God, or even, the self-revelation of God,[45] is no doubt a possibility, but may be too narrow (*theology* is not just *theo-logy*) or too broad (*theo-logy* covers all *theology*). For the NT itself it is certainly possible to assert that Jesus himself, or faith in Jesus as Christ and Lord, or some such formulation can serve;[46] all the NT documents are, after all, faith responses to what is sometimes summarily referred to as the Christ event. Though to assert that Jesus is the unifying centre of the Christian Bible as a whole simply re-poses the fundamental problem afresh.[47] And the way in which

Jesus functions as the center of the NT is itself hardly uniform. Diversity is as much constitutive of the NT writings and teachings on *Jesus* as the unity of shared beliefs, and the way in which Jesus is presented in these writings is equally diverse.[48] Above all, it should never be forgotten that the NT canon contains no less than four Gospels, not one, but four different Gospels. It was not one Gospel that was canonized, or a Tatian-like Diatessaron, as though there could be only one legitimate way of expressing the theological significance of Jesus. No less than *four* Gospels are counted Gospel, not just the often subtle variations between the Synoptics, but also the striking variation or alternative that is John's Gospel.

The kerygma, the common preaching of the first Christians, has frequently been put forward as the unifying bond.[49] So, in my *Unity and Diversity in the New Testament*, one of the tasks I set myself was to look for what might be termed the kerygma/gospel that forms the core unity of the NT, the core kerygma.[50] In summary, the points that came through there were

- that the core kerygma is an abstraction and never to be found as such in the NT, but
- only in the expanded forms made necessary as the particularity of different situations were addressed, that is,
- in the different forms that the different situations made necessary, and
- that the differences were *integral* to the proclamations in and to these different situations.

From this I concluded that any attempt to find a single, once-for-all unifying kerygma (the NT kerygma) is bound to fail. For concrete situations always call forth fuller expressions, and it is in the fuller expressions that the diversity, including differences and disagreements, lie.[51] This in turn means that a theological approach to the issue will always need to recognize a certain *beyondness*, an uncontrollability by any particular group or tradition of the core gospel, of the canon within the canon, of the Word within and through the words; and also an acceptance of the inevitability of different preached, written, and ecclesial forms of the gospel. In other words, the final unifying factor in the NT, or in NT theology, can never be reduced to a particular, far less a final formulation. At the same time, I should also repeat two other observations that I made in the same volume: that *the NT itself is the unity*, the unity within which the diversity is manifest—unity in diversity;[52] and that the NT itself indicates the *limits* of the diversity.[53]

The same is true of other attempts to find a single lens through which to read any group of NT writings. Is the common, unifying factor given by anthropology (individual "self-understanding"), as Bultmann maintained?[54] That would imply a degree of existentialist individualism, or even self-absorption that could be positively unhealthy.[55] Or should we find the unifying focus in the doctrine of justification by faith, the article by which the church stands or falls?[56] That too would run the danger of narrowing a broad channel of experience and language into a single metaphor.[57] Or should we find it in the church or a concept like apostolic succession? But "the church" was as diverse in the first century as the NT (writings), and apostolic succession is a concept won from one or two NT writings with more ingenuity than exegesis. And the more recently popular conception of a meta-narrative, presupposed by more or less all the biblical writers and binding them together,[58] simply poses the issue afresh: a single narrative or diverse narratives?

So the issue of NT theology as one theology or as several theologies cannot be ignored or sidelined and must be part of the agenda for any NT theology—which raises a fourth and final issue.

5. THEOLOGY OR THEOLOGIZING?

A prominent debate in biblical and NT theology has been whether the task is purely historical and descriptive,[59] as Gabler assumed and William Wrede and Heikki Räisänen so vigorously argued,[60] whether "what it meant" should be held sharply distinct from "what it means" (Stendahl).[61] It is itself a historical fact that the historical critical method, so fundamental to the emergence of biblical theology, was shaped to the pattern of scientific inquiry, exalting accurate observation and dispassionate objectivity into an ideal. Personal involvement in the subject matter, summarised as "faith," was to be bracketed out, as liable to distort perception. Description rather than prescription was the order of the day, and NT theology could be treated as a subset of a historical sociology of religion.[62]

An important first response to this trend is to observe that faith is itself part of the historical phenomena to be observed—the faith that Jesus' mission, death and resurrection excited is itself part of the data to be described.[63] So at least NT theology can be justifiably defined as a descriptive account of the theological thinking, of the faith of the first Christians.[64] But the real question is whether, or rather, the extent to which the NT biblical theologian allows herself/himself to interact with the text, to bring his/her own faith (of whatever character) into interaction with the faith expressed in the text.[65]

Bound up with the whole subject are classic hermeneutical issues, compounded in this case by the fact that the texts in view are not only historical writings but have functioned as scripture for faith communities, some of them for more than two millennia.[66] Is the NT biblical theologian to be concerned only with the *Sprache* (the wording) of the text, or also/more precisely with the *Sache* (the subject or substance) of the text?[67] Should biblical theology take into account the way the text has been understood throughout the intervening centuries (scripture *and* tradition), the way it has shaped the very presuppositions (linguistic, cultural) that most twenty-first-century readers bring to their reading of it?[68] To what extent does a reading today create the meaning heard from the text (the challenge of postmodernism)? Can the biblical theologian truly engage with the text without asking what it means for herself/himself and his/her community—above all, to believe in God or in Jesus as they believed? How different is a faith activist practicing a rigorous critical methodology from any critic seeking to enter into a text empathetically?[69] In short, can one "do" biblical or NT theology without theologizing with or in reaction to the biblical/NT writers as they theologized? Is the "a" in "*a biblical theology*" inevitable since the theology in question is unavoidably *my* or *your* biblical theology, rather than, in the most proper sense, the Bible's theology?

Symptomatic of the malaise is the fixation with the written text. Of course, the text is the focus of, and, inevitably and in large measure, the controlling factor in *New Testament* theology, that is the theology of the NT writings, that is, as attested by and expressed in their written texts. But it is possible to treat the text as a kind of idol, where our gaze fixes solely on the text and does not look through it. We can become fixated by the *Sprache* of the text and lose sight of the *Sache*. As in so many commentaries from the classic period of modernism, exegesis can be more or less reduced to word and syntax analysis. Or in a more literary-oriented era, narrative critics can become content with describing the text within its own textually determined (and restricted) world. Again, the interplay between different theologies within the biblical writings can be limited by being defined in terms of intertextuality, as though such interplay operated only in terms of one author's knowledge and use of other written texts. Or canonical criticism can seize on the moment of the canonical text and effectively discount all other forms of the text.

The alternative to a NT *theology* understood as primarily or even exclusively descriptive, and restricted by the nineteenth century Newtonian and historicist ideals of scientific inquiry, may be put in terms of NT *theologizing*, where the verbal noun (gerund) form is intended to bring some sense of movement into the understanding of the task.[70] This is partly a matter of taking seriously an understanding of theology as not merely "talk of God," and certainly not as simply consisting of theological statements or dogmatic pronouncements; but as also including the immediate corollaries of an active belief in God, the existential implications of understanding the world as *created,* of taking seriously the implications of divine revelation and a need for salvation, of seeking to live responsibly in human community and before this God, and so on.[71] But it is partly also a recognition that in order to enter into NT theology we need to see the text *as a testimony to and expressive of the flow and movement of experience, thought and praxis in earliest Christianity.* Of course all this is now frozen in the text, but what is frozen should not be seen as a final deposit of some interactions that happened long ago. The subject matter of NT theology should not be likened to an artifact retrieved by painstaking excavation from some archaeological tell. Rather the text is frozen theologizing, the process of engaging theologically with some subject or issue caught in a moment of an ongoing movement. In each case it was a climactic moment, presumably, the outcome of much reflection and use. But not an end point, for the context soon changed, and the reflection moved on. Apart from anything else, this is indicated by the fact that the text is not so fixed as is so often assumed. The recent work of textual critics has reminded us that the textual variations are not simply evidence of scribal carelessness, but evidence that the actual texts that functioned as scripture for different congregations were actually different texts.[72]

So the typical historical critical study of the text is only a *beginning* of the attempt to enter into the process of theologizing which the text both embodies and to which it bears witness. That includes some sense of the *depth* of the text—not only the allusions to and echoes of earlier theologizing, but also the ways of thinking and speaking as they had been shaped by the inherited traditions and culture. It includes some sense of the *width* of the text—of the usage and rhetoric of the time, of possibly intended ambiguities (should an exegete always assume that a single, sharply defined meaning was intended?), of comparative, alternative or even competing formulations, of what might have been said but wasn't, and (not least) whether the author might have expressed himself otherwise had he foreseen the inferences that would subsequently be drawn from what he wrote. And it includes not least a sense of *the text in historical context*, of the historical particularities that gave rise to the text, but also come to expression in the text, of the text as part of a developing insight or part of a dialogue, not something static and universal.[73] To enter thus into NT theology is to begin to re-experience theology as theologizing, to begin to immerse oneself in the stream of living theology that flowed from Jesus and the reactions to him, to read *with* the text rather than to assume that a hermeneutic of suspicion will always be more productive for contemporary interpretation.[74]

This approach does not assume or necessitate that the NT theologian can only approach the text effectively from a faith standpoint. Nor does it mean that the NT can be *heard* only by faith, or can only be understood within a church context.[75] I share with John Barton's recently expressed concerns, both his proper desire to "bracket out" (initially at any rate) the question of truth as one attempts to make sense of a biblical text, and also his perception of a danger of limiting or constricting the Bible within a faith community.[76] It is the latter thought, that the Bible could no longer speak to someone outside Christian faith, which is shocking to me.[77] On the contrary, a reader who attempts to achieve an empathetic reading (or better listening)—and at least a degree of empathy with the concerns and intentions expressed in a text I regard as almost indispensable to a fair evaluation of any text by any reader or hearer—should be able to hear the text responsibly.[78] And a degree of openness to what the text says may well result in many an initially agnostic reader being persuaded or even converted by what is read or heard.

For the NT theologian in particular, there is, however, a middle way between a neutral and committed approach, between a historical and a theological reading, between a modern and a nonmodern reading.[79] For NT theologians can and should read the text critically and with historical knowledge, but they will presumably also want to read with concern to learn empathetically or even to experience afresh what it was that made the text so important and so powerful for those who first heard it, and a willingness to engage with the major theological, social, and ethical issues that they find there. It is as NT theologians enter as fully as possible into the living situations of the NT texts that they learn how theology was done, how theologizing was effected in the earliest days of Christianity. In so doing they familiarize themselves with the models and precedents for dealing with issues theological and social and potentially learn how to handle similar or equivalent issues in the twenty-first century. They learn how to swim in the stream of theologizing that flows from (and through) the NT to the present day.

6. PAUL THE NT THEOLOGIAN PAR EXCELLENCE

A good test case for what has been set out above is the theology of Paul.[80] Here I need not elaborate the way in which Paul addresses the problems of continuity/discontinuity with his native Judaism. Or that so much of what he writes depends on the reader's awareness of the character of that Judaism, only accessible to us from the post-biblical Jewish writings. Or the issue of unity and diversity within Paul's writings themselves. All these aspects will be well illustrated and become clearer as we move into examination of the themes for chapters 3 through 6.

Here, however, I want to press the point about NT theology as theologizing, and it is precisely Paul who allows us to see most clearly the character of NT theology as something alive and moving. For he authored a number of letters that we still have.[81] And since J. B. Lightfoot's great nineteenth-century commentaries it has become standard practice to set each of these letters within their historical context of composition and reception, that is, to recognize the occasional character of the letters. So, inevitably, when one turns to these letters a sense is quickly given of a great theological mind addressing a sequence of different issues and situations. And because the issues and situations were different, Paul's theological response was and is different, that is, Paul's theology was and is different. It is only when we abstract texts from the particularities of their initial composition and reception that the variations of content and emphasis become problems as "inconsistencies" and "contradictions."[82] Rather, as with the variations in the triply told Jesus tradition (Matthew/Mark/Luke), we should see in such variations the expression of a living theology, not treat the letters as so many cadavers laid out in the pathology laboratory for dissection. It was in recognition of this living character of Paul's theology that several contributors to the decade-long seminar on the theology of the Pauline Letters at the annual meetings of the Society of Biblical Literature found themselves beginning to speak of Paul's *theologizing* in preference to Paul's theology.[83] Paul's letters show us theology in motion, living theology, theologizing.

A major disagreement surfaced in that seminar and was never resolved, or rather, no resolution achieved widespread consensus. The disagreement, already alluded to,[84] was as to whether a *Theology of Paul* written today could realistically deal with *Paul's* theology, or only with the theology of each of his *letters*. Is the subject matter the theology *behind* the letters, or the theology expressed *in* the letters? I was one of those who thought in terms of the former, that a description and analysis of Paul's theology could and should be attempted; though, mindful precisely of the problem of a moving stream of Paul's theologizing, I set myself to attempt to formulate Paul's theology at the time when he wrote his letter to the Christians in Rome.[85] My reasoning was and remains fairly straightforward and has already been indicated. Paul's letters were and are not abstract dissertations or treatises. They contain so many allusions to situations addressed, to formulations of other or earlier Christians, to the OT not least as it was being understood at his time, that it is impossible to enter into the theology of any single letter without taking these allusions into account and trying to engage with the warp and woof of the reactions and interactions they express. In terms of the present enterprise, any attempt to understand a letter of Paul in its own terms, in disregard of these allusions and of the particularity of its historical context, would be hard pressed to understand the theology of the letter as the theology of the Paul who wrote it with all these allusions alive in his mind. And when such an inquiry is pursued through letter after letter, one inevitably is drawn to an appreciation of the man who dictated or penned these letters and to appreciate his theologizing, and so also his theology, in however episodic terms.

Writing a theology of Paul, in other words, is like trying to listen to a sequence of varied dialogues, of which we can hear clearly only one side of the dialogue, but which we must understand as a dialogue, otherwise we will inevitably misunderstand what Paul says.[86] One cannot hope to write a theology of Paul except by listening to his letters as dialogue, overhearing, as it were, a great theological mind and spirit as it grappled with diversely challenging situations and questions. Put another way, Paul's letters are not just like erratic boulders left by some ancient glacier. Nor are they windows into a neatly rounded and complete theology of Paul; that would be *theologicism*, the theological equivalent to historicism, the assumption that the theology of Paul is like a complete and intact object accessed through and behind the letters, or like a solid artifact buried under the layers of his letters. Rather, in the letters we see and are privileged to overhear *theology in the making*, theology coming to expression, Paul theologizing.

In an earlier attempt to penetrate into Paul's theology (christology) I had attempted to remind readers that many/most/all of Paul's formulations are examples of "conceptuality in transition," and that we have to bear in mind the "limited horizons" within which he formulated his christology.[87] The point in both cases, of course, is that later readers of Paul's letters find it difficult to free their minds from the ways his formulations have been understood for so many centuries. The point was/is that formulations that naturally speak to later theology, for example, of a full-blown concept of pre-existence, or of hypostatization, may not have been so understood when first formulated. Hypostasis in its technical Christian sense, after all, was a fourth-century reminting to meet the problem of formulating a concept of God as Trinity; prior to that time, that sense had not been conceptualized.[88] Likewise, it is certainly likely that an *ideal* pre-existence had become thought of; but had the *real* pre-existence of a human person as such already entered the minds of those who spoke of someone sent by God? I don't want to defend here the particular views expressed in my *Christology in the Making*. The point is that recognition must be given to the at least strong likelihood that developing thought/theology meant also fresh conceptualizations and horizons being pushed back from what had earlier been perceived and articulated in many matters of theological concern and reflection. There were insights, ways of conceptualizing, theological arguments that came to expression for the first time in Paul's letters, perhaps in an exploratory way and with Paul unaware of their potential as resources for further theologizing. However the point is put, the point is that descriptions of the theology of Paul should not treat his letters as the cold and petrified remains of a volcanic eruption that took place centuries earlier, but as lava streams still hot and moving, still capable of scalding and burning.

When we see Paul's letters as his theologizing, as expressions of living theology, it also becomes easier to take proper account of the post-Pauline letters and of the representation of Paul's theology (and of Paul) in Luke's Acts. Here the parallels provided by the OT and the Jesus tradition become relevant. As already suggested, it is important to recognize so many OT writings as the product not of a single act of composition but as the outcome of an often lengthy traditioning process, and not as a complete and closed outcome, as the LXX, Targumim, and "the oral law" of the Pharisees and rabbis remind us. Similarly the Gospels are not best understood as created *de novo* by individuals but better as the congealing of a living Jesus tradition (editorially shaped, of course) into (various) written form(s). So Paul's theology, the movement of Paul's theologizing, did not end with his close imprisonment or his death. If the work of later tradents contributed to and shaped Torah that no doubt began with Moses, wisdom that began with Solomon, teaching that goes back to Jesus, then we should not be surprised to find that disciples of Paul continued to theologize in the spirit of Paul, as the stream of theologizing that began with Paul continued to roll forward.[89] And too little appreciated is the fact that Acts gives us the possibility of seeing Paul as others saw him, of hearing the (or an)other side to Paul's relationships with Jerusalem, a different take on his assertions of independent apostleship. None of this exempts the twenty-first-century theologian from evaluating these different kinds of Pauline theologizing, or even from taking sides with one or other on disputed questions. On the contrary, so to recognize such factors—the fact that the lava continued to flow after Paul's departure from the scene, the fact that Paul's theologizing about his apostleship and his relations with Jerusalem provide only one side of a more complex historical reality—is to enter into the dialogue ourselves, to engage theologically with the various theologizings that the Pauline and post-Pauline and Lukan material represents. A historical description of the various theologies is only the beginning of the process of doing NT theology.

THE DETERMINING
FACTORS

1. INTRODUCTION

N T Theology, the theology of the NT writings, is principally determined by two, if not three chief factors. I list them in chronological sequence rather than by priority in influence.

1. The first was the writings already regarded as sacred and authoritative by the first Christians, that is, what Christians came to
know as the Old Testament, or less anachronistically, the
Hebrew Bible or the LXX. As already indicated, for the NT writers biblical theology would have been the theology of OT/LXX.

2. The second was what Paul described as "the revelation of Jesus
Christ" (Gal 1:12). I use the phrase to embrace everything from
the impact made by Jesus during his life and mission, and particularly the impact of his death and resurrection as perceived by his
first disciples.

3. The third, to the extent that it can be distinguished from the second, was the impact of fresh experience of God, attributed to the
Spirit of God, bringing new insight and revelation.

The dynamic of NT theology begins precisely with the tension
between these three determining factors, between what was generally

agreed already to be revelation, but older revelation, and what was claimed to be new revelation. Each factor requires further elucidation and reflection.

2. NT THEOLOGY AND THE OT

A. The OT as Divine Authority

It bears repeating that integral to NT theology is the interaction with the Old Testament. In C. H. Dodd's words, the NT's use of the OT provides the "substructure" of NT theology.[1] We need think only of the regular quotations from the (Jewish) scriptures that pepper the pages of the NT.[2] The appeal to a specific scripture or scriptures is a regular feature in the Gospels, in Acts, in Paul, in Hebrews, and in James and 1 Peter. "As it has been written" (*kathōs gegraptai*) is a regularly occurring formula, as a claim is made for the present by citing the authority of Israel's sacred writings.[3] Matthew in particular, but he is not alone, makes great play with his fulfillment quotations: certain events happened "in order that it might be fulfilled," and the relevant text is cited.[4] Prominent examples of narratives and arguments that depend entirely on the scriptures cited include the accounts of Jesus' crucifixion in the Gospels, constructed as they seem to be round several psalms, particularly Psalm 22,[5] Romans 9–11, Hebrews,[6] and 1 Pet 2:6-9, though we, should also note how strained some of the use made of scripture can be.[7]

What becomes very clear from even a brief familiarity with such material is that the NT writers depended heavily on the OT. It was essential for them that they should be able to claim, and claim validly and effectively, that what they were writing was wholly in accord with their scriptures. The Tanakh was not in any sense the scriptures of another religion; Torah, Prophets, and Writings were *their* scriptures, on whose revelation of God and his will they depended entirely.[8] We need instance only passages like Luke 24:44 and Gal 5:14 for the point to be clear: without the support of the OT, the NT writers themselves would not have been able to make claims that were central and essential for their faith and praxis. It is simply inconceivable that the NT writers would have pressed ahead with their claims and paraenesis had they thought they were running counter to what the Bible (Hebrew Bible or LXX) said. Had the first Christians been unable to validate their beliefs and practices from the OT they would have become something quite other than they became, more like a Gnostic group that disowned or wholly disregarded the OT. However a modern biblical theology may evaluate the relation and continuity and discontinuity of OT and NT, there can be no doubt that for the NT writers, the OT was a major and determining factor in their own theologizing.[9]

However, for a biblical theology of the NT it is not simply a matter of identifying where and considering how the NT authors work with the OT;[10] the OT is not to be likened to a quarry from which texts, motifs, and themes have been mined for subsequent use.[11] Nor can it be limited to the much more subtle issue of the extent to which the NT writers allude to or echo OT passages.[12] Still more important is the way in which the OT has influenced and shaped the writing of the NT, no doubt often subconsciously.[13] Of course, there is an intangibility about much such influence. But unless we begin to sense the way in which the scripture of the first Christians formed and shaped their own theologizing, we will again mistake the character of NT theology.[14] We will see below good examples in Paul's talk of "the righteousness of God"; another is the way James draws on the Jewish wisdom tradition.[15] But to appreciate what is involved here one has indeed to be so immersed in the material, both OT and NT, that one's hearing becomes attuned to motif and movement of thought as well as the more perceptible allusion and echo.

B. The OT as Ongoing Revelation

It is equally important to recognize that what we call the OT was itself not a fixed reference. For example, we know that the Pentateuch was the product of a long process, no doubt going back to Moses as the fountainhead, but only given its determinative shape by Ezra, and still fluid enough to allow a controversial reference like Acts 7:16, or for Jesus to pull out a single sentence (Lev 19:18) and give it a new primacy for conduct. As we shall see below (#6) the interpretation of the Torah (the Halakhah, the "oral Torah") was a lively issue of debate and disagreement between the Pharisees and Jesus. We also know, for example, that the Psalms were not yet a closed book, with fresh psalms attested among the Dead Sea Scrolls. We know that writings like Jubilees and the Qumran Temple scroll (11QT) were in effect rewritings of biblical material. We know that the translation of the Hebrew Bible into Greek (the LXX) did not rest with simply translating what had already been written, but also elaborated old writings and included new writings. Similarly the Targumim, like all translations, did not, could not simply provide straightforward translations, but took the opportunity to elaborate and explain.[16]

So when we talk about the NT's use of the OT, what do we mean? Certainly not simply a familiarity with and use of some texts fixed in writing several centuries earlier. Nor can such usage be reduced to a simple promise-fulfillment process, or typological analysis, as though the OT functions only as a foil to the NT. I say this without in any degree wishing to deny or diminish the crucial importance of the *gegraptai* and "in order that it might be fulfilled" motifs in so many NT writings. Still less can the OT be allowed to function in NT theology only as background to fill in otherwise obscure motifs in the NT. Rather, the NT's use of the OT has to be seen more as an engagement with the moving, developing traditions of thought and praxis expressed *in and through* these texts, always, of course, in the light of the revelation the first Christians experienced through and in reference to Jesus the Christ. That includes an acknowledgment of the scriptural authority of the texts of the Hebrew Bible, certainly. But also an entry into the process that gave birth to these texts, a process that did not finish with their fixation in written (canonical) form, but continued (the same process) in the attempt to understand these texts, to fill out their meaning, to explain their relevance. The NT use of the OT was the beginning of NT theology.

Here I take seriously James Sanders's understanding of "canonical criticism" as distinct from that of Brevard Childs[17]—that is, recognizing that the traditions and material that made up the Hebrew Bible were canonical not because the final text was later decreed to be such, but were canonical because at each stage of the process the traditions that lasted, which were prized and preserved carried their authority "in their face."[18] What we see in NT theologizing, I suggest, is the recognition of that authority and the attempt to hear and understand its implications—a task and challenge, of course, which they shared with Qumran commentator and Pharisee, and subsequently with sage and rabbi. The Jesus who disputes with the Pharisees on Sabbath observance[19] and speaks against Qumran priorities,[20] and the Paul who talks of "works of the law" in terms now recognizable from 4QMMT,[21] or who shows knowledge of targumic elaborations of scripture,[22] were themselves part of the living flow of tradition, engaging in the art of theologizing, which consists of wrestling with the proper understanding and proportions of scripture in the changing circumstances of their time.[23]

This is why the NT theologian should not treat the OT as a closed book, as a fixed entity,[24] still less imply that by evaluating parts of it, by picking and choosing within it, the NT authors abused or rejected it. The Gospel/Law antithesis that has been so dominant in so much Reformation theology treats the latter too much in effect as a bounded entity, something complete in itself. In so saying I am not referring simply to the fact (noted earlier) that there was as yet no fixed, far less closed canon in the time of Jesus and Paul. My point is much more that the translations of LXX and Targumim, and the formulations that resulted in NT and Mishnah were themselves part of the same creative, inspired process of theologizing that had earlier come to expression in the writings that now make up the Hebrew Bible. So the theologizing which debates the relevance of the laws of clean and unclean, which claims the advent of the new covenant, which disputes the relevance of circumcision is not foreign to or essentially something different from and other than the traditioning processes that culminated in the Hebrew Bible. The processes that crystallized in the writings of the OT continued and crystallized again in further writings. And just as the earlier writings required evaluation and prioritizing in order to continue to speak to changing circumstances (for example, the shift from nomadic and agrarian society, the hellenization of culture, the destruction of the Jerusalem temple), so the first Christians and the NT writers in particular were evaluating and prioritizing within their sacred scriptures and theologizing with the effect that their writings became (in due course) the NT.

The point that emerges from this is important for a NT theology written within the context of biblical theology. The point is that *unless a NT theology both recognizes and brings out the degree to which the NT writers saw themselves as in continuity with the revelation of the OT and as at least in some measure continuing or completing that revelation, it can hardly provide a faithful representation of what they understood themselves to be about.*[25] Unless the NT writings can be understood as a valid addition to or even completion of the then not yet closed canon of the OT, the NT theology that results can hardly be described as authentically biblical theology.[26] Or to pose the point as a question: can the NT writings be regarded as valid an interpretation and elaboration of the Hebrew Bible as the Mishnah?[27]

It is the tension that such a claim and such a question set up that has to provide the major stimulus for a biblical NT theology. How to correlate such different emphases—not least, for example, the different attitudes to the importance of circumcision, or the laws of clean and unclean, or the Sabbath? Or more centrally, how to incorporate the claims made for Jesus within the scope of the revelation of the OT? How to integrate the choice of Israel out of all the nations, with a gospel for all who believe? Are these questions already integral to the diversity of the OT writings? Are the issues debated with the Pharisees and "the Jews" in the Gospels and other NT writings simply part of the debate regarding the meaning of the previous revelation of Israel's scriptures? Or did "the revelation of Jesus Christ" mean a fundamental breach with both that older revelation as well as the terms in which it was being understood in Second Temple Judaism?

In short, the OT is a fundamental factor in the making and shaping of NT theology. The sense of and claim to fulfillment and completion was foundational. No NT theology can ignore the OT or the profundity of its influence on the NT.

3. THE REVELATION OF JESUS CHRIST

A. The Impact of Good Friday and Easter

The most important determinative factor for NT theology is Jesus, particularly the impact of his death and resurrection. It was the *earliest wrestling with the shocking fact of Jesus' crucifixion* that transformed the first disciples' understanding of the scriptures—classically expressed again in the account of Jesus' appearance to two disciples on the road to Emmaus and how "beginning with Moses and all the prophets, he interpreted to them the things about himself in all the scriptures" (Luke 24:27). The story well expresses the sense of a dawning of a whole new light illuminating and causing a complete reappraisal of traditional ways of reading the OT. Jesus was indeed Messiah, and not despite his having been crucified; rather his suffering was proof of his messiahship, as a fresh awareness of passages like Isaiah 53 brought home to them.[28] The death of their leader gave his closest disciples a whole new perspective on their scriptures.

Even more so with the *resurrection*.[29] Quite why the first disciples came to understand what had happened to Jesus as "resurrection," rather than as his being raptured to heaven and thus vindicated, is probably beyond the reach of historical inquiry.[30] The theological fact, however, is that they *did* so think of it as resurrection. And not only as an isolated resurrection of an individual, far preceding the end-time resurrection of the dead; the latter was an expectation familiar in Second Temple Judaism since Dan 12:1-2. Astonishingly, however, the first disciples evidently understood Jesus' resurrection as the *beginning of the resurrection of the dead itself.*[31] Here was an amazing shift in perspective—usually summed up in the term eschatological.[32] They believed that the climax of all human history was in process of being realized. And that gave them a wholly new perspective on everything else. The resurrection of Jesus became a fulcrum point on which their perception of reality turned on to a new plane. However difficult it is for a reader two millennia distant to appreciate these heady days of earliest Christianity, however difficult it is to give a fully existential import to a term like *eschatological*, unless the present-day NT theologian attempts to do so, and does so with some success, the resulting NT theology will seriously lack the dynamic of its first formulations.[33]

Certainly not to be downplayed, or simply merged into the resurrection faith, was the further conviction that Jesus had not only been raised from the dead, but also *exalted* to heaven (Jesus' "ascension"). If ever a scripture helped shape Christian perception, it is Ps. 110:1—"the LORD said to my Lord. 'Sit at my right hand'"—as we shall see in more detail below, when we consider the transformation in the first Christians' apprehension of Jesus himself (#3.3e). Faith in Christ was not simply belief about an event that had happened some time before, but a sense of Jesus as risen and exalted, as Lord, in their ongoing daily living—including their theologizing.

What needs to be appreciated, then, is that the risen and exalted Jesus became a lens through which the first Christians viewed scripture and indeed everything else. Jesus was the Son through whom God had spoken with a fullness and completeness that rounded off all previous revelations through the prophets (Heb 1:1). He was the one who had made the invisible God visible (John 1:18; Col 1:15). He was the one who unveiled the significance of the past, of scripture (2 Cor 3:14). He was the one who was unfolding the future (Rev 5). *It is this sense that everything makes sense finally in the light of Jesus that makes Jesus such a crucial determinative factor in NT theology.* It was this sense or recognition that with Jesus a whole new chapter had dawned, a whole new age had arrived, a new revelation which did not dispense with the previous revelation, but brought it to

completion and illumined its ongoing significance, which was so fundamental and determinative for the first Christians and their theology.

Of course the issue still stands for biblical theology: whether the NT
writers were right, or better, justified in claiming that continuity and fulfillment, or were twisting scripture to their own ends in the light of their
apprehension of Jesus? The actual claims made by several at least of the
NT writers—for example Matt 2:23, or Paul's expositions in Galatians 3
and 4, or Hebrews' use of the same Psalm 110 to advance his presentation
of Christ as a "priest according to the order of Melchizedek" (110:4)—
certainly give scope for a very vigorous biblical theological debate on the
subject. But the key point here still stands: that for NT theology the centrality of Jesus, Jesus as the fulcrum point on which the history of salvation turns, Jesus as the lens through which scripture is to be read, is
indisputable.

B. Is Jesus' Own Mission and Message Part of NT Theology?

It is thus easy to see the creative and formative effect on NT theology
of Jesus' death, resurrection and exaltation. But what about Jesus' own pre-
Good Friday message and pre-Easter mission? Should that be counted part
of NT theology? Rudolf Bultmann famously answered that question nega-
tively in the opening words of his *Theology*.[34] Alternatively put, is there a
marked lack of continuity between Jesus' own mission and the Easter faith
of the first disciples? Did the first Christians make claims for Jesus that he
did not or would not have entertained for himself? It has been claimed
more than once that Paul is the real founder of Christianity, or that of the
two founders, Jesus and Paul, Paul was actually the more influential.[35] If
the role of the OT within or in relation to NT theology, and the continuity of OT with NT are major problems for a NT biblical theology, the
role of Jesus' own proclamation and teaching within NT theology has
been even more contentious. The issue is of no little importance for
Christian theology. For if there is a lack of continuity between Jesus and
Christian faith, if Jesus did not and would not have thought of himself in
the terms which came to be used of him, if what happened in the beginnings of Christianity was wholly discontinuous from Jesus' own mission,
then that must be of some considerable concern for believers.

It is true that Bultmann's dismissal of Jesus' own theology from the arena
of NT theology has had to be heavily qualified. For the Gospels themselves
are certainly central within NT theology, and Jesus' own mission is central
to their subject matter.[36] The significance of Easter entailed a looking back

to Jesus' own earthly mission; only so can we understand why the Gospels were written.[37] The issue cannot be handled with the old antithesis between the Jesus of history and the Christ of faith[38]—as baleful an antithesis in the twentieth century as the Gospel/Law antithesis has been for much longer. As OT/Torah cannot be regarded as a finished entity to be set over against the gospel, for both law and gospel are expressions of the same inspired/theologizing process, so the Jesus of history does not belong to some irrelevant back room whose door was closed with the event of Easter and ever after remains inaccessible to us, blinded as we are by the light of Easter faith. For the Gospels are *gospel*. And as gospel they contain rich accounts of Jesus' teachings and deeds, of Jesus' own theology as lived out and taught.[39] Their traditions were part of both the pre-Easter and the post-Easter theologizing of the first disciples. I will develop this point at some length, drawing on other of my recent work, since it is so important to the task and challenge of NT theology/theologizing as I see it.

Some commentators seem to think that (or at least act as though) there was a hiatus between the incidents in which Jesus spoke and acted and the recollection and recording of them—a hiatus that lasted at least up to and beyond the first Good Friday and Easter day, but which, to all intents and purposes, lasted until the traditions were written down, by Q or Mark or whoever. As though individuals simply heard and witnessed what Jesus said and did and stored the information away in their memories, waiting for the Easter event, or the inquiring tradition-collector, to jog their memory and bring it back to the surface, to be (only then) attested and recorded.[40] I cannot find any credibility in such a reconstruction. For almost certainly—the point can be stated in *a priori* terms—the first disciples talked together about what they had seen and heard, what it was that had drawn them into discipleship, into a shared discipleship. And almost as equally certain, such talking and sharing of their most immediate and vital memories of Jesus, of the impact he had made on them, was the beginning of what we now call the Jesus tradition. This talking and sharing, and then repeating (performing) and communicating these traditions is part of the earliest Christian theologizing, to inform not least their own paraenesis and conduct.[41] The point is that such performing and communicating inevitably involved an element of interpretation, an element of the spin that is unavoidably involved in selecting, placing emphasis, and grouping. And very quickly the first Aramaic remembrances were translated into Greek, with the inevitable transformation as well as communication which that involved.

What appears now in our Gospel texts, then, is not a straight transfer of a word or deed of Jesus "untouched by human hand" (as we might say) into the scroll of a Q or Mark. It is what Jesus was heard to say, and seen to do, filtered through the memories and performances and teachings of the earliest apostles and teachers. It is an expression of their appropriation of and reflection on the tradition. It is their theologizing on Jesus, on what he said and meant, on what he did and its ongoing significance. How can we begin to handle the disagreements in content and emphasis between the Gospels unless we recognize that they are examples of this living process? It is the varied character of the theologizing that lies behind the Gospels that comes to expression in these differences and divergences. So, for example, it is idle to enquire whether Mark or Matthew is more accurate or more authentic in their diverse presentations of Jesus vis-à-vis the law (as in Mark 7/Matt 15). For what they exemplify is the different ways Jesus was heard, the different voices in which the teaching of Jesus was remembered. The business of theologizing the Jesus tradition cannot be adequately characterized as some later Christian/author redacting or editing some already fixed tradition for his own ends. For the tradition was not fixed. That is the point! It was fluid, moving, living, coming to expression in one form of words at this point, and in another form of words at another point. And to appreciate it we have, so far as is possible, to get inside that process, to theologize rather than simply describe the theology.

In my recent *Jesus Remembered,* on which I draw for the above reflections, two points became particularly important for me.[42] One was to refute the assumptions already referred to, both that faith *prevents* a properly historical perspective on Jesus,[43] and that the only faith we have to take account of in the Gospels' portrayal of Jesus is Easter faith. Of course I have no wish to deny that the Gospels are gospel precisely because they present Jesus in the light of Easter faith, climaxing as each of them does in the passion and resurrection of Jesus the Christ. My point is rather to protest against the inference that the process of theologizing the Jesus tradition began only *after* Easter. On the contrary, it was the first disciples' attraction to Jesus that caused them to become disciples. A discipleship in which they abandoned their other responsibilities (to earn a living and care for their families) was already an expression of faith, of trust in this Jesus as God's spokesman, and a commitment of life to following him. Not yet Easter faith, to be sure; but certainly fully deserving of the description *faith,* trust, and commitment.[44]

My point here is that so much of the Jesus tradition reflects that faith, so many of the individual traditions reflect a pre-passion setting and a Galilean context,[45] that we can fairly conclude that the Jesus tradition must have begun to take shape in the pre-Easter Galilean discipleship of the first disciples. Indeed, I am prepared to argue that much of the tradition was given its form in that very early, even pre-Easter period, a form that has endured into our Gospels.

What is striking, then, is that for the Synoptic tradition at least, that pre-Easter faith was not discarded nor was it retained only in a reworked form, reworked by Easter faith. John's Gospel, and the apocryphal so-called Gospels, show clearly what might have happened had Easter faith simply ridden rough-shod over the expressions of the impact made by Jesus in his pre-Easter mission. From which I conclude that the first Christians saw *an immediate continuity between these early recollections of Jesus and their full Easter faith*—a continuity of theologizing. Moreover, it would seem that they could fully integrate these early impressions made by Jesus and remembered by those who had been his disciples "from the baptism of John" into their full gospel understanding of Jesus and of his significance. They did not make a dichotomy between his mission in life and his saving death and resurrection. They were all of a single piece. And—here, again, is the point—their theologizing on this Jesus was a continuum, stretching from the first impact made by Jesus to the Gospel of John, a moving, living stream.[46] How this bears on the question of christology, on whether the first Christians understood Jesus in terms he would have disowned or failed to recognize, is a subject to which we will return in chapter 3.

The other point that became important for me as a result of the work leading to my *Jesus Remembered* is the difference it makes when we can see most of that living stream of tradition, of which the Gospels are frozen moments, as *oral* tradition.[47] NT scholars have allowed themselves to become too fixated on the written tradition, or, to be more precise, on the Jesus tradition as written. It is this, more than anything else, which has clouded our perception of the tradition as living and moving, and prevented us from seeing NT theology as theologizing. For the written text is indeed fixed,[48] certainly in comparison with oral tradition. And that fixity encourages us to think of the Jesus tradition as a kind of solid and firm entity that is added to or subtracted from. We think of layers of tradition on the analogy of editions of a book, or of strata in an archaeological dig. We assume that there is a firm something deep down in there, like a solid, physical artifact to be attained by digging down through the layers.

But oral tradition is different. An oral performance is not like another edition of a book. With a book we can pause for reflection, or check back a few pages, or anticipate by turning over a few pages. We can take the book away and refer to it later. Or we can edit it, even modestly, by eliminating infelicities, improving style, adding clarifications. None of this is possible with an oral tradition that lives only in oral performance. That is essentially evanescent. And the performer (apostle, teacher, elder, disciple) will by no means necessarily store up the tradition in memory as something fixed, to be parroted forth on each occasion. In oral tradition, typically, the story—the *same* story!—is variously retold, with different emphasis, and different details; and the teaching—the *same* teaching!— is re-taught, in different groupings, and with different nuances and interpretative clarifications or elaborations suited to the occasion—much as we find when we look at the Jesus tradition synoptically!

Perhaps most important of all is the insistence of oral traditionalists that we who study the Jesus tradition as oral tradition must abandon the critical assumption of an *"original version."*[49] This is precisely the blinkeredness that our literary mind-set imposes on us. For in a culture of the written word it is natural to inquire after the original edition, in order to check how subsequent editions have changed from the original. But in oral tradition there is no original; or, alternatively expressed, every performance is an original. In the case of Jesus, of course, we can take it for granted that there were teachings he gave and deeds he was witnessed as doing. But today we are all too well aware that witnesses of the same event invariably produce different, even divergent accounts of that event. In effect, there was not one event, but several events, that is, the event as seen (differently) by different witnesses. And the same is true of at least much of Jesus' teaching material. For it would have impacted different disciples differently. And if Jesus gave the same or similar teaching on several occasions—as of course will have been the case—then what would be remembered and reflected on would be different from the outset.

The corollary, of course, is that *the assumption of a single and singular original version of what Jesus said and did is a highly misleading perspective that perverts the whole enterprise of NT theology/theologizing.* For it immediately implies that the only authentic version of the Jesus tradition is the original version, and that every other version is somehow less authentic and less valid. In contrast, my point is precisely that only by abandoning the myth or ideal of the original version can we begin properly to appreciate the process of hearing or seeing, reflecting, expressing in words, performing and communicating, which was (and is) the traditioning process, or in terms of the present volume, the process of theologizing that has resulted in the written texts that now form our Gospels.

Not only so, but recognizing the oral character of so much of the traditioning process of the Jesus tradition frees us from assuming that the only reference points for other NT and early church writers was the written text of one or more of the canonical Gospels. We are freed immediately to recognize and give fuller weight to the many echoes of and allusions to Jesus tradition in the letters of Paul, James, and 1 Peter, not to mention the Didache and others of the apostolic fathers.[50] We are freed, that is, to recognize that they too were part of the stream of theologizing that sprang forth from the mission of Jesus. The Paul who simply absorbs Jesus' teaching into his own paraenesis shows us one facet of the theologizing process.[51] But so also does the Paul who finds it necessary to *elaborate* the tradition of Jesus' teaching on divorce (1 Cor 7:10-16) and to *disregard* Jesus' teaching on the support which apostles like him could expect (1 Cor 9:14-18). The flow of oral tradition was not transformed without remainder when the written Gospels were produced, nor did it dry up because the written Gospels made the oral tradition dispensable. It was too much alive to be fixed so finally in particular writings. At the same time, we need to recognize that the particular written expressions that became the canonical Gospels did thus come to function as determinants of the type and extent of diversity that the Jesus tradition could express and tolerate without becoming something else—the Gospel of Thomas being deemed a divergence too far. But that should not prevent us from proper recognition of the rich and living character of the theologizing that remained within the accepted boundaries—John's Gospel being the obvious case in point of one who "sailed close to the wind."

It is precisely the character of the Jesus tradition as we see it in the NT writings (and beyond) that makes it so important to see the Jesus tradition as integral to NT theology. For *it is the Jesus tradition, in the diversity of its presentation in all four Gospels, and in the mostly hiddenness of its substructural influence on the theology of the other NT writings, which highlights dimensions of NT theology that we dare not ignore.* For as the Jesus tradition was not a fixed artifact that subsequent writers observed clinically and described scientifically, but a living tradition that they shaped even as it shaped them, so the writer of a NT theology has to maintain a sense of the movement and interactive character of all the subject matter. Otherwise NT theology assumes the character of a clinical pathology that deals only with cadavers.

4. THE EXPERIENCE OF THE SPIRIT

The Christian doctrine of the Trinity underscores the fact that the first Christian theologians did not simply collapse or subsume all previously recognized modes of God's revelation into the revelation of Jesus Christ; that would have been to adopt a more binitarian model. The Spirit of God remained for them a characteristic mode of divine revelation, correlated with the revelation of and through Christ of course ("the Spirit of Christ") but still distinct, and a crucial correlative factor in determining NT theology. It is important, therefore, that its distinctiveness be recognized and given appropriate emphasis.[52]

A. The Impact of Pentecost

If the revelation that God had raised Jesus from the dead was the primary determinative impulse to the new movement that emerged after the death of Jesus and became Christianity, a second is well indicated by the account in Acts 2 of the outpouring of the Spirit at Pentecost. Luke's account probably reflects in a fair degree the event of what has sometimes been referred to as "the first mass ecstasy" in the beginnings of Christianity.[53] Whether or not that is a satisfactory historical description, the fact remains that experience of the Spirit, or experiences attributed to the Spirit of God, the Holy Spirit, were a central feature of the first Christian congregations. So much so, and evidently of such intensity, that a story like that of Pentecost (Acts 2:1-11), had it not already existed, would have had to be created in order to express the depth and intensity of these experiences. We need only think of such passages in Paul's letters as Rom 8:15-16 and Gal 3:1-5 for the point to become clear—or elsewhere of Heb 2:4, John 4:14, and 7:39. And we certainly should not forget John's own unique take on the gift of the Spirit from the crucified-and-risen Christ, "the Johannine Pentecost."[54] It has always struck me as of particular significance that the nearest Paul comes to a definition of a Christian is in terms of "having the Spirit": "Anyone who does not have the Spirit of Christ does not belong to him" (Rom 8:9). For Paul in particular, the gift of the Spirit was the beginning of the process of salvation that would climax in the resurrection of the body,[55] the Spirit as the *arrabōn* ("first installment, guarantee") and *aparchē* ("first fruits") of the complete inheritance still to come.[56]

The same is true elsewhere in the NT. It was the renewal or re-emergence of prophecy, in John the Baptist, Jesus, and the first disciples,[57] when the Spirit of prophecy seemed to have long been withdrawn, which demonstrated that the age long expected was now being inaugurated. And certainly it is clear from the Gospel accounts that the Spirit coming upon Jesus was what gave his mission its kick-start (Mark 1:10-11 pars.), just as it was the fact that Jesus performed his exorcisms by the power of the Spirit that demonstrated that the kingdom of God had come upon them (Matt 12:28 par.). Likewise, it was having the Spirit, having been given and having received the Spirit, that was evidently the *sine qua non* of being a Christian, as Luke clearly implies in his accounts of where the Spirit was lacking.[58] In Hebrews the Spirit is the first taste of the powers of the age to come (Heb 6:5-6). And in 1 John one of the key "tests of life," of Christ abiding in the first believers and they in him, is the Spirit he has given them.[59] So the gift of the Spirit was as foundational and determinative for the beginnings of Christianity as was the resurrection of Jesus.[60]

A point that has not been given the weight it should have been given in most histories of Christianity's beginnings, and in the formation of a distinctive Christian theology, is the fact that *the reception of the Spirit was determinative in the expansion of infant Christianity beyond the bounds of Second Temple Judaism.* I will deal with the point in more detail later (#5). However, here it is crucially important to appreciate that it was the wholly unexpected fact that the Spirit had been given to uncircumcised Gentiles, and without any expectation of their being circumcised, which brought about the breakthrough of the Gentile mission. The same gift to Gentile as to Jew was sufficient to convince even skeptical traditionalists that the acceptance of uncircumcised Gentiles was God's will.[61] If it is true that Christianity would not have begun without the resurrection of Jesus, *it is equally true that Christianity would have not become a religion for non-Jews without the outpouring of the Spirit.*[62]

Not least of importance was the fact that these experiences could be identified with what several of the prophets had prophesied for the advent of the age to come. The account in Acts 2 sees the Pentecost experience as fulfillment of Joel's prophecy: that "in the last days it will be, God declares, that I will pour out my Spirit upon all flesh. . . ."[63] The talk of the Spirit being "poured out" elsewhere in the NT implies a wider knowledge of the Joel prophecy and claim to its fulfilment.[64] The obviously deliberate echoes of other famous S/spirit prophecies[65] in 2 Cor 3:3, and 1 Thess 4:8 make the same point. Somewhat differently, 1 Pet 1:10-12 links together the ancient prophecies inspired by the Spirit with the good news inspired by the same Holy Spirit now being proclaimed. Again differently, the description of Jesus breathing the Holy Spirit on his disciples, with the words, "Receive the Holy Spirit" (John 20:22), is another deliberate echo, noticeably both of the description of the first breath of life (Gen 2:7) and of the means by which Ezekiel's prophecy brought life to the dead bones of the house of Israel (Ezek. 37:5-10).[66] And of course, a central belief regarding Jesus was that he was the one anointed by the Spirit of God, as Isa 61:1-2 had predicted.[67] Here again we may deduce that without such a vivid correlation between such key scriptural prophecies and their actual experience, the infant Christian movement would have been unable to sustain its belief that it was a fulfillment of Israel's hopes.

Integral in all this, of course, was the conviction that it was by the Spirit that the correct interpretation of the scriptures was possible. In the key passage on the subject (2 Corinthians 3) Paul sets the life-giving power of the Spirit over against the death-dispensing effect of the old covenant taken at a surface level (the visible "letter") (3:3-6); and then he goes on to expound Exodus 34 to the effect that only when one turns to the Spirit ("the Lord, the Spirit") is the veil removed, the veil that prevents the appropriate understanding of the significance of the old covenant (3:12-18). What 2 Peter indicated was no doubt a conviction generally held within earliest Christianity, that to properly interpret scripture it was necessary to be granted the same inspiration as had first produced the prophecy (2 Pet 1:21). As a more general principle, it was the gift of the Spirit, Paul maintained, which enabled the first believers to understand the gifts bestowed on them by God, to interpret spiritual truths and to discern the will of God and the things that matter.[68]

So the gift of the Spirit is a if not *the dynamic factor* in the beginnings of Christianity. As such, it was as foundational and determinative for NT theology as the revelation of Jesus Christ.

B. The Importance of Experience

Too little appreciated is the further fact, already implicit, that when we speak of the Spirit in biblical theology, we are speaking in the first instance about *experience*. Before ever the Spirit was a subject of belief, let alone a dogma, the Spirit was a fact of experience.[69] The original term *ruach* denotes the breath of life, the life force from God. *Ruach* was conceived as an animating power, analogous to or even continuous with the force of strong wind,[70] a power that could invigorate or be invigorated in exceptional circumstances.[71] Common to the range of usage was evidently the sense of an invisible, mysterious, awful force. The word itself (*ruach*) is onomatopoeic—the sound of the wind. Thus coined, *ruach* became the common deonominator to denote analogous experiences of mysterious, otherly power, including a sense of the numinous quality of life itself.[72]

This basic sense continues to adhere to the Christian use of the Greek equivalent, *pneuma*—as is reflected in the fact that it too could carry a similar range of meaning. In the NT this is most evident in the wordplay on *pneuma* as "wind" and "Spirit" in John 3:8 and in the "Johannine Pentecost" of John 20:22 referred to above (at note 66). It is not for nothing that the Nicene Creed describes the Spirit as "the Lord and giver of life," picking up characteristic language of the NT.[73]

The basically experiential character of biblical pneumatology deserves more emphasis than it has traditionally been given. In Christian tradition it has become customary to think of the gift of the Spirit as a deduction to be drawn from a confession or from a properly administered sacrament. In dogmatic treatments of the Holy Spirit it has often been regarded as sufficient to discourse on the themes of the divinity, personality, and procession of the Spirit, as though little more needed to be said on the subject. But for a NT theologian that simply will not do. The Spirit as first experienced, with the experience then reflected upon, is much more the pattern for NT writers and their theology.[74]

Although the Gospels do not present the descent of the Spirit on Jesus as an experience of Jesus, such is implied by Mark's description (Mark 1:10-11). The Gospels do not hesitate to describe the events following in terms of almost ecstatic experience: "the Spirit drove him out into the wilderness."[75] And the account of Jesus' casting out demons by the Spirit of God similarly implies a self-consciousness on the part of Jesus that marked off his exorcisms from those of other Jews (Matt 12:27-28).

The experiential character of the reception of the Spirit is particularly marked in Acts—the regular feature of glossolalia and inspired prophetic speech giving evidence of the Spirit's presence.[76] Luke certainly understood the coming of the Spirit as an event in individuals' lives that they could not be unaware of or mistake (19:2). It is the same with Paul: "Did you receive the Spirit by doing what the law demands or by hearing with faith?" (Gal 3:2, 5). The impact of the Spirit was evidently often marked by visible effects and moral outworking. Hebrews and 1 John evidently thought in the same terms.[77] Paul often mentions the powerfully affective impact of the Spirit in and through his preaching[78] and various emotions that the Spirit stirred within his converts: love (Rom 5:5), joy (1 Thess 1:6), love, joy, peace... (Gal 5:22).[79] The regular experience of the Spirit crying "Abba! Father!" in early Christian worship was evidently rather intense.[80]

Particularly noticeable is the typical use of water imagery in reference to the Spirit, wholly understandable in a Middle East context—the Spirit experienced as a rainstorm on a parched land, as a draught of cool water quenching a raging thirst.[81] John makes great play of the imagery in John 4:14—the experience of fresh water quenching thirst, as of a spring of water bubbling up as it were in people (John 4:10, 14), subsequently identified explicitly with the reception of the Spirit (7:37-39). And Paul draws on the same imagery in 1 Corinthians: what united the believers as one was the experience of being given to drink, as it were, of the same Spirit (1 Cor 12:13).

To draw attention to such features of the NT witness can make some people uneasy.[82] The history of Christianity, as of religion generally, is littered with examples where emotions have been given free rein with disastrous consequences. The dangers of "enthusiasm" (Schwärmerei) have been appreciated in western Christianity since the excesses of the spiritual or radical Reformation, and are still evident today in various sects.[83] From a historical and NT perspective, however, two things need to be appreciated. One is that earliest Christianity, certainly as attested by Luke and witnessed to in part at least by Paul, had an enthusiastic character itself. An element of "enthusiasm" is inescapable within the NT, and should therefore be regarded as part of the data with which a NT theology has to wrestle.[84] The other is that Paul, arguably the most experienced and most perceptive in this area of all the NT writers, shows himself well aware of the dangers of giving way to the impulses of enthusiasm. The care he took in his treatment of ta pneumatika, "the things of the Spirit," or specifically "spiritual gifts," to warn against such excesses[85] and to underscore the priority of love, of contributions that addressed the head as well as the heart (1 Corinthians 13 and 14), should be a salutary reminder to all who are inclined to follow uncritically Luke's portrayal of the earliest Christian mission.[86]

In fact NT biblical theology will always find itself caught in what should be a creative tension but is frequently a dispiriting or even destructive tension. I refer to the tension between a certain hard-headedness, which is the heritage of the priority given by the Enlightenment to objectivity and dispassionate scrutiny of data, and a desire to feel again the inspiration and emotion of the singer or the poet, of the song or the poem, which is the heritage of the Romantic Revival. For myself, the tension can be entirely creative: there is no reason why a musical performance should not display both technical expertise and the deep passion that the music stirs up. Without the former the performance would be unsatisfactory; but without the latter even a technically efficient performance could never be wholly satisfying.

The point I am making is that the NT bears eloquent witness to the formative and transformative effect of what we may describe simply as "religious experience."[87] To be clear on the point, I do not want to argue for a simple process in theologizing, as *from* experience *to* theology. I am fully aware that there is no such thing as a "pure" religious experience, that, for example, the conceptualization of an experience as a "religious experience" already presupposes a degree of traditioning that shapes even what we perceive as happening to or in ourselves. My point is simply that there was an experiential and emotive dimension (or dimensions) in the beginnings of Christianity that contributed to and was part of the self-understanding, social evaluation and theologizing that emerged as Christianity. It was almost certainly the *experience* of the preaching about Jesus as "good news'"(*euangelion*, "gospel") and as "grace" (*charis*) that caused Paul to draw these words from other usage and to give them the weight and force that they have enjoyed in Christian thought ever since.[88] The experience was not constrained by or limited to earlier usage but could find adequate expression only in such terms freshly minted. It is that crafting of new speech forms, the quickening of senses to fresh awareness, the opening of eyes to different horizons, to which the NT bears testimony, and to which the NT is itself testimony.[89] And that fresh impulse, the "new creation" dimension of the NT perspective and writings, no NT theology can afford to lose.

5. THE CENTRAL SUBJECT MATTER OF A BIBLICAL THEOLOGY OF THE NT

How, then, to go about the task of writing or doing NT theology? As already noted, it would be quite possible to follow the dominant pattern of NT theologies of the last fifty years and examine each NT writing or group of NT writings in sequence.[90] And if the subject matter was a single theme, christology, soteriology, ecclesiology, ethics, that would be a sensible way to proceed. But if what has already been said is valid, then it follows that the structure and content of any NT biblical theology will be decided by the way the questions of continuity-discontinuity and unity-diversity are handled. And in this introduction to the subject of NT theology within a biblical theology framework I want to focus on *the themes that provide the most demanding challenge to a NT biblical theology.* That means identifying the central features of the religion and traditions of Israel/Second Temple Judaism, or if it be preferred, the key distinctive features of OT theology, and analyzing how the NT writers handle them, interact with them or transform them.

I suggest that these central features and key distinctives can be grouped under four heads—a variation of what I refer to elsewhere as "the four pillars of Second Temple Judaism."[91] For the purposes of this volume, these are

1. God: God as one
2. Salvation: how God saves
3. Israel: the elect nation
4. Torah: how the people of God should live

The fundamental issue for a NT biblical theology is whether the message of Jesus or the gospel about Jesus introduced a radical disjuncture with these central features of what we may fairly call Israel's biblical theology.

One of the interesting and important features that became increasingly apparent to me as I drafted the following chapters was just how integrated all four themes were—and are. God, the one God, creator of the cosmos and the nations, has committed himself to be Israel's God, to save and sustain Israel as his people, and has given them the Torah to show them how they should live as his people. This means that none of the themes can be treated in isolation from the rest, as we shall see. More to the point, it means that any disruption that the NT brings to one of the themes is bound to have repercussions on the rest. Can, for example, continuity be maintained in the first two if it is broken in either of the last two?—if God's covenant with Israel has been superseded or is irrelevant to the church(es) of the NT, or if the law no longer applies to Christians and obedience to the law is no longer relevant to the final judgment of believers in Messiah Jesus? A NT biblical theology simply cannot duck or avoid such questions. On the contrary, they form the major items on the agenda of any NT theology set within the framework of biblical theology.

These four themes form the agenda for the other volumes in the sequence of the Library of Biblical Theology, with three volumes dedicated to each theme (OT, NT, and systematic theology). Consequently in this introductory volume, having posed the problems and indicated the factors that determine the NT theologizing on these themes, my primary concern is to review some of the basic data and pose the questions that will call for fuller discussion in the subsequent volumes.

THE THEOLOGY OF GOD

1. INTRODUCTION

The most obvious opening theme, if not the principal theme for any theology is *God*. Theology is first and foremost *theo-logy*. This is not simply because the term theology means in the first instance, "talk about God." Nor, in the case of NT theology, is it because the NT writers focus much of their attention on God, or write at great lengths in defense of belief in God, far less that they speculate extensively about God's being and nature. It is rather because *God is the basic presupposition in all they say*, the axiom on which all their propositions, teachings, and exhortations depend, the foundation on which everything else is built, the first principle from which everything else follows.

In point of fact, "God" (*ho theos*) is the most frequently occurring noun to be used in the NT, surpassed only by personal pronouns, particles, and one or two common prepositions and conjunctions. "God" in effect forms the warp with many other themes forming the weft in the tapestry being woven by the NT writers. It is not possible to appreciate or to begin to understand the theology of the NT without taking into account the writers' beliefs about God and the consequences that they drew from these beliefs. One need consider only the language of the letter openings and the various doxologies that appear in the letters.[1] These should not be regarded as mere formalities, as though they were similar to the use of *God* in the exclamations (and swearing) of so many today who never darken the door of a church or mosque or synagogue. Rather such prayers and doxologies express the instinctive habits of a vibrant piety that informed and determined daily living.

The inexplicit character of the NT writers' beliefs in and about God helps explain why so many expositions of NT theology or the theologies of individual NT writers so often forego a section on God and jump at once into other aspects, often an analysis of the human condition.[2] But it is imperative that a NT theology tackle this subject and make explicit the inexplicit; otherwise the rationale underpinning so many other beliefs and practices will have been lost to view. Without an appreciation of the axiom, the consequent propositions will lack persuasiveness. Without an awareness of the foundation, the logic of the superstructures will be unclear, and the superstructures will seem all the less secure.

Here more than anywhere else in NT theology we need to be aware that the NT writers have simply taken over what was more explicitly expressed in the OT. It is because the NT writers simply assumed the faith of their fathers,[3] and could assume that for the most part these assumptions were equally axiomatic for their audiences, that they evidently felt it unnecessary to spell out these beliefs afresh.[4] Here NT theology in large part is indeed a subset of biblical theology. One can only write the *theo-logy* of the NT writers by referring their presuppositions back to the OT and filling them out from the OT. Even where the NT writers go beyond the scribes and sages whose writings make up the Hebrew Bible and LXX, the full significance of what the NT writers say can only be filled out by referring to that which they have gone beyond. And always the question has to be, whether what the NT writers say about God simply develops what was being developed anyway within the Hebrew Bible and LXX (and beyond in the "inter-testamental" literature), or whether they were so changing the terms of Israel's *theo-logy* as to make it into something else.

The *theo-logical* givens inherited by the NT can be briefly reviewed under six heads:

A. God as Creator and Judge
B. God as one
C. The God of Israel
D. God as transcendent and immanent (Spirit)
E. Angelic intermediaries
F. God's wisdom/word

The major factor that enters into the biblical *theo-logy* and begins to transform it is, of course, *the Christ event,* that is, the mission of Jesus, and what was believed to have happened to him on Good Friday and immediately thereafter, at Easter. A NT *theo-logy* must, therefore, include consideration of the impact made by Jesus—an impact that can be measured to a considerable degree by considering some of the key titles by which the first Christians used for him and some of the language and imagery they drew upon to make sense of what they believed had happened to him and what he embodied:

A.   Teacher and prophet
B.   Messiah
C.   Son of Man
D.   Son of God
E.   Lord
F.   Wisdom/word of God
G.   The worship of Jesus

The reason above all why christology becomes fundamental and central to Christian *theo-logy* is that Jesus is seen from very early on within embryonic Christianity not only as the bearer of God's revelation, the spokesman for God, but as uniquely the revelation of God's love and commitment to his saving purpose, not only as revelation *from* God but as the revelation *of* God.[5] In what follows, then, I will not be concerned simply to outline either a complete *theo-logy* or a complete christology, but will focus attention on the challenge of making sense of Jesus (christology) in relation to *theo-logy.*

2. THE INHERITED *THEO-LOGY*

A. God as Creator and Judge

The concept of creation and of a creator, or at least of a divine architect, could easily hold its place within the spectrum of Greco-Roman religion and philosophy. Plato's *Timaeus* was a fundamental text in Greek intellectual thought,[6] and Philo's portrayal of creation in *De Opificio Mundi* was heavily influenced by middle Platonic thought.[7] Paul also shows no inhibitions in taking up what, in terms of usage, was a typically

Stoic formulation—of the cosmos as "from," "through," and "to"—as in Rom 11:36, 1 Cor 8:6, and Col 1:16-17.[8]

However, the principal influence on the NT writers came undoubtedly from the Hebrew Bible's depiction of God as creator, evident, for example, in the direct influence of the creation narratives of Genesis 1–2 in passages like John 1:1-4, Col 1:15-18, and Heb 1:2-3.[9] The Jewish understanding of *creatio ex nihilo* (creation out of nothing) is clearly reflected in the description of God as "he who calls things that have no existence into existence" (Rom 4:17). And Paul it is again who draws directly on the image, so familiar from Jeremiah in particular, of the divine potter making different vessels for different uses (Rom 9:19-22).[10] Likewise the concept of the breath or Spirit of God giving (new) life to the human form[11] draws directly on the second creation narrative and Gen 2:7 in particular.[12] We should also probably recognize a distinctively Jewish influence in Paul's exclusive use of *ktizō/ktisis* ("create/creation") for the act and fact of *divine* creation, reflecting the same exclusiveness as in the Bible's use of the Hebrew *bara'* ("create"),[13] in contrast to the less discriminating usage of Greek thought.[14]

Even more striking is the more *positive* Hebrew understanding of creation, that is, of the physical and material, than in the characteristic Greek disparagement of the material, expressed classically in the tag *sōma sēma* ("the body is a tomb [of the soul]") and in the much-quoted saying of Empedocles about "the alien garb of the flesh."[15] Here the contrast with Genesis 1's repeated appraisal of each stage of creation, "And God saw that it was good,"[16] is noteworthy. An integral feature of Paul's anthropology, too little appreciated, is the degree to which his concept of the "body" (*sōma*) reflects this more typically positive evaluation of the created body: he distinguishes "body" from "flesh," *sōma* from *sarx*,[17] piles the more negative (Greek) overtones on the latter, and insists that believers may look forward to a resurrected *sōma*, the "spiritual body" of resurrection (1 Cor 15:44-46).[18] Despite Genesis 3, humankind is still the image of God (1 Cor 11:7), and 1 Timothy speaks for most of the other NT writers in affirming that "Everything created by God is good" (1 Tim 4:4). In turn, the story of Adam's disobedience, although determining a more pessimistic assessment of the human condition,[19] does not draw the NT writers' evaluation of the created order toward the negativity of Greek anthropology, but simply underlines the degree to which the earliest Christian theologizing worked within the framework determined by the OT. The corollaries for a responsible attitude towards creation need to be drawn out in a full biblical theology.[20]

Also distinctive of Jewish *theo-logy* was the belief in a *divine purpose*, in Jewish apocalyptic thought a purpose hidden from the ages, but now revealed to the prophetic seer.[21] The motif is taken up in the Jesus tradition's talk of "the mystery of the kingdom" (Mark 4:11 pars.), and particularly in Paul's claim that the mystery of the divine purpose was his intention to include the Gentiles within the promised blessing of Abraham.[22] That this purpose would climax in a *day of judgment* was also characteristically and distinctively Jewish. The idea of divine judgment itself was familiar in Greek thought, but particularly prominent in the Jewish tradition,[23] and the last day as a "day of judgment,"[24] or a "day of wrath,"[25] were themes again taken up by Paul but also other NT writers.[26] The fullest exposition of the theme, in Rom 2:1-16, is notable in that it takes as axiomatic two principles enunciated in the OT: that God "will render to each according to his works" (2:6),[27] and that "there is no partiality with God" (2:11).[28]

B. God as One

The basic Jewish creed was (and is) the *Shema,* the confession of divine unity: "Hear O Israel: The Lord our God is one Lord" or "the Lord our God, the Lord is one" (Deut 6:4).[29] On the basis of Deut 6:7, a devout Jew, such as Jesus and Paul, would have said the *Shema* twice a day. Similarly the decalogue, the most basic statement of Jewish obligations, begins with the unequivocal charge: "You shall have no other gods beside or before me" (Exod 20:3). In a full-scale biblical theology, concerned with tracing the diachronic development of this fundamental belief, we would have to discuss how Jewish monotheism emerged, and whether, in particular, it was only a post-exilic development.[30] For a NT theology, however, it is sufficient to know that in the first century C.E. the affirmation that "God is one" was a universal creed for all Jews,[31] and that it was a firm presupposition inherited by the first Christians.[32]

The evidence is direct on this point. Jesus is recalled responding to the question as to which is the first commandment by citing the *Shema* in full (Mark 12:28-30), and, when tempted, refusing to worship Satan by citing the sequel to the giving of the *Shema*: "you shall worship the Lord your God and him alone shall you serve."[33] The center and burden of his message was the kingdom of God.[34] Paul draws one of his major gospel principles directly from the *Shema* (Rom 3:29-30), and other references show

how central Israel's creedal affirmation continued to be for his theology too.[35] And James equally takes it for granted that "God is one" (Jas 2:19).

Tied into this axiom was the conviction that God is *invisible*, or, more precisely, *un-image-able* (Exod 20:4) and unlookable-on (Exod 33:20).[36] Hence the implacable hostility in early Judaism to idolatry, already classically expressed in Isa 44:9-20, the Wisdom of Solomon 11–15, and the Epistle of Jeremiah.[37] Paul here again shows how deeply these convictions were rooted in his own theology and how unremitting was his own continuing condemnation of idolatry: "flee from idolatry" (1 Cor 10:14).[38] At this point the portrayal of Paul's hostile reaction to the idolatry evident in Athens (a "city full of idols"—Acts 17:16,29) is borne out by his indictment of human idolatry in Rom 1:23 and his delight in recalling how the Thessalonians had "turned to God from idols" (1 Thess 1:9). The invisibility of God is equally a given for Paul,[39] and the insistence of the Johannine prologue that "no one has ever seen God" (John 1:18) is characteristically and distinctively Jewish through and through.[40]

Whether the English term *monotheism* expresses adequately the Jewish belief in God as one has recently been debated,[41] and a degree of reserve is called for before declaring that Israel's was a monotheistic faith *simpliciter*.[42] This caution is not simply a consequence of the Christian qualification of Israel's monotheism as "christological monotheism," a subject crucial in any serious attempt to unfold the NT *theo-logy*.[43] As we shall see, the issue also arises within the framework of Israel's monotheism itself.[44] But let us proceed one step at a time.

C. The God of Israel

No less fundamental to the convictions inherited by the first Christians was the axiomatic belief that *God had chosen Israel to be his own*. This was a major part of the offence of Jewish monotheism: that Yahweh was not simply the national manifestation of the supreme God such as *all* peoples could claim for themselves.[45] On the contrary, Israel alone had been given the true perception of God, because the one God had given Israel the special revelation of himself through the patriarchs and because out of all the nations God had taken only Israel for himself. Similar claims for the favored status of their own city or state were familiar in Greek and Roman history, but Israel's universalistic monotheism gave their claim a distinctive character: the God of all the nations had chosen Israel to be his own (Deut 32:8-9). It is more appropriate to develop this point in #5 below, particularly the tension between Israel's particularism (God as the God of Israel) and its universalism (the one God creator of all), and the consequences for NT theology. Here we simply pause to note that where the tension becomes most explicit in the NT it is seen as a *theo-logical* problem. Is God God of the Jews only? Or is he also God of the Gentiles, with a similar concern for them? In his most thorough treatment of the issue (Romans 9–11) Paul attempts to square the circle by integrating his own commission to the Gentiles (11:13) into his hope and conviction that all Israel will be saved (11:11-16, 25-26). What is striking is that he sees the issue to be one of the faithfulness of God (3:3-4): Israel's rejection of the gospel is an issue precisely because God's call of Israel is "irrevocable" (11:29); the word of God cannot have failed (9:6).[46]

D. God as Transcendent and Immanent (Spirit)

One of NT theology's most obvious take-overs from Second Temple Judaism's *theo-logy* has been Israel's conception and understanding of *the Spirit of God*. NT writers do not have to explain that God has or is a spirit; John 4:24 ("God is a spirit") is more an appeal to first principles than an explanation. The confident assumption when the Spirit of God is spoken of is that audiences will know what is being referred to, not only from their own experience—that certainly[47]—but also from their knowledge of Jewish convictions on the subject. Their experience of the divine Spirit could be simply assumed to be experiences of the Spirit of the one God, creator and God of Israel. What should be noticed here, however, is that part of the heritage was the recognition that to speak of God's Spirit was to speak of *God*, God in his outreach to his creation and people.

So far as we can tell, Israel's theologians and sages were conscious from early days of *the otherness of God*. Hence the refusal to countenance any image of God, the insistence on the invisibility of God, and the insistence equally that God was not like and did not act like human beings.[48] The word that perhaps best expresses this fundamental instinct of Israel's *theo-logy* is *transcendent*. Yahweh was a god like no other. The term actually used by Israel's writers was "holy," a word indicating the otherness of God, marking the qualitative difference and distance between the creator and his creation, and signaled by the frequent reference to the holiness of God's name; "Yahweh's holy name contrasts with everything creaturely."[49] God's holiness means that any place to which he attaches himself is itself holy,[50] and any infringement of that holiness, of that wholly otherness of God by mere mortals was likely to be fatal.[51]

At the same time, the same writers had no doubt that God was also *immanent*. The term that came to express most frequently this active presence of God in creation and in his human creation in particular was *spirit*. The Spirit of God was the presence of God throughout the world: "Where shall I go from your spirit? Or where can I flee from your presence?" (Ps 139:7).[52] God had acted to create; God had shaped the dust of the earth to form man (Gen 2:7); it was God's breath breathed into the nostrils of the clay man that provided him with, which *was* for him the breath of life (Gen 2:7). The spirit of God was the creative force in creation,[53] the spirit of God the life-force within animal as well as human,[54] in pointed contrast to the idol.[55] The fact that the Hebrew *ruach* had a range of meaning from "(storm-)wind," through "breath" to "s/Spirit" was not simply a literary curiosity or coincidence.[56] Rather it expressed the experience of the ancient Hebrews of a life-force both visible in creation and bubbling up within them that they could only explain both as given by God and as a manifestation of the divine within the human.

Characteristic (though again not distinctive) of Israel's religion was the experience of particular individuals especially equipped by this more-than-human life force. In its early history this was recalled as true of various charismatic leaders, like Gideon, Samson, and Saul, Israel's first king.[57] The fact that such leaders need not be distinguished for their high morality heightened the non-rational and even amoral character of such experiences of enhanced power.[58] Even more characteristic was the recognition of certain individuals, by no means always of high social status, as prophets, as inspired by God and given access to the divine council.[59] Highly noteworthy is the fact that the two central planks of Israel's scriptures are the Torah and the Prophets. So central to and characteristic was prophecy in shaping Israel's religion that the Spirit of God came to be understood most typically as "the spirit of prophecy."[60]

It is hardly surprising, then, that central and integral to the beginnings of Christianity are the claims made concerning the Spirit. It can be simply stated, but stated as a key to appreciating the significance of Jesus' mission, that he had been anointed by the Spirit, and therefore did and was able to do what he did.[61] The account of Christianity's beginning with the outpouring of the Spirit (at Pentecost) is explicit only in Acts 2 but in effect is assumed everywhere else in the regular appeals made to the believers' experience of the Spirit.[62] Central to their understanding of their experience as experience of God's Spirit is the claim that this had happened in fulfillment of the prophets' expectation of an outpouring of the Spirit "in the last days," explicit again in Acts 2:17-18, but once again presupposed elsewhere.[63] More striking is the degree to which the Spirit's power has been recognized to have an integrally ethical quality; in the NT the Spirit is regularly described as "the Holy Spirit."[64]

Most striking of all is the way in which the Spirit is *correlated with Jesus*. The revelation experienced by the first Christians through Jesus and in relation to Jesus is nowhere allowed to become something independent of Israel's understanding of God active in his world and his people in and through his Spirit. It is not simply, as already noted, that Jesus' mission was regarded as inspired by God's Spirit. More than that, the character of the Spirit comes to be perceived more clearly through (and as) the character of the mission that the Spirit inspired in Jesus. As the first Adam became "a living soul," so Christ, the last Adam, in his resurrection became "life-giving Spirit" (1 Cor 15:45).[65] The Spirit is to be recognized precisely now as "the Spirit of Jesus" (Acts 16:7), "the Spirit of Christ,"[66] "the Spirit of God's Son" (Gal 4:6). In John's Gospel the Spirit (Paraclete) is to be in effect the presence of the absent Christ.[67] In view of the way the NT writers took over the other modes used by Israel's sages to express the nearness of God, as we shall see, the claims implied here move beyond mere rhetorical flourish.

E. Angelic Intermediaries

The tension between conceiving God as both transcendent and immanent was present in Israel's *theo-logy* from the first. And, confusingly, it was wrapped up with the ambiguity integral to some of the early talk of God. Early Christian attempts to formulate a Trinitarian understanding of God made much of the plural in Gen 1:27 ("Let us make humankind in our image") and the account of the three heavenly visitors to Abraham in Genesis 18.[68] But later theology has made more of the different names used of God—El Elyon, Elohim (plural!), and particularly YHWH (Exod 3:13-16), with the explanation of Exod 6:3, that "I appeared to (the patriarchs) as El Shaddai, but by my name YHWH I did not make myself known to them." In recent years such passages have been the basis of challenges made to the belief that Israel was a monotheistic religion,[69] but that probably gives too little credit to the theological acumen of even the early Hebrew theologians.

What I have in view is already evident in Israel's early *angelology*—angels being understood to be messengers from God (Heb, *mal'ach*;

Greek, *angelos*), and particularly in the early Hebrew talk of "the angel of the Lord."[70] For the language used indicates a degree of ambivalence between the angel of the Lord and God himself. For example, Hagar, having encountered the angel of the Lord, exclaims: "Have I really seen God and remained alive after seeing him?" (Gen 16:13). In Jacob's dream the angel of God says, "I am the God of Bethel" (31:11-13). And in Judg 2:1 the angel of God says, "I brought you up from the land of Egypt.... I will never break my covenant with you." The ambivalence arises, presumably, not because the early Israelites' understanding of God was confused, but because they wanted to express the reality of God's presence and communion with favored individuals without detracting from his otherness. An angelic messenger who could wholly represent God and express the will of God fully and intimately was as good a solution as they were able to come up with. Similarly the conception of the heavenly council, of God supported by a range of "the (angelic) sons of God," such as we find in Job 1–2, was no doubt primarily a way of highlighting the uniquely exalted status of God by means of the less than perfect parallel of the oriental monarch surrounded by an extensive and expensive court of officials and advisers.

The same is basically true in regard to early Judaism's subsequent burgeoning angelology, and not least of the emergence of archangels and supreme angels, like Michael and Gabriel, "the angels of the presence."[71] For example, in the DSS, Melchizedek seems to be depicted as a heavenly figure among the Elohim (11QMelch). And in *Apoc. Ab.* 10 an interpreter angel Jaoel is described as "a power in virtue of the ineffable name that is dwelling in me" (referring to Exod 23:21). Here too there was the possibility, for the visionary, of confusing such a glorious heavenly being with God himself.[72] But that was in large part because the range of language to describe such glorious visionary beings was itself limited. And the writers typically hasten to refute any suggestion of confusion. For example, in *Apoc. Zeph.* 6:15 the angel says, "Take heed. Do not worship me. I am not the Lord Almighty, but I am the great angel, Eremiel." And in *Apoc. Ab.* 17 "the angel knelt down with me [the apocalyptist] and worshipped" (17:2). So here again, the best way to appreciate what such language was intended to do, is probably to conclude that these were ways both of stressing God's involvement (through his emissaries) in the world of the visionary, and of highlighting the awesome otherness of God, by depicting even his messengers and angelic agents in as glorious terms as vision and language allowed.

When similar language is used by the Christian apocalypse (Revelation) the same possibility of confusion is evident and is indeed heightened (cf. Rev 1:13-14; 10:1)—a fact that makes the apocalypse of John one of the most intriguing texts for NT biblical theo-logy.[73]

F. God's Wisdom/word

Other means by which the immanence of God was experienced include God's *name*, as just instanced (Exod 23:21), the name representing the very person of God. God's awesome presence was also indicated by his *glory*, the shudderingly awe-ful manifestation of his holiness. And subsequently the rabbis found in the reference to the Shekinah a more fruitful way of speaking of the divine presence.[74] But the most sophisticated of early Jewish attempts to speak of God's dealings, in creation, revelation, and redemption, without actually speaking of God as such, was probably the concept of God's *wisdom*, and, alternatively, of God's *word*. In the conceptualization of a divine force present and active throughout the world, sustaining the world and its order, the thought was similar to the Stoic understanding of the same divine reason both as the divine tissue of the world's being and as implanted within man.[75] But again the Jewish conceptuality had its distinctive features.

The earliest developed expression is found in Prov 8:12-31. In Proverbs the wisdom essential to sensible and successful living is depicted as a beautiful lady, the Jewish alternative, probably, to the enticing attractions of Astarte (Prov 1–9).[76] But in the poem of Proverbs 8 the personal terms used of "wisdom" are taken further: Lady Wisdom speaks in "I" language; she reflects on her role in guiding kings, her creation as "the first of (God's) acts," "before the beginning of the earth"; and she ends the poem by likening herself to "a master-worker" (or "little child") at God's side when the heavens and the earth were made (8:30-31). And this vivid representation is taken further in a further hymn of self-praise in Sir 24:3-22: "I came forth from the mouth of the Most High ... I dwelt in the highest heavens... I grew tall like a cedar of Lebanon" and like other fruit-bearing trees and bushes. Similarly, though in third person terms, in Bar 3:9-37. What is particularly striking is that in the Wisdom of Solomon it is to Wisdom that the acts of God are attributed, from Abel onwards and including the divine enactment of the exodus and throughout the wilderness wanderings (Wisdom 10–11).

There is sustained debate as to the status of this figure of divine wisdom. Does this provide further proof that Israel's monotheism embraced more than one person or personality? Is Wisdom a second divine being,[77] or does she fill an intermediate status best described as a "hypostasis"?[78] Or is this simply vigorous poetic language to describe the manner in which God has acted in his creative role and particularly in directing his people.[79] My own view is that the last option is the most faithful to what the sages of Israel intended by this language. Their language was poetic and full of imagery; they could press their metaphors beyond what we today might think appropriate.[80] Ben Sira, for example, likens wisdom to a range of fruit-bearing trees. And the Wisdom of Solomon assuredly did not intend to present Wisdom as Israel's savior in any degree of distinction from God as such. In fact, both ben Sira and Baruch make explicit that this very wisdom of God was not just to be found in the Torah, but *was* the Torah: "All this is the book of the covenant of the Most High God..." (Sir 24:23); "She is the book of the commandments of God..." (Bar 4:1). The claim was in effect an apologetic one: that those who desired the wisdom from above required for living as one should, should look no further than Israel's Torah. Here was God's wisdom. *The Torah was no threat to or qualification of Israel's monotheism!*

We should probably think in the same terms of the Word of God. The *logos* was a more common way of speaking of the divine rationality (*logos*) evident in the structure and order of the world and was the more favored term in Greek philosophical reflection on the subject. In Israel's religion it was not so prominent, but it could certainly be used to express Yahweh's agency in creation—naturally, following from the divine *fiat* of Genesis 1 ("God said...")[81]—and so express basically the same thought as elsewhere is expressed in terms of Spirit or Wisdom.[82] Likewise, the thought can embrace the healing word (Ps 107:20); and in Wis 18:14-16 the "powerful word" of God, leaping down from heaven, does the work of the killing angel in the last of Egypt's plagues, equivalent to the protecting Wisdom of the earlier chapters.

The most striking Jewish use of *logos theo-logy* is by Jesus' older contemporary, Philo of Alexandria. Here the vividness and vigor of the metaphor becomes very clear: the Logos can be described as God's "chief messenger, highest in age and honor" (*Heres* 2-5), as "the ruler and steersman of all" (*Cher.* 36), as God's "firstborn Son...like the viceroy of a great king" (*Agr.* 51), and even as "the second God" (*Qu. Gen.* 2:62). But even in this case we should hardly conclude that Philo had abandoned his Jewish monotheism and believed in two gods in heaven.[83] His theologizing is far too profound to be reduced to such simplifications. A more adequate appreciation of his logos *theo-logy* starts with the recognition that *logos* could mean both the unspoken thought and the spoken word—the *logos endiathetos* and the *logos prophorikos*.[84] The point is that while a clear distinction can be made in principle between the thought and the word that expresses it, in reality it is quite hard to do so.[85] So the *logos* can represent the idea or the mind of God, and also the expression of that idea in concrete events. So the *logos* is the mind of God, God in his thinking and intending, and God's enacting of his mind and intention in his dealings with creation and his people (*Mos.* 2:127-129). This also means that to function at the level of the mind, of rationality, of *logos*, is to draw near to God. But Philo also makes clear that to encounter the Logos is not to encounter God as such, the one "who is in very essence God."[86] Here, in other words, we find *the most sophisticated attempt within Second Temple Judaism to maintain the tension between the transcendence and the immanence of God.* The Logos is not God as such, but is the mind of God coming to expression in ways that humans can apprehend. The Logos is not God as such, but to encounter the Logos is to encounter God in his creative, revelatory, and redemptive outreach to his people.

What emerges from all this is the richness of early Judaism's reflection on the ways in which the one God whom they worshiped interacted with his creation and with the people he had chosen to be especially his own. It was not that their ideas were clear cut or wholly consistent with one another. It is rather that their sages and theologians recognized that the immanence of God is a reality that escapes neat formulation and definition. Their search for appropriate language and images was ongoing and still in process when the impact of Jesus began to be felt as an additional factor that some Jews found necessary to include in such reflection.

3. MAKING SENSE OF JESUS (CHRISTOLOGY) IN RELATION TO THEO-LOGY

We will soon see that there are NT passages and language about Jesus that were (subsequently) understood to require some sort of revision or refinement of Israel's understanding of God. But before turning to them we should note the other more obvious (less-controversial?) terms with which Jesus himself operated and in which the significance of Jesus was initially grasped at or became apparent to those who believed in him.

What should not be ignored is that *the language used are precisely the categories and terms already given definition in the scriptures of Israel*. The question, and challenge, of NT christology in relation to biblical theology is whether the significance of Jesus could be sufficiently or wholly grasped by these categories without disturbing the heritage of Israel's conceptualization of God.

A. Teacher and Prophet

There are two titles that were given to Jesus during his mission, and Jesus acknowledged, at least to some extent. These should be noted but, it should also be noted, they did not carry over very far into earliest Christian reflection on Jesus' significance.

The title accorded to him most frequently, if we follow the Gospels themselves, is *teacher*.[87] And there is no doubt whatsoever that Jesus was and was remembered as a highly insightful and memorable teacher, noted both for his aphorisms and parables in particular.[88] Moreover, it is very probable, though disputed, that Jesus' teaching continued to provide guidance for the early Christians in their own relationships and conduct;[89] in particular the wisdom teaching of the letter of James shows how the teaching of Jesus could be and was seen to stand within and in full continuity with Israel's wisdom tradition.[90] Not only so, but in terms of Jewish-Christian relations the thought of Jesus as a Jewish sage or rabbi provides quite an attractive meeting point or starting point for further discussion.[91] The key point for us, however, is that the title is never used for Jesus in the NT outside the Gospels; even for the first Christians, the title *teacher* was simply inadequate to express the significance of his person and his work.[92] So for such a discussion between Jew and Christian to prosper it would soon have to move on.

A second category that was obviously much canvassed during Jesus' own lifetime was *prophet*. This seems to have been the obvious label for those struck by Jesus' mission and trying to define it.[93] Jesus himself evidently thought the category was appropriate to his mission (Mark 6:4 pars). There is a surprising degree of consensus among those engaging in "the quest of the historical Jesus" that in terms of his own mission Jesus is best depicted as the eschatological prophet of Israel's expectation.[94] And there are certainly strong indications that one of the terms initially drawn on to make sense of Jesus was Moses' promise that "the LORD your God will raise up for you a prophet like me from among your own people" (Deut 18:15, 18); most noticeably the passage is cited in reference to

Jesus twice in the sermons of Acts (Acts 3:22; 7:37). Here too one can readily imagine how setting Jesus within the history of Israel's prophets could open a fruitful avenue of dialogue between Christian and Jew, and indeed with Muslim also. But again, elsewhere in the NT itself, the category of prophet seems to have been avoided as less than sufficient for Jesus. For example, Hebrews begins by contrasting God's less adequate revelation through the prophets with the fullness of divine self-manifestation in his Son (Heb 1:1-4); Moses was a servant, Christ a son (3:2-6). And in John's Gospel, "prophet" is presented as an expression of the crowd's inadequate apprehension of who Jesus is (John 6:14, 26), with the bread from heaven given by Moses presented as only a foreshadowing of "the true bread from heaven," Christ himself (6:31-35). That Jesus saw himself as transcending the category of prophet is entirely arguable on the evidence available.[95]

B. Messiah

The name by which Jesus came to be known and now is almost universally attached to the name of Jesus is 'Christ'. 'Christ', from the Greek *christos,* is simply the Greek translation of the Hebrew "messiah" (*mašiah*). *Messiah* means "anointed one" and refers to the evidently widespread Jewish expectation in the three or four centuries around the turn of the years (B.C.E. to C.E., or B.C. to A.D.) that one or more anointed figures would be sent to deliver Israel. Most prominent was the hope of a royal figure, in line of descent from king David. The hope was that the ancient promise given to David would be fulfilled (2 Sam 7:12-16): that David would have a son, who would build the temple that David had desired to build, and that David's house and throne and kingdom would be established forever. The hope had been maintained in the dark days leading to and through Judah's exile to Babylon,[96] and revived in the two centuries before Jesus' appearance. The most obvious manifestation of it was in *Pss. Sol.* 17:21-24 and in the expectations that featured in the Qumran community, for whom the prophecy of 2 Sam 7:14 remained a fervent hope.[97]

It is sufficiently clear from the Jesus tradition that the possibility of Jesus fulfilling the role of the anointed son of David was canvassed during his life, though whether Jesus himself accepted the title for himself, given its popular connotations, is less clear.[98] It is virtually certain, however, that Jesus was condemned to death and executed by the Roman authorities as a messianic pretender, one who claimed to be "king of the

Jews" and who might therefore be presented to the authorities as posing a threat to Roman rule.[99] This is more likely than the alternative thesis that Jesus only came to be regarded as Messiah after his death. The latter is given some credibility by Acts 2:36: the resurrection made Jesus both Lord and Christ. But the former provides a more coherent explanation for Jesus' execution than any other. And there is no obvious reason why the first believers would have concluded that a crucified leader was messiah otherwise. Whereas, it was presumably the difficulty in reconciling the pre-Easter claim that Jesus was (or even might be) God's Messiah with what then happened to him (crucifixion) that caused the first believers to search the scriptures afresh, there to find substantial evidence that suffering would be the lot of the anointed one.[100]

What is very striking about the NT evidence at this point is that the title "Messiah/Christos" quickly became so established in the earliest Christian circles, that already by the time of the earliest Christian writing (the early 50s), "Christos" was already functioning more as a proper name, "Jesus Christ," rather than "Jesus the Christ."[101] What is so striking about this is that for the title to have become so fixed probably means that it was not (or quickly ceased to be) controversial in Jewish circles. The Christian claim that Jesus was the Christ was evidently not so remarkable that Jewish authorities and synagogue leaders found it necessary to sustain an attack on the new sect as apostate. The key data here is that the Christian Jews in Jerusalem (the Jerusalem church) remained largely undisturbed, at least subsequent to the stoning of Stephen, despite their conviction that Jesus was Messiah; according to Acts, many priests (6:7) and Pharisees (15:5) had joined the sect; indeed there were myriads of believers, "all zealous for the law" (21:20).[102] And Paul's letters contain only one reference to and another hint of Jewish opposition to the claim that God was fulfilling his purpose through a crucified Christ.[103]

The point here is that to designate anyone as Messiah/Christ may have been controversial within Second Temple Judaism, but it did not constitute any challenge to Jewish understanding of God as one and God of Israel. Two generations later it was the claim that Bar Kochba was Messiah who united Israel in its second fruitless revolt against the might of Rome (132–135 C.E.). And in his dialogue with Justin, Trypho the Jew makes it clear that the Messiah was expected "to be born as a human being from a human being" (*Dial.* 49). So, for the first Christians to claim that Jesus was Messiah was in no way un-Jewish, and though it necessitated a reassessment of the way God was fulfilling his purpose, it did not require a reconfiguration of Israel's belief in God itself.

There were other anointed figures in Israel's hope for the climax of God's purpose for his people, particularly for *an anointed priest*. The hope came to expression in the Qumran sect (1QS 9:11). But there is no indication that Jesus was seen as fitting that category during his lifetime (he was not of a priestly family).[104] The only NT writer to make anything of this category is the author of Hebrews, but he could only do so by distinguishing a unique category of priesthood, "according to the order of Melchizedek" (5:6). And as the category involves the imagery of Jesus offering sacrifice in the heavenly temple and as appearing "in the presence of God on our behalf" (Heb 9:24), presumably the category of Melchizedek priesthood did not infringe the holiness of the one God.

C. Son of Man

At first sight, at least as viewed from later Christian doctrine, the two terms "Son of Man" and "Son of God" can be taken as neat summaries of the classic creedal Christian claims for both Jesus' humanity and his divinity. And indeed "son of man" is an Aramaic idiom to speak of man, or of humankind, as many would prefer to say. The idiom is easily grasped: prophets may be described as "sons of the prophets";[105] a Pharisee as "a son of Pharisees" (Acts 23:6). So "son of..." could denote simply "belonging to" or "displaying the characteristics of."[106] That Jesus used the phrase "son of man" himself, and of himself, should be recognized as almost certain, though some have disputed it.[107] The evidence could hardly be clearer: the phrase in effect appears only on Jesus' lips, and the self-reference is for the most part evident, if implicit.[108] As such the phrase in itself would carry no great christological, or *theo-logical* implications.

The subject becomes more complex when the issue of whether Jesus' usage of the phrase reflected a particular reference to the "one like a son of man" in Dan. 7:13-14. This too is hotly disputed, many arguing that such an influence only entered the Jesus tradition after Easter.[109] The more important issue for us is what significance such a drawing on the vision of Daniel 7 would have carried. Here we encounter yet another controverted issue: whether the man-like figure of Daniel's vision had already been interpreted as a particular individual, a heavenly redeemer figure; and whether this figure had been already identified as Messiah, transforming the earlier hoped for Messiah into a heavenly being.[110] For myself I think it unlikely. There is no documentary evidence that can be securely dated prior to Jesus that makes such an identification.[111] And had there been such an expectation abroad at the time of Jesus, we would most likely have seen signs of it within the Jesus tradition, in questions put to or about Jesus ("Are you the [expected] Son of Man?"), or confessions to the effect that Jesus was indeed the expected Son of Man. In the absence of such evidence it is wiser to conclude that the thought of a heavenly Son of Man redeemer figure had not yet emerged within Second Temple Judaism by the time of Jesus' mission. And the likelihood is surprisingly strong that it was *Jesus himself who drew Daniel's vision into play* in finding in it reassurance of his own vindication (Mark 14:62 pars).

In any case, it is noticeable that there is virtually no sign of what might be designated a "Son of Man christology" outside the Gospels; Acts 7:56 is the only exception.[112] The simple fact seems to be that the talk of Jesus as son of man/Son of Man did not survive in Christian reflection of Jesus and his significance—presumably because the Aramaic idiom was meaningless beyond Palestine. Knowledge of the Similitudes of Enoch may have influenced the later editing of the Jesus tradition at this point by Matthew;[113] and John's further elaboration of the "son of man" idiom in the Jesus tradition to talk of "the Son of Man" as "the one who descends from heaven" (John 3:13) suggests similar influence.[114] But when developing their own christologies the other NT writers evidently did not regard the "son of man/Son of Man" motif as opening a major thoroughfare for them. Its impact on the subject of *theo-logy* is negligible. This may be significant in that so much of early expectation of Jesus' coming (again) from heaven seems to have been built on Daniel 7's vision of one like a son of man coming on/with the clouds of heaven.[115]

D. Son of God

With "Son of God," however, we come to the foremost way of referring to Jesus within the classic creeds of Christianity. When Christianity came to grapple with defining Jesus' relationship to God, it was Son of the Father that emerged as the consensus way of doing so.[116] Why so?

The first part of the answer must be because *Jesus was remembered as having so spoken or as so expressing himself.* Examination of the Gospel tradition at this point is illuminating.[117] For there does seem to have been a trend to multiply the instances in which Jesus spoke of himself as God's son, with the latest of the four Gospels, John, showing much the most frequent usage, and the earliest of the written Gospel tradition (Q and

Mark) evincing a much less common motif.[118] This strongly suggests that Jesus was initially remembered as not speaking very much on the subject. However, there is the further indication that Jesus was remembered as praying to God as Father, addressing him as "Abba," using the language of family intimacy.[119] The usage as such is attested within the Gospel tradition itself only in Mark 14:36. But Paul shows that the usage was familiar within Christian prayer, and *precisely as attesting a share in Jesus' sonship*—the implication obviously being that they were praying as Jesus prayed and experiencing the same sense of sonship that "Abba" expressed.[120] At the very least, then, the more explicit talk of Jesus as God's son is best seen as both *a recognition of and expression of the relationship that Jesus himself was remembered as experiencing.* The Gospel tradition on this point therefore highlights two features. One is that *the belief in Jesus as God's son goes back in large measure to Jesus himself*, that is, to Jesus expressing himself and (we may hazard) thinking of himself in those terms. Second, from very early days this way of speaking about Jesus appealed to the first Christians, whose own faith in Jesus as God's Son is expressed in the elaboration of the Jesus tradition on this point.

How did such talk impact *theo-logy*? The answer may be, initially not much. For "son of God" was not a very narrow or tight category in the first century. In Jewish scripture the term could be applied collectively to Israel[121] or individually to the king.[122] In the Qumran scrolls the expected royal Messiah is thought of as God's son.[123] But in Israel's Wisdom literature the righteous think of themselves as "sons of God"[124] and pray to God as "Father."[125] And particular attention has been focused on the Jewish traditions of two charismatic rabbis, one before Jesus (Honi "the circle drawer"), the other from the generation after (Hanina ben Dosa), who prayed to God as a son to his father.[126] So presumably the initial talk of Jesus as God's son need not have amounted to a very significant claim being made for Jesus—hugely significant in one sense, but in its implications for *theo-logy* not necessarily of great moment or consequence.

However, it is clear that from the beginning of Christian reflection on the status of Jesus, Son of God was a much more expressive way of speaking of Jesus than any of the previous titles or referents. Belief in the resurrection evidently gave a boost to this language, however precisely we reckon the significance of passages like Rom 1:4 and Acts 13:33, as indicating either a new status newly bestowed or an enhanced or formally acknowledged status.[127] Other passages, which seem to be citing already older formulations, imply that it quickly became very natural to speak of

Jesus as Son in terms of a mission from heaven: 1 Thess 1:10—the Thessalonians had converted "to wait for his Son from heaven"; Gal 4:4 and Rom 8:3—God sent forth his Son, born of woman, in the likeness of sinful flesh.[128] Son of God, in other words, made the transition from Gospel tradition to independent early Christian reflection that Son of Man failed to make.

So the more elaborate Son of God christologies of the other NT writers are not surprising. Matthew, for example, presents Jesus in his birth narratives as fulfilling both Isa 7:14 ("'Behold, the virgin shall conceive and bear a son, and they shall call him Emmanuel,' which means 'God with us'") and Hos 11:1 ("Out of Egypt have I called my son") (Matt 1:23; 2:15); Jesus the Son who brings the presence of God to immediate reality.[129] In its opening sentences, Hebrews elaborates the climactic character of the revelation through Christ in powerful imagery: "in these last days (God) has spoken to us by a/the Son, whom he appointed heir of all things, through whom he also created the worlds. He is the reflection of God's glory and the exact imprint of God's very being, and he sustains all things by his powerful word" (Heb 1:2-3), language on which we will have to reflect below. And in the opening to the Fourth Gospel John has no qualms about climaxing his opening statement by reminding his readers that "No one has ever seen God. It is the only-begotten God,[130] who is close to the Father's heart, who has made him known" (John 1:18). Typical of John's presentation of Jesus is the thought that Jesus is the Son who has been sent from heaven by the Father,[131] whose glory Isaiah saw in the temple,[132] who identifies himself with the "I am (he)" of Second Isaiah,[133] and who makes the Father visible to mortal eyes (particularly John 12:45; 14:9).

In the NT writings, therefore, the way is well prepared for what became the principal language to express the relation between God, as Father, and Jesus, as Son. It was always appreciated by the leading theological thinkers, of course, that the language was analogical or metaphorical, since one could hardly imagine what the equivalent to physical conception and birth would be among heavenly and spiritual beings. Jesus was not literally the son of God in the literal sense of familiar usage. No one can say precisely(!) what it means to confess that Jesus is the Son of God. Nevertheless *the image and metaphor indicate an intimacy of relationship of Jesus with God that could find no better or more fitting expression*, and so it has endured into the classic confessional formulations and beyond. Not least of the importance of this christological motif is that *it can be rooted back within Jesus' own mission and even his own experience*; the continuum begins with Jesus himself.[134]

E. Lord

All the titles and terms used of Jesus thus far reviewed had their roots in Jesus' own mission, in that all were used or canvassed, or indeed articulated in some form by Jesus himself. But "Lord" as a title denoting heavenly status seems to have been accorded to Jesus only after the events of Easter.[135] It is interesting to note, for example, how the title is used in Luke's Gospel: whereas Luke as narrator himself freely refers to Jesus as "the Lord,"[136] he seems to have taken some care to avoid quoting the title on the lips of Jesus' own contemporaries—until, noticeably, after Jesus' resurrection (Luke 24:34).[137] The belief that in or by virtue of his resurrection Jesus had been designated Lord seems to be well rooted in NT thought, as indicated by two passages where the earliest NT writer, Paul, seems to be drawing on statements of faith formulated earlier and expressive of more than simply his own views. One is Rom 10:9, where Paul may well quote a baptismal confession: "If you confess with your lips that 'Jesus is Lord,' and believe in your heart that God raised him from the dead, you will be saved." Indeed, it is very likely that "Jesus is Lord" was one of the earliest Christian confessions.[138] The other is what most regard as a pre-Pauline hymn (Phil 2:6-11), which climaxes with the assertion that God exalted the one obedient to death "and gave him the name that is above every name, that at the name of Jesus every knee should bow...and every tongue confess that Jesus Christ is Lord, to the glory of God the Father" (2:9-11).

In this case we can trace some of the earliest Christian theologizing. For it is fairly obvious that an OT passage played a key role in formulating this confession. As already indicated, it is entirely probable that the first believers in Jesus searched their scriptures with great energy in order to find indications of what had happened to Jesus and why. One of the passages that evidently caught their attention was Ps 110:1: "the LORD said to my Lord, 'Sit at my right hand until I make your enemies your footstool.'" The frequent quotation of and allusion to this passage in the NT writings is a clear indication of its influence on earliest Christian theologizing.[139] Here was a scripture that envisaged the Lord God addressing another as "Lord" and inviting him to sit at his right hand. One can readily understand why the first disciples would find this text so instructive, and why they would conclude that it was not enough to think of Jesus as having been raised from the dead; he had also been exalted to God's right hand. The quotation of Ps 110:1 in Acts 2:32-35 and the allusion in Rom 8:34 simply make explicit what is implicit in the other references to the Psalm: both raised from the dead *and* exalted to God's right hand![140]

Still more striking is the way in which several OT passages that speak of *God* as "Lord" are used by NT writers of the exalted Jesus.[141] The most striking examples come from the same two passages already cited. In Rom 10:9-13 the quotation of Joel 2:32, "Everyone who calls upon the name of the Lord shall be saved," is clearly used in reference to Jesus as Lord. And in Phil 2:10-11, the confident expectation that "every knee will bow . . . and every tongue confess that Jesus Christ is Lord" clearly echoes Isa 45:23, one of the most unyielding monotheistic passages in the whole Bible: "There is no other god besides me, a righteous God and a Savior; there is no one besides me . . . To me every knee shall bow, every tongue shall swear" (Isa 45:21-23). If anything, even more striking is Paul's confession in 1 Cor 8:6: "for us there is one God, the Father, from whom all things and we for him, and one Lord Jesus Christ, through whom all things and we through him." What is so striking here is that Paul seems to be taking up the Shema, Israel's creed that "there is no god but one" (8:4). As already noted, in its fuller form the Shema confesses "the Lord our God, the Lord is one" (Deut 6:4). But *Paul seems to have pulled apart the confession of one God as one Lord into a twofold confession of one God, the Father, and one Lord, Jesus Christ.*

What are we to make of this? On the one hand Jesus as Lord features alongside God as Father in the opening blessings and closing benedictions of Paul's letters.[142] And Jesus as Lord shares in the honor that is due to God alone (Phil 2:10-11). On the other, Paul confesses the oneness of God alongside his confession of Jesus as Lord (1 Cor 8:6), and does not hesitate to speak of God as "the God and Father of our Lord Jesus Christ"[143]—*Jesus as Lord, still has God as his God!* Not only so, but in his most explicit statement of the exalted Jesus' relation to God, using the imagery of Ps 110:1 (1 Cor 15:24-28), Paul speaks of the exalted Christ surrendering his exalted share in divine rule back to God and concludes unhesitatingly that "when all things have been subjected to (Christ), then the Son himself will also be subjected to the one who put all things in subjection under him, so that God may be all in all" (15:28).[144]

How then should Christ's exalted status as Lord be designated? That Paul sees the Lord Christ as sharing in God's rule, as worthy of the same subservience is clear. But does that amount to sharing in the very being (or identity) of the one God?[145] Did Paul think of the one Lord as YHWH, the one God, or as God's vice-regent or plenipotentiary? Here is a topic worthy of the closest and most careful consideration in any biblical *theo-logy*.

F. Wisdom/word of God

The very early Christian reflection regarding the exalted Christ did not hesitate to attribute roles to Christ that would seem to be *appropriate to God alone*. One was participation in final judgment, and in the role of judge (particularly 2 Cor 5:10). But Second Temple Jewish theologizing had already envisaged such figures as Abel and Enoch functioning in this role;[146] Jesus himself is remembered as promising such a role to his twelve disciples (Matt 19:28/Luke 22:30); and Paul speaks similarly of the saints judging the world (1 Cor 6:2). So perhaps not too much should be made of this.[147] More striking is the claim that the exalted Christ *has poured out the Spirit of God* (Acts 2:33). That God gives his own Spirit could be taken for granted.[148] But John the Baptist had provided some precedent for one other than God "baptizing in Spirit" (Mark 1:8 pars.). And this seems to have been the trigger for the Acts formulation.[149] Even so the depiction of the exalted Christ as the heavenly source of the divine Spirit is extraordinary.

The most striking exercise of a divine role attributed to Christ, however, is his participation in the act of creation. Heb 1:2-3 and 1 Cor 8:6 have already been cited.[150] Equally we could refer to "the Colossian hymn" (Col 1:15-20): "He is the image of the invisible God, the firstborn of all creation; for in him all things in heaven and on earth were created . . . all things have been created through him and for him. He himself is before all things, and in him all things hold together." And to John 1:1-3: "In the beginning was the Word, and the Word was with God (*ho theos*), and the Word was God (*theos*). . . . All things were made through him, and without him was made nothing that was made."

It is generally recognized that the NT writers here were drawing on and in effect carrying forward the theologizing about the Wisdom of God and the Word of God, sketched out earlier.[151] The claim is sometimes disputed,[152] but it is hard to avoid the implication that follows from the various parallels between what had been said of Wisdom and Word and what is said of Christ. Wisdom and Word are both characteristically spoken of as the "firstborn" of creation[153] and as divine agents in creation, "through whom" God made the world,[154] and through whom the world is sustained.[155] As for the distinctive terms used of Christ in Heb 1:3—"the radiance (*apaugasma*) of God's glory and the stamp (*charaktēr*) of his very being"—the former is used of Wisdom in Wis 7:26 ("She is the radiance of eternal light, a spotless mirror of the working of God"); and both are characteristic of Philo's manifold treatment of the Logos, the corona round the sun on which humans can look when they cannot look at the sun directly, the stamp that impresses the divine character on created being.[156] The Johannine prologue's identification of the Word with light (John 1:4—"in him was life and the life was the light of humankind...") was equally familiar with regard to Wisdom (Wis 7:26, 29) and Logos.[157] And the thought of the Word coming to Israel and not being received there (John 1:10-11) is drawn directly from Israel's narrative of Wisdom being given its dwelling in Israel (Sir 24:8; Bar 3-4) but finding no dwelling place among humankind (1 Enoch 42). We can even see that the thought of the Word as God (John 1:1), indeed as "only-begotten God" (1:18) had already been anticipated in Philo's talk of the Logos: Philo in fact provides a commentary on John 1:1's distinction between *ho theos* and *theos*, the former appropriate only to "him who is truly God," while the latter is appropriate to the Logos (*Som.* 1:227-230); and, as we have already seen, Philo could speak of the Logos as "the second God" (*Qu. Gen.* 2:62).

It is hard to avoid the conclusion, therefore, that the earliest Christian theologians latched on to the trend in Jewish theologizing evident in Israel's Wisdom tradition and characteristic in Philo and found in it a fruitful way to make sense of the significance that had become increasingly apparent in Jesus' mission[158] and in his resurrection and exaltation. The vivid poetic imagery used in the Wisdom tradition to speak of God's action in creation and sustaining, in revealing and redeeming, was an obvious resource on which the first Christian theologians were able to draw freely.[159] We could even say that the speculation within Second Temple Judaism as to how God reveals his will and himself to his people reached its climax in the early Christian conclusion that Jesus was the climax of that self-revelation. Where Israel's sages found the climax in the *Torah*, the Torah as the embodiment of the divine wisdom that permeates all creation and enlightens the human searcher after God, the earliest Christians found an even richer and fuller climax in *Christ*. As Baruch had taken up the language of Deut 30:12-14 to underline the point that the much sought after wisdom had been given to Israel in the Torah (Bar 3:29-30, 3:36–4:1), so Paul used the same language to argue that the same wisdom is now to be found in Christ and in "the word of faith" (Rom 10:6-10).[160] For the Fourth Evangelist, the Word had become flesh in Christ (John 1:14); the Word of God did not just appear among humankind, nor simply inspire prophets, nor was just to be allegorically represented in patriarchal figures like Sarah,[161] but *became* a particular human being, one in whom "the whole fullness of deity dwelt bodily" (Col 2:9).

The question left hanging, then, is once again whether these earliest Christian theologians were simply extending the theo-logizing of their Second Temple Jewish predecessors and peers, or were they transforming it into saying something different about God?

G. The Worship of Jesus

The further question as to whether the first Christians thought of Jesus as God (or god) seems at first to take the discussion a step further. But in fact it does not. For just as "son of God" had a much wider range of usage in the first century, so too *theos* could cover a range of divine status. Philo was able to take up Exod 4:16 and 7:1 (Moses to be as God to Aaron, with Aaron as his prophet) and say such things of Moses as "(God) appointed him as god" (*Sac.* 9), as one "no longer man but God" (*Prob.* 43). In John 10:33-36 Jesus is able to respond to the charge that he was making himself God by citing Ps 82:6, "I say, 'You are gods, children of the Most High, all of you'" (referring probably to rulers and judges). And we have already observed twice that Philo did not shrink from describing the Logos as a "second god." So the few NT passages where the term "G/god" is used of Jesus may not be so significant as they are often assumed to be.[162]

The more penetrating question is whether Jesus was worshiped as God. A firmly positive answer seems to be required by John 20:28, though we should also note that the risen Jesus whom Thomas worships had said to Mary Magdalene a week earlier, "I am ascending to my Father and your Father, to my God and your God" (20:17).[163] But in the book of Revelation the worship given to the Lamb seems to be unequivocal (Revelation 5). A noticeable feature of the Apocalypse of John is the crucial distinction drawn between angels and the exalted Jesus. In continuation of the apocalyptic tradition, the angelic guides of the seer spurn any attempt to offer him worship (19:10), whereas *worship is given to the Lamb unreservedly* (5:13; 7:10).[164] Equally striking is the fact that the seer is given visions not simply of two thrones, one for God and one for the

Lamb, but (also) of one throne, the Lamb apparently sharing the throne of God (7:17; 22:1, 3) and worthy of the same sort of worship as given to God.

Yet a slight hesitation may be called for, since like some of our other terms, *worship* is quite a broad category. The term[165] can embrace everything from polite acknowledgment of a superior,[166] through less weighty terms like *reverence* and *veneration*,[167] to the full worship appropriate only to God. It could well be argued that in the first century the key characteristic of worship in that full sense was its expression in ritual sacrifice.[168] Indeed, it was the absence of any sacrificial cult dedicated to Wisdom in Second Temple Judaism that makes clear the distinction between Israel's Wisdom *theo-logy* and its nearest parallel in the polytheistic religious environment.[169] Similarly, it was the fact that offerings were made to the imperial figures within the imperial cult already firmly established in the eastern Roman Empire that made the challenge of emperor worship so real and pressing for the first Christians as well as for Jews generally. Here it is important to note that the absence of a sacrificial cult and sacrifice-offering priesthood within first-century Christianity actually prevented the practice of worshipping Jesus from becoming an issue for Christians still claiming to worship one God. Jesus was revered more as the sacrificial victim who had made atonement for others, and not as the one to whom sacrifice should be made. And even when the language of sacrifice re-emerged in talk of offering what came to be described as "the sacrifice of the mass," it was a re-enacting or re-offering the sacrifice that was and is Jesus, rather than offering a sacrifice *to* Jesus. The question of whether the first Christians worshiped Jesus (as God) is therefore rather more complex than many recognize.[170]

Larry Hurtado has argued strongly that it was the *cultic devotion offered to Jesus* from the very earliest days of Christianity that was decisive in moving Christian *theo-logy* beyond the *theo-logizing* of Second Temple Judaism about supreme angels and divine Wisdom.[171] He can point to data in the earliest NT writings (of Paul), such as the invocation of Jesus in 1 Cor 16:22—"Maranatha," "Our Lord, come"—already formulated in the earliest Aramaic-speaking community; or Paul's appeal to the Lord (Jesus) for relief from his "thorn in the flesh" in 2 Cor 12:8; or again the linking of the Lord Jesus Christ with God the Father in benediction.[172] At the same time, however, we need to note the care with which Paul uses his normal worship terms.[173] His thanks (*eucharistein, eucharistia*) are always addressed to God and never to Christ or "the Lord"; Christ is again more the content than the recipient of his thanksgivings. The normal prayer terms (*deomai, deēsis*) are usually addressed to God and never to Christ. The term "glorify" (*doxazō*) never has Christ as its object; properly speaking, for Paul, only God is to be glorified. The same is true of *latreuō*, "serve (religiously, cultically)," and *latreia*, "service, worship," and his one use of *proskyneō*, "worship, reverence" (1 Cor 14:25). In Paul's worship, Jesus is typically the content of the worship; such hymns as Phil 2:6-11 and Col 1:15-20 (if they are hymns) are not addressed *to* Christ, but give praise to God *for* Christ. And overall, it is more characteristic of Paul's understanding and practice of worship that it is offered *through* Christ rather than *to* Christ.[174] So there is a reserve here that if not noted may be lost to sight, leaving us with an imperfect appreciation of Paul's *theo-logy*.

4. CONCLUSION

These reflections have consumed more space than I bargained for. Perhaps that was inevitable, since Jesus and the sense of Jesus still present and active after his death have been so central to the emergence of Christianity as a distinct religion, and since the significance attached to Jesus within Christianity has been one of the most puzzling and troublesome features in Christianity dividing it from the other Abrahamic faiths. What we have found, however, is that *the complexity of Second Temple reflection on God's immanence and the subtlety of the first Christians' apprehension of Jesus in relation to God cannot be reduced to over-simple slogans like "Jesus is God" without losing that subtlety and losing sight of the diversity of imagery and language actually used by the NT writers.* That the diversity is hard to encapsulate within any single slogan is simply a reminder that the apprehension of God and of God's dealings with his creation in and through Christ, as also earlier, through prophets, sages, and visionaries, escapes simple formulation in words. Any such formula will have to be balanced by other such formulae, not always compatible with each other (otherwise they could be reduced to a single all-embracing formula). Christianity has always recognized this, both in the diversity of scriptures and scriptural language that it acknowledges as canonical, and in its creeds with their assertions that Christ was and is both true God and true man. Here biblical theology provides resources, both inspirational and cautionary, which have not been as fully appreciated and drawn on in subsequent theologizing as they might have been.

On the big underlying issues of biblical theology (#1), however, we should note by way of summary:

1. The high measure of continuity between the revelation of God and of God's dealings with creation and humankind and the claims made for Christ; *the earliest christological reflection is consistent with and belongs within the* theo-logical *reflection of Second Temple Judaism*; the high christology of the NT writers (more or less from the first) was made possible by the templates and precedents available to them from their Jewish forebears. Christians claim that this early Christian reflection on the significance of the revelation of Jesus Christ remains within the monotheism of the Jewish scriptures (the OT), while at the same time providing a clearer understanding of that monotheism (christological monotheism). Whether that claim can ever be accepted by Jews in Jewish-Christian dialogue is one of the most fascinating agenda items in biblical theology/theologizing.

2. I have not focused attention on the diversity of christological claims made regarding Jesus. But the restraint of the Synoptic Evangelists in their portrayal of Jesus should not be ignored. Nor should the striking contrast between the Synoptic portrayal and that of John's Gospel. The sermons in Acts embody a good deal of very early christology that does not seem to have been much developed;[175] and I noted that "teacher" and "prophet" did not survive far into earliest christological reflection. The high priestly christology of Hebrews is unique in the NT (with the sole exception of Rom 8:34). And Revelation's apocalyptic treatment is likewise unique. On the other hand *the unifying focus on Christ as both the name round which the first Christians gathered and as revealing the ways of God and the character of God more fully than ever before* has been clearly drawn out above.

3. Equally clear has been the fact that the theologizing of the first Christians did not begin with themselves. They remembered a Jesus who had prayed to God as his Father and who had found in the vision of Dan 7:13-14 a source for his expectation of vindication. *They did not need to abandon or to transform his teaching to make it serve as gospel for them*; it was quite sufficient for the Jesus tradition to be held within a framework beginning with the bap-

tism of John and climaxing in Jesus' death and resurrection. The theological reflection about Jesus became more extravagant, in talk of virginal conception (Matthew) and heavenly dwelling with the Father prior to his mission on earth (John), but it can certainly be argued that that was an unfolding of a significance rooted in and already present in Jesus' own mission, rather than that it was a later addition drawn from other systems of philosophy. NT christology (or christologizing) began with Jesus. Here too is plenty of grist for NT theologizing.

4. The understanding of God as Trinity is only to be found in the NT itself with hindsight, foreshadowed in passages like Matt 28:19, 1 Cor 12:4-6, and 2 Cor 13:14. What can be said more firmly, however, is that the understanding of God, or at least of God's self-revelation as requiring complex language and imagery, was not a NT or Christian creation. Long familiar talk of the angel of the Lord and the Wisdom and Word of God remind us that earliest Christian reflection on Jesus as the one who reveals God most clearly both had and drew on such precedents. The NT also provides the language (with its meaning-content) for subsequent christological and trinitarian reflection (Logos and Son). And it is precisely the tension (if that is the appropriate word) between a christology that absorbs Wisdom and Word *theo-logy*, but a christology from which pneumatology remains distinct (even when the Spirit of God is also spoken of as "the Spirit of Christ"), that provides the driving force in subsequent theologizing towards an understanding of God as Father, Son, and Holy Spirit.[176] Christology is both theology and *theo-logy*.

F O U R

THE THEOLOGY OF SALVATION

1. INTRODUCTION

Salvation has long been established as the summary word to refer to the range of human dependency on God. It arises out of a common sense of the fragility of life, constantly threatened by an endless sequence of dangers—illness and disease, bad harvests, famine and flood, hostile armies and banditry, injustice and oppression, human failing, greed and spite, accidents, old age, and on and on. The term *salvation* sums up the help needed, the rescue hoped for, and so, in the end, the condition and situation of one who has survived all such perils and attained to a state beyond such threatening dangers—the state of having been saved. Because so many of these dangers are beyond human control, the word inevitably has a religious dimension, as looking to God for a help or rescue that no human individual or institution can provide. And so, also, the final salvation, a state delivered from the vulnerabilities of daily human living, is conceived as a state beyond daily human living, given by God, some kind of utopia or heaven.

I have sketched the outlines of salvation in broad terms in these opening sentences precisely because the biblical language of salvation displays the same breadth in both Testaments, and as it becomes a predominantly theological term, the imagery encapsulated in the term is drawn from that breadth of usage.[1] It is important to be aware of this from the outset, otherwise the term can become too narrow too quickly, a technical term of only limited reference. But in any case, whatever term we choose and however it is defined, it points to an area of major importance for any biblical theology.[2]

Here too NT theology is entirely continuous with and dependent upon its inheritance in the scriptures of Israel. The givens of Israel's theology of salvation can be summed up under five heads:

- A. God as savior
- B. God's initiative
- C. God's faithfulness
- D. The means of atonement
- E. Hope for the age to come

And here too it is the impact made by Jesus, his mission as one of healing (salvation), and particularly the effect of his death and resurrection, which reshapes the elements inherited from Israel and poses questions for the continuity of the biblical concept:

- A. Realized eschatology
- B. The new covenant
- C. Sacred space and atonement
- D. Diverse images of salvation
- E. The hope of salvation

2. THE INHERITED THEOLOGY

A. God as Savior

A striking feature of the biblical usage is the recognition that only God can provide the salvation needed. It was well enough understood that salvation can come through human agency: the early leaders of Israel were remembered in Israel's history for the deliverance (salvation) they brought;[3] and it is taken for granted that one of a king's roles is to rescue his people from oppression.[4] But even there it is firmly asserted that God took the initiative in raising up these early deliverers; it was Yahweh who saved through the hand of the judges (Jdg 6:36-37). For Israel's prophets, it was precisely Yahweh's power to save that marked him off from idols of wood and stone.[5]

Characteristic of Israel's trust in God, then, is that it is *to God alone that Israel looks for deliverance;* he alone is Savior. Particularly in the Psalms and Isaiah God is consistently hailed as the God of salvation: "The Lord is my light and my salvation" (Ps 27:1); "He alone is my rock and my salvation, my fortress" (Ps 62:2,6); "Surely his salvation is at hand for those who fear him" (Ps 85:9). "I am the LORD your God, the Holy One of Israel, your Savior.... I, I am the LORD, and besides me there is no savior" (Isa 43:3, 11); "Turn to me and be saved, all the ends of the earth! For I am God, and there is no other" (Isa 45:22).

The NT usage is broader, with the verb (*save*) often used, particularly in the Gospels, for being healed (saved from disease or death); Jesus is remembered as typically saying, "Your faith has saved you (made you whole)."[6] Sometimes the NT writers too speak of individuals as the mediators of salvation.[7] But in the Gospels it is typically Jesus who heals or saves, or through whom God saves. And it is noticeable that, in the Pastorals in particular, the title of Savior is used of God[8] as much as of Christ.[9] The regularly used passive, *be saved*, should probably be taken as a divine passive, the unidentified savior being God. Here we should probably see the same sort of development as that examined in chapter 3: Jesus understood to be the medium of God's saving power, as bringing about *God's* salvation.

The concept of salvation as requiring divine intervention and help from beyond one's own resources was, of course, widespread in the ancient world. By the time of Paul, the title *Savior* (*sōtēr*) was already long familiar in reference to various gods, notably Asclepius, the god of healing,[10] and had became prominent in Emperor worship, though it was used also of individual heroes, statesmen, and others.[11] So the claim made by the first Christians for Jesus—by Peter in Acts 4:12 ("There is salvation in no one else, for there is no other name under heaven given among mortals by which we must be saved"), and by Paul in Acts 16:31, in answer to the question "What must I do to be saved?" ("Believe on the Lord Jesus, and you will be saved")—was a bold one and indicated early Christianity's entry into the market place to promote its gospel in the face of all other offers of and invitations to healing, wholeness, and salvation.

B. God's Initiative

At the heart of Israel's theo-logy is the conviction that creation is the free initiative of God, summed up in the repeated phrase of the creation narrative in Genesis 1, "God said, 'Let there be,'" the divine *fiat*.[12] Without God so willing it and bringing it about, nothing else would exist. John's Gospel makes the affirmation explicitly, speaking of God's word, in direct echo of the Genesis narrative: "All things came into being through him, and without him not one thing came into being" (John 1:3). This conviction that it all goes back to God and all depends on the divine will that there should be beings other than God is fundamental to Israel's theology as a whole.

It is hardly surprising, then, that when *the story of salvation* makes its real beginning, with the story of Abraham, it begins with the same insistence on the initiative of God—the implication being that without such divine initiative the history of human beings would be as colorless and as negative as it had been prior to Noah (Gen 6–9) and as confused as it had become following the episode of Babel (Gen 10–11). Its effective beginning is the commission and promise that God made to Abraham implicitly on his own initiative entirely, the oath that God freely swore to Abraham, the covenant he made of his own accord with Abraham and his descendants: "The LORD said to Abram, 'Go from your country and your kindred and your father's house to the land that I will show you. I will make of you a great nation, and I will bless you, and make your name great, so that you will be a blessing'" (Gen 12:1-2). The point was clearly seen as of central importance for those who formulated Genesis, since the promise is repeated regularly through the narrative, repeatedly to Abraham and to each of Abraham's descendants.[13] And it is precisely this theme that is picked up when the story of salvation is resumed in the account of Israel's deliverance from slavery in Egypt—the exodus—the new chapter beginning when "God remembered his covenant with Abraham, Isaac, and Jacob" (Exod 2:24; 6:4-5). Similarly the hope held out to an Israel repentant over future (inevitable) iniquity and failure is that God will remember his covenant with the fathers (Lev 26:40-45). And Deuteronomy in particular makes the point repeatedly that Israel's inheritance of the land (of Canaan) was not because of any virtue in themselves or anything they had done, but solely because God was remembering the covenant he had made with Abraham, Isaac, and Jacob, because of God's love for their ancestors.[14] Understandably, both the exodus and the experience of exile and return from exile were seen as emblematic expressions of God's saving purpose for Israel—the classic expressions of each being Deuteronomy and Second Isaiah.[15]

The character of God's freely accepted covenant commitment is well summed up in the two words, *chesed* (*"loving kindness"*) and *mercy*. The first in particular characterizes the love of God for the patriarchs and Israel as steadfast, loyal, and faithful, enduring in spite of their disobedience and failure. "The most important of all the distinctive ideas of the Old Testament is God's steady and extraordinary persistence in continuing to love wayward Israel in spite of Israel's insistent waywardness."[16] Its significance is summed up in the prayer of Jacob: "I am not worthy of the least of all the steadfast love and all the faithfulness that you have shown to your servant" (Gen 32:10). The psalmist continually praises God for the same steadfast love.[17] And the amazing imaging of God's *chesed* in the story of Hosea, the enduring, unyielding love of God for adulterous Israel, speaks more powerfully than any other; God solemnly affirms, "I will take you for my wife forever; I will take you for my wife in righteousness and in justice, in steadfast love, and in mercy" (Hos 2:19). God's steadfast love is "forever."[18]

One of the words most frequently linked with *chesed* is *mercy*; God's *chesed* and mercy are two sides of the same coin.[19] The passage that most clearly sums up Israel's appreciation of the God they worshiped is Exod 34:6-7—the closest Moses came to grasping the character of God: "The LORD passed before him and proclaimed, 'The LORD, the LORD, a God merciful and gracious, slow to anger, and abounding in steadfast love and faithfulness, keeping steadfast love for the thousandth generation....'" The fact that this passage is repeated in several variations throughout Israel's history is a clear indication that Israel cherished this insight into their God more than any other as lying at the very heart of their experience of God and their grasp of the significance of their relation with him.[20]

The point about Israel's recognition and affirmation of the divine initiative in initiating the process of salvation needs to be stressed, since much Reformation theology encouraged the idea that the Jewish precursors of Christianity were essentially legalistic in character. The sharp Lutheran antithesis between law and gospel allowed the impression to gain strength that Judaism understood salvation as something achieved by means of law obedience. That the law indeed stood at the center of Israel's religion and early Judaism is certainly the case, and we will explore the role of the law within Israel's understanding of its responsibilities and obligations as God's people in #6 below. But what needs to be underlined here is *the total graciousness of God's initiative in first calling*

Abraham and binding himself to Abraham and his descendants by a solemn oath.[21] The starting point was nothing that Abraham had done or achieved.[22] The starting point was God's sovereign choice to make covenant commitment to Abraham and his descendants, to promise his steadfast love and mercy without prior condition. The story of Israel's salvation is to be found in nothing in themselves and in nothing they were doing or could do as a slave people, but solely in the grace of God remembering the covenant he had made with the patriarchs.

The NT word that best captures this axiom of the biblical theology of salvation is *grace* (*charis*), and Reformed theology caught this emphasis well in its concept of the covenant of grace as already operative in the Old Testament.[23] For "grace" is another term for the covenant choice, steadfast love, and mercy of God. It was Paul in particular who took up a word that was much used in the context of benefactions, *charis* as "favor" bestowed, and gave it the profoundly theological and religious weight that it still retains in Christian theology.[24] And it should occasion no surprise when Paul seeks to resolve the dilemma of Israel's future in God's plan of salvation by appealing finally to the mercy God displayed in first choosing the patriarchs and calling Israel (Rom 11:28-32). *The NT understanding of God as gracious is rooted deeply in Israel's understanding of God's covenant love and mercy.*

C. God's Faithfulness

Other terms emphasize the enduring character of God's favor and commitment once given. The emphasis is already evident in the frequent talk of God's *chesed*, but the reinforcement of the emphasis with alternative and almost as equally important language underlines just how important the theme was for Israel's sages and theologians.

Two examples are the terms *'emeth* and *'emunah* both from the root *'mn*, denoting "constancy" (of things) and "reliability" (of persons), with the former acquiring the meaning of "truth" and the latter conveying more the idea of "conduct that grows out of reliability," hence "faithfulness" (in the LXX translated as *pistis*).[25] Central for Israel's theo-logy is the affirmation that Yahweh is *'el 'emeth*, "faithful God" (Ps 31:5), one who can be utterly relied on. "The faithfulness of God endures forever" (Ps 117:2).[26] So, for God as creator: God "keeps *'emeth*," and humankind can rely on God forever (Ps 146:6). Here it is important to recall that the first covenant made by God is the covenant with Noah, never again to destroy the earth and humankind by flood (Gen 9:8-17); the subsequent covenant commitment to Israel presupposes the prior commitment to creation.[27] But it is the thought particularly of God's faithfulness to his chosen people, Israel, which most captivated psalmist and prophet. Thus the psalmist celebrates that God "has remembered his steadfast love and faithfulness to the house of Israel"(98:3). In Micah 7:20, the prophet ends with the note of assurance: "You will show faithfulness to Jacob and unswerving loyalty to Abraham, as you have sworn to our ancestors from the days of old." And in Hosea 2:20 Yahweh says to Israel, "I will take you for my wife in faithfulness; and you shall know the LORD."

Another member of the word group embracing "steadfast love," "mercy," and "faithfulness" is a little more surprising—"righteousness." The surprise is because "righteousness" has traditionally been understood in terms of conformity to a norm; the one who measures up to the norm is righteous. And in terms of Israel's history, that norm is usually taken, quite naturally, to be the law. So we find ourselves left with a basic concept of righteous as law-abiding, or law-fulfilling. This is certainly an important part of what righteousness in biblical usage embraces. But it misses, or misses out an important aspect of the early Hebrew understanding of the term. For the early sages of Israel, "righteous" was understood in relational terms—*righteousness as fulfilling the obligations arising out of a relationship.* The king was righteous when he fulfilled his obligations to his subjects. The judge was righteous when he administered justice to rich and poor impartially.[28] Consequently, fundamental to Israel's understanding of God's righteousness was the relationship that God had taken upon himself in choosing Israel to be his people. *God was righteous in that he fulfilled his commitments as Israel's God*—to watch over his people and grant them security and prosperity. In other words, it was of a piece with the other terms already noted. The psalmist is confident that "steadfast love and faithfulness will meet; righteousness and peace will kiss each other. Faithfulness will spring up from the ground, and righteousness will look down from the sky" (Ps 85:10-11). He prays: "Give ear to my supplication in your faithfulness; answer me in your righteousness" (143:1). And God promises through Zechariah: "They shall be my people and I will be their God, in faithfulness and in righteousness" (Zech 8:8).[29]

A most striking testimony to this understanding of God's righteousness as his acting on Israel's behalf in fulfillment of his covenant obligations is to be found in a recurrent usage in the Psalms and in Second Isaiah. For in a sequence of passages it is clear that the writers saw God's righteousness as his acting to restore his own and to sustain them within their covenant relationship with him. So, for example, the psalmist prays, "In your righteousness deliver me" (31:1; 71:2); "Vindicate me, O LORD, my God, according to your righteousness" (35:24). And Isaiah regularly puts "righteousness" and "salvation" as complementary or synonymous concepts.[30] Indeed, in several cases the Hebrew term *righteousness* is better translated as "deliverance" or "salvation" or "vindication,"[31] as modern translations show. And one of the most astonishing features to emerge from the Dead Sea Scrolls, astonishing at least in face of the traditional Christian disparagement of Jewish "legalism," was the language of 1QS 11:11-15:

> As for me, if I stumble, the mercies of God shall be my eternal salvation. If I stagger because of the sin of the flesh, my justification shall be by the righteousness of God which endures for ever.... He will draw me near by his grace, and by his mercy he will bring my justification. He will judge me in the righteousness of his truth and in the greatness of his goodness he will pardon all my sins. Through his righteousness he will cleanse me of all the uncleanness of man and of the sins of the children of men. (Vermes)

Here the line of continuity from Hebrew Bible (through Second Temple Judaism!) to NT is even more direct, for in what is set out as the most sustained exposition of the gospel, Paul evidently took it for granted that his audiences in Rome (churches he had never visited) would know what he meant by "the righteousness of God." The phrase spoke not of God's righteous judgment in punishing the wrongdoer—the meaning that initially caused Luther so much anguish. It spoke rather of God's *saving* righteousness, the righteousness that the gospel reveals, the gospel that Paul and his audiences had already experienced as the saving power of God (Rom 1:16-17). Even more interesting is the way Paul was able to play on the associated themes of God's faithfulness, God's truth (*'emeth*), and God's righteousness (Rom 3:3-7). And again in the final summary of his exposition, linking God's truth (*'emeth*), in confirming the promises of the fathers, and his mercy (Rom 15:8-9).[32] Whether his Greek-speaking audience in Rome would have picked up the word associations that grew out of the Hebrew is less to the point. The point is that Paul saw the gospel as integrally expressing the same affirmations of God's faithfulness and righteousness that had been so fundamental to Israel's soteriology.

D. The Means of Atonement

A central part of the obligations that Yahweh laid on his covenant people was the provision to ensure the maintenance of the relationship between God and his people. This essentially focused on the temple in Jerusalem, the provision of a holy place where the holy God could dwell in the midst of his people.[33] Hence the importance of priests within Israel's religion, to mediate between the holy and the normally profane. Hence too the importance of ritual purity and the laws to ensure the cleanliness of those seeking to enter the holy space, the presence of the holy God.[34]

Equally integral to Israel's whole temple theology was the sacrificial system. Indeed, the temple existed primarily to provide a, or rather, the place where sacrifice could be made that was acceptable to Yahweh. The Hebrew Bible bears testimony to the struggle to establish the Jerusalem temple as the one place where sacrifice would and therefore should be offered, but from a NT perspective that was already a firm given.[35] The rationale of the sacrifices is far from clear, and included the daily *Tamid* offering, two male yearling lambs, one in the morning, the other in the evening, paid for from the temple tax (one half-shekel) contributed by adult male Jews all over the world. Also the individual burnt offering (Lev 1), probably thought of as a gift to God, the "grain offering" (Lev 2), part of the provision, with tithes and first-fruits, made for the benefit of the priests, and the "peace offering," whose function remains unclear (Lev 3).[36]

Most significant, however, was *the divine provision for Israel's failure* to live in accordance with the law, the means provided to ensure that Israel's sins and transgressions did not prevent access to God or disrupt or break the covenant bond between God and his people. This provision focused in the sin offering (Lev 4–5) and the annual Day of Atonement ritual (Lev 16). There is some dispute as to whether the sin offering and the Day of Atonement ritual were intended primarily as a purification offering (purifying the altar and the sanctuary) or as an atonement sacrifice (atoning for the individual's and nation's sins).[37] We may well have here a case of both-and, since purification is certainly one aspect of the whole.[38] But the repetition of the formula in reference to the sin offering, "the priest will make atonement for him/for his sin and he will be forgiven,"[39] assuredly indicates that "atonement" as removal of the cause of offence between Yahweh and his people was (also) fundamental. In both cases the sacrificial blood made possible the continuation or restoration of the relation between God and his people ruptured by sin and/or prevented by human impurity.

Once again the biblical theologian experiences some frustration, in that the theological logic of the sin offering is never clearly expounded in the biblical texts. The most obvious way of understanding the mechanism—but it is much disputed—is as follows:[40] that the sacrificial animal in some way represented the guilty or sinful person; that the offerer laid his hand on the head of the animal, thereby signaling his desire that the animal should represent him in his sin;[41] and that the animal's death served in place of the destructive effects of the offerer's being out of relation with God, or indeed destroyed the corrupting sin itself. Here is a case where the theological given inherited by the NT writers is far from clear, and yet it was presumably taken for granted by the NT writers in their treatment of Jesus' death in terms of sacrifice. There is, undeniably, something dubious or even hazardous in trying thus to reconstruct an unexplained element in Israel's theology of atonement. Yet the death of Jesus was to become so central to NT theology that it is difficult to make sense of the theology of atonement in the NT without drawing some inferences regarding the givens that the NT writers inherited.[42]

Though many Israelites fell into the trap of thinking that divine forgiveness operated as a ritual mechanism, Israel's law-givers, prophets, and sages never forgot that it is Yahweh who forgives, who removes or pardons sin, as the much reflected-on Exod 34:6-7 emphasized in its fuller version: "keeping steadfast love for the thousandth generation, forgiving iniquity and transgression and sin. . . ." It is God's forgiveness for which Abraham pleads on behalf of Sodom (Gen 18:24-26), and for which Moses pleads on behalf Israel (Exod 32:32). Notably at the consecration of the temple itself, Solomon prays for God's forgiveness for future transgression and disaster.[43] And the psalmist regularly recalls or pleads for God's forgiveness.[44]

Since the NT heritage from Second Temple Judaism has been sometimes misrepresented, as though Pharisaical Judaism thought only in terms of merit-accumulation and had reduced the religion of the OT to a fine-tuned process of credit-debit calculation, and as though forgiveness was something which Jesus introduced to a dead religion of legalism, *the centrality of the provision to deal with sin and transgression within the religion of Jesus and his contemporaries needs to be re-emphasized.* Neither Israelite nor Jew was expected to avoid sin, or to live a perfect (that is, sin-less) life; and the contraction of impurity was a daily occurrence.[45] The grace of God was fundamental for both Israelite and Jew, not simply in the initial making of the covenant with Abraham and his descendants, but also in making it possible for a constantly sinning people to be sustained within that covenant relationship. Repentance and forgiveness, sacrifice and atonement were part of the language system that the first Christians inherited.

E. Hope for the Age to Come

For most of the Hebrew Bible one cannot properly speak of an end-point of salvation, or indeed of a future final salvation of the individual. The covenant promises relate to *the people* and hold out the promise of length of years in the land (the covenant people sustained through ongoing generations) and prosperity in the land.[46]

As a religious hope, the hope was for *a more effective relationship with God*. The more penetrating of Israel's prophets and theologians always recognized the danger of superficiality in Israel's religious observance. "The Lord said, '... these people draw near with their mouths and honor me with their lips, while their hearts are far from me, and their worship of me is a human commandment learned by rote'" (Isa 29:13). It was well appreciated that the ritual act of circumcision represented (or should represent) a much more profound commitment than the excision of flesh; what was really required was for the *heart* to be circumcised.[47]

In the face of repeated failure, of exile and of domination by foreign powers, the hope grew that in a new age things would be different, would be as they should always have been. God in his covenant faithfulness would vindicate and save his people, he would restore Israel's scattered exiles to the land and grant Israel a prosperity that it had never known before, freedom from pestilence, disability, and oppression, a restoration indeed of paradise.[48] He would pour out his Spirit upon them and grant them the flourishing well-being of peace.[49] He would give his people a new heart and spirit to enable them to live in accordance with God's rules for life (Ezek 36:26-27). He would make a new covenant and write his law in their hearts so that they might be enabled to live in accordance with it instinctively (Jer 31:31-34). He would forgive their sins, presumably in some final or complete sense.[50]

This vision of hope regularly, but not always, included an agent who would maintain God's cause and prosecute his will effectively. The figure or figures are characterized variously, as we saw earlier (#3.2a-b), but can be grouped without too much simplification under the heading of "messianic expectation." It is important to appreciate, however, that much of the hope outlined above was never correlated with such messianic expectation or attributed to the messianic figure. *The NT focusing of Israel's hope so closely and exclusively on Jesus was a major and largely unprecedented development.*

It is only in the later books of the OT, and the post-biblical (post-OT) apocalyptic writings of Second Temple Judaism, that the thought of finality, of an end-point in the divine purpose for Israel emerges. Various prophets speak of "the days to come" or "the latter days."[51] But only with Daniel do we hear talk of "the time of the end,"[52] "the appointed time of the end" (8:19; 11:27), "the end of days" (12:13), with the kingship and dominion given to the saints of the Most High understood (implicitly) as final (7:27). Other post-biblical writings speak of "the final age," "the end of days," "the time of the end," and "the end of the age."[53] And here the thought of salvation embracing the individual beyond the grave begins to feature too. Previously existence beyond the grave was envisaged in the shadowy terms of Sheol.[54] But with Daniel and with the Maccabean martyrs there emerges the hope of resurrection, the participation of the dead and martyred saints in the life of the age beyond this one, the age to come.[55]

This last is a classic case of material that is not part of OT theology as such, but is part of a continuum from Hebrew Bible to NT and without which so much of what the NT writers assume could hardly begin to be comprehended. The givens for NT theology, which include familiarity with eschatological expectation and the hope of resurrection, are not given by OT theology as such, or only barely. But they are givens nonetheless, the givens of a biblical theology that includes the continuum between Hebrew Bible and NT.

3. THE NT THEOLOGY OF SALVATION

What difference did the mission, the death, and resurrection of Jesus make?

A. Realized Eschatology

It is hard to avoid this as starting point. Not because, as we have just seen, eschatology was a prominent feature of Israel's theology, a prominent given from the OT. Rather because the eschatological emphasis becomes immediately apparent in the NT's recollection of Jesus' message, and because the central claims of NT theology regarding the resurrection of Jesus and the outpouring of the Spirit are integrally and unavoidably eschatological in character.

Mark's Gospel makes a point of striking the eschatological note at the very beginning of Jesus' mission: "Jesus came into Galilee preaching the gospel of God and saying, 'The time is fulfilled, and the kingdom of God has drawn near'" (Mark 1:14-15). Luke strikes a similar note by reporting Jesus' sermon in Nazareth, in which Jesus claims to be the one upon whom the Spirit of God had come, anointed to act out Israel's hopes of good news for the poor, release for the captives, recovery of sight for the blind, and freedom for the oppressed—the year of the Lord's favor.[56] That the kingdom of God, God fully exercising his rule on earth, was still to come was, and remained implicit in the prayer taught by Jesus, "May your kingdom come."[57] But *the really distinctive feature of Jesus' preaching,* and clearly as it was remembered, *was his claim that the blessings of salvation hoped for in the age to come were already being realized in Jesus' mission.*[58] This was a feature that marked out Jesus from earlier prophets, including John the Baptist: their hope was for the blessings of God's favor to be restored in an as yet unknown future; whereas Jesus spoke and lived as one who was seeing and enacting these blessings already in his mission— the blind receiving their sight, the lame walking, the deaf hearing, the dead being raised, the poor having good news brought to them.[59] Probably most striking of all were the claims Jesus is recalled as making regarding his exorcisms, that they were evidence that the final defeat of Satan was already happening, were proof (since they were effected by the Spirit of God) that the kingdom of God was already upon them.[60]

Those who are familiar with these passages need to pause and attempt to hear them again as for the first time. The claim being made was indeed an astonishing one. Without other signs of renewed material prosperity, of liberation from Roman domination, or spiritual revival across the land, Jesus nevertheless proclaimed the realization of many of Israel's most cherished hopes. And without priestly, far less royal anointing or author- ization, in his table-fellowship with the despised and irreligious,[61] and in his pronouncing sins forgiven,[62] Jesus was enacting the reality of God's hoped-for favor for his people. *Eschatological salvation was now.*

As already noted in #2, the same point needs to be appreciated in regard to Jesus' resurrection and the outpouring of the Spirit at Pentecost. The hope of resurrection was indeed one of the givens shared by the

Pharisees and the first Christians. But that was the hope for resurrection at the end of the age, resurrection in the age to come—as assumed in Jesus' discussion with the Sadducees on the subject (Mark 12:18-27 pars.). There was no real or widespread conception of an individual being resurrected prior to that final event; an individual being restored to life, perhaps, but not resurrected as such. Yet this is just what the first Christians claimed for Jesus. To be sure, the initial thought was that Jesus' resurrection was the beginning of the general resurrection, the (first-fruits) beginning of the harvest of the dead.[63] But even when the end-events did not continue to unfold in the final resurrection, the first Christians continued to confess, as fundamental to their understanding of the gospel of salvation, that God had raised Jesus from the dead.[64] If the resurrection of Jesus is indeed the most distinctive part of NT theology within a biblical theology, then it is also true that an inescapably escha-tological element lies at the heart of NT theology.

We must return to consider the further ramifications of this eschatol-ogy below.

B. The New Covenant

Closely correlated with such claims was the belief that undergirds the very talk of a *New* Testament. For important also for the first Christians was the conviction that they were direct heirs of the covenant promise of God to renew his covenant, the promise of a new and more effective covenant.

The *continuity* of covenant is indicated by several of the NT writers: for example, the birth of Jesus was God acting in remembrance of his holy covenant, the oath he had sworn to Abraham (Luke 1:72-73); the gospel was preached to the Jerusalemites as heirs of the covenant given to their ancestors (Acts 3:25); Paul's hope for Israel was rooted in the promise of God's covenant (Rom 11:27); the law had not annulled the covenant promise made to Abraham (Gal 3:17); the ark of the covenant is still within the heavenly temple (Rev 11:17).

However, even more striking is the conviction that the first Christians were recipients of the *new* covenant. It was not a distinctive claim, since Qumran also made a similar claim.[65] In the case of infant Christianity the claim is implicit in the way the last supper of Jesus with his disciples was recalled and celebrated, as sharing in the blood of the covenant, as the new covenant in Jesus' blood.[66] The claim is explicit in 2 Corinthians 3, where Paul elaborates his contrast between the ministry of Moses and his own ministry in terms of a contrast between the old covenant and the new (2 Cor 3:6, 14).[67] And Hebrews presses the contrast still more sharply: there is a degree of continuity between old and new, but the new underlines the inadequacy of the old covenant as now passé and obsolete (Heb 8:6-13; 9:15-22).

As again already noted in #2, we find a correlative emphasis in the claims made by the first Christians to have experienced the outpouring of the Spirit promised for the last days. This is explicit in the Acts account of the Day of Pentecost (Acts 2), where the assertion is made in so many words that the prophecy of Joel regarding "the last days" had now been fulfilled (Acts 2:16-21). But it is implicit also in Paul's equation of participation in the new covenant with experience of the life-giving Spirit. Here Paul draws together two strands of Israel's hope, new covenant and new spirit: the new covenant is written not on tablets of stone (as was the covenant through Moses), but with the Spirit of the living God on tablets of the human heart, a covenant no longer of deadening letter but of life-giving Spirit (2 Cor 3:3, 6). Hebrews characterizes believers as "those who have been enlightened, have tasted the heavenly gift and shared in the Holy Spirit, and have tasted the . . . powers of the age to come" (Heb 6:4-5).

A further correlative emphasis is Paul's claim that the hope of a circumcised heart had been realized in the first Christians. They had experienced the circumcision of the heart, in Spirit not (or no longer simply) in letter (Rom 2:28-29). They were "the circumcision," in that they worshiped by the Spirit of God (Phil 3:3). A claim so integrally related to law-keeping and to a people defined by the law cannot escape being cross-matched with Paul's understanding of the law and of its continuing function for believers and with his talk of Christian conduct as being led by the Spirit; but we will leave following up that aspect of Paul's theology till #6 below.

In the play between old and new covenant a key player is the term *pistis*. For in the OT and Second Temple Judaism its dominant sense is "faithfulness"—the faithfulness of God to his people, and the faithfulness he demands of his people. But in the NT the dominant sense is "faith, trust," and Paul in particular makes a point of marking off this latter sense ("faith") from the former by his insistence that the term be read in reference primarily to Abraham's act of believing God's promise,[68] and, by implication, not also by reference to Abraham's subsequent obedience ("faithfulness"), which was the prevailing interpretation of the day.[69]

Here the tension in biblical theology is encapsulated in the fact that *pistis* can be understood in both ways, and is to be worked out in the search for the proper balance between the two meanings, an issue to which we will again have to return in #6 below. More to the point here, is that *pistis* in the sense of *trust* is presented both as the attitude that receives the healing power of God,[70] and as the attitude that glorifies God as God, the attitude of the creature conscious of its dependence on the Creator for all good (Rom 1:21).

C. Sacred Space and Atonement

A primary testing point of continuity between Hebrew Bible and NT is the role of the temple and temple cult. For that was central to Israel's understanding of how the relationship between Israel and its covenant God was to be sustained (#4.2d). But when we turn to the NT the picture becomes somewhat confused.

The ambiguity begins with Jesus. Did he regard the temple as of continuing central significance? He is remembered as attending the temple on his visit(s) to Jerusalem, and to do so must have observed ritual purity in accordance with the law. He is remembered as criticizing the abuse made of the temple in the so-called cleansing of the temple (Mark 11:15-17; pars.); but allusion to Isa 56:7, the temple as "a house of prayer for all the nations" (Mark 11:17 pars.), would seem to imply some continuing role for the temple. He is remembered also as predicting the destruction of the temple (Mark 13:2 pars.), a prediction that evidently formed the central thrust of the accusations laid against Jesus when he was put on trial (Mark 14:58; par.). But whether he also spoke of rebuilding the temple, or thought of his circle of disciples as forming a new temple community, as the Qumran community thought of themselves,[71] remains unclear.[72] John's Gospel certainly points the talk of a renewed temple away from the Jerusalem temple itself (John 2:21; 4:21-24). And the image of the early Christians as a temple community is probably implicit in the talk of the "pillar" apostles (Gal 2:9) and of individual believers as "pillars" in God's temple (Rev 3:12).

How such self-designation correlated with the Jerusalem temple itself is not clear. Certainly the fact that the earliest Jerusalem congregation remained in Jerusalem is a significant fact here. For the only reason to remain in Jerusalem was to be near the temple. This presumably included participation in the temple cult, as is implied in various passages,[73] though the primary concern may have been the expectation that Jesus would return to the temple—perhaps in accord with Mal 3:1 (cf. Acts 3:19-21). When the data is so unclear there should be some question about including such an element within NT theology, even though the expectation of Jesus' return is a major element in earliest Christian theology and has been retained into the classic creeds despite its failure to be realized within the first generation of Christians, as they seem to have assumed it would be.[74]

What is clearer is that the Hellenist Stephen was remembered as critiquing the temple and denying that it should be seen as God's dwelling place (Acts 7:48); also that the Jerusalem temple plays no part in the theology and lived religion of the NT letter writers. A repeated contrast is between the heavenly reality that God intended and the inadequacy of the earthly substitute or copy.[75] More striking is the effective abandonment of the idea of the temple as a particular, geographically limited sacred space, a turning from the temple implicit in Stephen's speech. Now it is the bodies of the believers that are to be seen as temples, temples of the Holy Spirit;[76] the community as a whole is "a holy temple in the Lord" (Eph 2:21). Likewise Hebrews makes the point forcibly that there is no role for the mediating priest: the only effective priest is Christ; a special order of priests within the worshiping community is part of the old covenant that is passé and obsolete and has no place within the congregations of the new covenant (Heb 7–9).[77] So also both 1 Peter and Revelation revive the idea of the people of God as a whole and individually or conjointly as "a kingdom of priests" offering spiritual sacrifices through Jesus Christ.[78] And Paul in particular does not hesitate to see everyday service of the gospel in priestly terms[79] or the offering (in sacrifice) of one's whole bodily personality and relationships in daily living as the full equivalent to what previously only the priest could do within the sacred space (Rom 12:1). Similarly for Paul in particular, the rituals of purity, including the observation of the laws of clean and unclean, were no longer necessary and had been transcended by a concept of spiritual purity.[80]

This is a feature of NT theology deserving of more notice than it has usually received. It is noteworthy in that it parallels to some extent what became true of rabbinic Judaism, following the destruction of the Jerusalem temple. The transition from Second Temple Judaism to rabbinic Judaism is marked precisely by the loss of the Jerusalem temple as a living part of their religion. It is true that the whole edifice of temple cult and purity law remained important (the Mishnah!), but it was the law itself that replaced what had previously been law and temple, and the teacher/rabbi in effect replaced the priest. In contrast, the NT had no sooner been completed than the language of priesthood and sacrifice began to re-emerge, soon to be followed by the reassertion of the importance of a priestly order—a striking retreat from earliest Christianity's eschatological self-consciousness back into the pattern set by the old covenant rather than the new.[81] Here is a good test-case for the interaction of NT theology with subsequent dogmatic theology.

The issue is sharpened if we ask the question whether it is or should be somewhat the same in regard to the two universally regarded Christian sacraments. To what extent does Christian baptism have the same function within a theology of salvation as circumcision? To what extent does the Lord's Supper or Eucharist have the same function within a theology of salvation as the Passover? Or was circumcision fulfilled and superseded by the circumcision of the heart, the gift of the Spirit?[82] Alternatively, is or should the Lord's Supper be seen primarily as a commemorative shared meal? The larger issue is that of NT theology within biblical theology: is it primarily a matter of continuity, of development along an unbroken continuum? Or does the entry of Jesus Christ form a break in the continuum and an integrally different new beginning? We will return to this issue below in the following chapters.

The most sensitive topics in this subject area are the issues of atonement and of *Christ's death as atonement*. For Christ's death is variously imaged in the NT[83]—including the fate of prophets,[84] the death of a martyr (Rom 5:6-8),[85] vindication after unjust suffering,[86] the price of redemption from slavery,[87] the reconciling act,[88] the victory over hostile evil powers,[89] and the conquest of the power of death.[90] But the most extensively used image is that of sacrifice. Here too there is variation, including covenant sacrifice (as at the last supper), and Passover sacrifice (1 Cor 5:7). But the most powerfully enduring image is that of atoning sacrifice, *sacrifice for sins*.[91] Here it is clear that the theological point can only be effective if the theology of sacrifice operative in Israel's sacrificial system is assumed: unless the sin offering and Day of Atonement offerings were effective in dealing with sin, why would they have been used to make sense of Jesus' death? The most sophisticated handling of the subject, in Hebrews, resolves the issue by seeing the sacrifices of the old covenant as only foreshadowing the one and only effective sacrifice of Christ (Heb 9–10). But it remains hard to see why earlier Paul would have used the imagery of an ineffective sacrifice to express his understanding of what God had accomplished through Christ's death. So we may ask to what extent the first Christians saw the death of Christ as a sacrifice that superseded and rendered unnecessary all such future sacrifices (as Hebrews did)? Was the abandonment of atoning sacrifice simply another aspect of the more general turn away from the Jerusalem cult? Or was the understanding of Jesus' death as atonement so central to earliest Christian theology that resorting to cultic sacrifice was simply unimaginable?

Such questions are important for the historical concerns of NT theology, given, not least, as already observed, that the mother church of Christianity seems to have continued to participate in the temple cult (Acts 21:20-26),[92] probably right up to the outbreak of the Jewish war in 66. And given that the Jewish Christianity, which formed some degree of continuity with the first generation Jerusalem church, continued to retain its loyalty to the law,[93] one can only wonder whether there is a piece of NT theology that has been broken off here and ought to be reconsidered as part of the spectrum of NT theology.

This leaves the intractable questions of what the NT writers thought actually happened in the death of Jesus. Did they think of it as an actual sacrifice, of sin metaphysically heaped upon the spotless lamb from Nazareth, and the sin expiated and/or the wrath of God literally assuaged? Presumably in all this we are in the linguistic territory of metaphor—of language indicating reality but not in literal terms. The debate has been popular on whether "expiation" or "propitiation," "substitution" or "representation" are the more appropriate terms to describe this central act in the NT theology of salvation.[94] However, too little consideration has been given to the facts both that the metaphor cannot be lost without losing some vital grasp on the reality thus referred to, but also that if the metaphor is taken literally the reference is equally lost.

It should perhaps also be noted that when thought of incarnation emerges (John 1:14), it is not depicted as itself a saving event (the Logos redeeming the flesh by becoming flesh), though becoming flesh makes it possible for Christ to provide atonement.[95]

D. Diverse Images of Salvation

Israel's sacrificial system certainly gave the first Christians one of their most powerful metaphors of salvation and how it had been achieved. But Israel's history and theology gave several others. In the metaphors of *redemption* and liberation, Israel's redemption from slavery in Egypt is strongly echoed.[96] The metaphor of *inheritance*[97] goes back to the promise of land given to Abraham as part of the covenant. The proclamation of *good news* is drawn directly from Second Isaiah's vivid hope for the return from exile (Isa 52:7-10).[98] *Reconciliation* (note 87 above) probably reflected the many comings together of Yahweh with his people when they repented of their waywardness. *Repentance* itself is a powerful image, not simply of changing one's mind, but, in its Hebraic form (šub), of turning round, converting, returning to the Lord[99]—although, rather interestingly, Paul and John largely ignore it and prefer to use the language of faith and trust.[100] And the metaphor of being *transferred* into another kingdom in Col 1:13 probably reflects the origins of the Jewish communities in Asia Minor, established by Antiochus the Great when he settled two thousand Jewish families in Lydia and Phrygia to help stabilize the region.

Others were more humdrum, like waking up (Rom 13:11), night giving way to day (Rom 13:12), "putting on or off" clothes (Col 3:9-10). Or sowing and watering (1 Cor 3:6), the downpour of rain on a thirsty land (1 Cor 12:13), the harvest (Rom 8:23), the seal of transferred ownership,[101] the laying of a foundation (1 Cor 3:10-11). Or major turning points of life like birth,[102] adoption,[103] engagement and marriage,[104] and death.[105]

Reformation theology has given particular prominence to the metaphor of *justification* used by Paul, but anticipated, or echoed, in the Jesus tradition at least in the parable of the Pharisee and toll collector (Luke 18:14). More to the point, Paul's usage, as already noted, is drawn directly from the Hebrew Bible's understanding of God's righteousness as saving righteousness.[106] The metaphor is drawn from the law court, justification as acquittal, the pronouncing of the person under charge to be innocent. Paul's talk of God's acquittal as "justifying the ungodly" (Rom 4:5) on the face of it runs counter to Israel's perception of what was expected of a judge—that he should on no account justify the ungodly.[107] But Israel had had plenty of experience of God acting with partiality towards Israel, of maintaining faith with Israel despite Israel's apostasy, so Paul could present the gospel by posing the paradox of God's covenant love, of his saving righteousness in just these terms, not least because it was so true to Israel's experience of God's *chesed* and mercy.

Another important way of speaking of the saving relationship entered into by God with those who trusted him was expressed in the language of *indwelling* or *participation*. The language of being "in Christ" is a particular feature of Paul's soteriology,[108] as is the thought of *mutual indwelling* in the Johanine writings.[109] The image is not entirely clear, involving as it does the language of physical location.[110] But in all talk of relation with the divine, metaphor and analogy are unavoidable. And as is the nature of metaphor the reality envisaged may not be capable of expression in non-metaphorical language. We might say, then, that the reality envisaged includes the thought of being within a sphere of power or force field, or under the formative influence of the divine power that characterized the mission of Jesus. But that would lose the sense of intimacy, of intimate relation between believers and their Lord, of a dependency for being and for meaningful existence, which is evidently wrapped up in such imagery.

The same point is evident when we include the other principal way of speaking of the effect of entering a positive relationship with God and/or Christ—*the gift of the Spirit.*[111] For it even more clearly has power implications—a transformative influence working from within, a new and effective motivation and enabling to do the will of God[112]—but the intimacy of personal relationship with God through his Spirit is fundamental too.[113]

Insufficient recognition has been given to the *diversity* of the NT's soteriological language and to the *metaphorical force* of its imagery. In particular, there has been a tendency to play off metaphors against each other, with a dispute, for example, as to whether Paul's forensic language is more important than his participationist language.[114] *But Paul and the other NT writers do not seem to have been concerned about the diversity of the imagery they used and whether the metaphors could be neatly integrated with one another.* On the contrary, their concern seems to have been rather to bring to as vivid expression as possible the existential reality of their varied experience of saving power, even when it meant ransacking the range of imagery available in order to bring out the different ways in which it had impacted individuals. Equally, there has been a woodenness in the interpretation of the Spirit's working, as though the water imagery so characteristic of biblical Spirit talk has to be taken somehow literally, so that the Spirit is seen as a kind of refined material or physical substance in which believers have been baptized or that they have ingested by drinking (1 Cor 12:13).[115] But *the metaphorical force of such water imagery should be almost self-evident,* drawn particularly from the experience of a rain-shower on a parched land, and the thirst-assuaging drink of water for a thirsty traveler. The same point is evident with other Spirit-imagery drawn from the experience of the mysterious, powerful wind (John 3:8) and the experience of life itself.[116]

In all this we should bear in mind, once again, that the NT teaching on salvation was not a theory or axiom taught and learned so much as *an attempt to make sense of what had been and was being experienced.* From Jesus' proclamation that the kingdom of God was already operative in what he and those he ministered to were already experiencing, through the experience of seeing Jesus after his death, the experience of being forgiven and accepted by God ("peace with God"), and the experience of the Spirit, whether in crying "Abba, Father," or in speaking in tongues, or in motivation to serve or preach, what is consistently in view are experiences of new relationship and new life enabled by Jesus or the first Christian preachers. Being saved was first an experience before "salvation" became a dogma or a subheading of NT theology.

E. The Hope of Salvation

A consistent aspect of the NT teaching on salvation is that it is a three-phase *process,* with a beginning, or decisive initiating event, an ongoing experience, and an end, the outcome to be attained.[117]

We have already noted the realized eschatology so characteristic and distinctive of Jesus' teaching and (it would appear) of his own self-understanding. Here what needs to be stressed is that an equally characteristic feature of his proclamation was the still future emphasis. Not only did he teach his disciples to pray, "Your kingdom come" (Matt 6:10/Luke 11:2). But he also warned of an imminent crisis and of the need to endure[118] and spoke of a future coming of the Son of Man (to heaven, or back to earth?).[119] The Evangelists soften the resulting tension between the realized and still future eschatological perspectives in various ways,[120] but they do not remove it. And even John, more noteworthy for his "realized" emphasis, retains a clear future element in his presentation of Jesus' teaching (for example John 5:25-29). The difficulty of holding the two emphases together has encouraged various attempts to deny or remove the present/future eschatological tension in the Jesus tradition,[121] but it is inescapable, both at the level of the historical Jesus and of the enduring biblical text.

The same tension is present elsewhere in the NT. The equivalent realized emphasis in the belief both that the resurrection of the dead had begun with Jesus' resurrection and that the eschatological Spirit had been poured out, is fully balanced by expectation of Jesus' *parousia.* Acts 3:19-

21 may be the earliest recalled expression of that expectation, perhaps even the earliest recorded post-Easter christological affirmation.[122] And the belief in a (second) coming of Jesus is one of the most prominent motifs in the NT,[123] yet surprisingly much less frequently engaged with theologically than others—the relative lack of interest betraying a sense of the difficulty in handling it within biblical theology, and perhaps also a Christian embarrassment at the fact that Christ *has not* (yet) come again.[124] As a challenge to theologizing with the NT it has no equal. Insofar as it aroused attention in the twentieth century it was principally as the "the delay of the parousia" providing a clue to the dating of NT documents. But the discussion arising has not made much progress, simply because "the delay of the parousia" does not seem to have been much of a problem for the NT writers (except for 2 Pet 3:8-10).[125]

Another way in which the tension came to expression was with the experience of love, joy, and peace[126] balanced by the experience of *hope* yet to be realized. *Hope* is another common expression of the psalmist's faith,[127] which is taken up spasmodically outside the Pauline corpus— notably Matt 12:21 ("in his name the Gentiles will hope"),[128] Acts 23:6 and 28:20 (Paul's message and mission as the fulfillment of Israel's hope), Heb 6:11 and 19 ("the full assurance of hope," "a sure and steadfast anchor of the soul"), and 1 Pet 1:3 ("a new birth into a living hope through the resurrection of Jesus Christ from the dead"). But it is in Paul that we find the clearest articulation of the character of Christian hope: it is one of the three great characteristics of the Christian community, together with faith and love;[129] it is faith as it looks to the future rather than to what has already transpired in the past (Rom 8:24-25); its confidence in God is not shaken, only matured by experience of suffering in the present (Rom 5:2-5), because it is hope in God and in his Christ and not in circumstances or in oneself;[130] in the Christian armory it is "the helmet of salvation" (1 Thess 5:8).

Paul's understanding of salvation as a process has frequently been summed up as a tension between the "already" and the "not yet." The process character is clear from the consistent way he speaks of salvation itself as *a goal still to be attained*, the final good (Rom 5:9-11). Believers can be described as "those who are (in the process of) being saved";[131] complete salvation is "not yet." The image of redemption can be used both for what has already been accomplished[132] and for what is still to be accomplished.[133] The balance between "already begun" and "yet to be completed" is well caught by Gal 3:3 and Phil 1:6; or in the double use of the metaphor of adoption within consecutive paragraphs, already effected in the gift of the Spirit, but still awaited as the redemption of the body (Rom 8:15, 23); or in the Spirit itself as the "first installment and guarantee" of salvation or the "first fruits" of the harvest of the resurrection.[134]

An important aspect of this is that of *personal transformation*, explicitly signaled by Paul in the present tenses of 2 Cor 3:18 and Rom 12:2 (salvation as the process of "being transformed").[135] In the Pauline corpus the transformation is explicitly understood as a *being conformed to the image of God in Christ*,[136] including an ongoing sharing in his sufferings and a growing conformity to his death in sure hope of being finally conformed to his resurrection.[137] Thus what is implicit in the gospel elsewhere in the NT and comes to different expression elsewhere[138] is made explicit by Paul: the salvation promised by the gospel is no primrose path or recipe for material success, but rather a process of refinement and maturing. The theology of the cross (*theologia crucis*) is not simply an attempt to describe what happened to Jesus and to explain the various images and metaphors used in the NT in reference to Jesus' death. It certainly includes the complete reversal and transformation of the usual values that determine social and personal living, as 1 Cor 1:18-31 in particular makes clear.[139] But it certainly also includes the complete transformation of the person of the believer, the dying of which Jesus also spoke (Mark 8:34-35 pars.) as well as the sharing in his risen life, not just the judgment of "Not guilty" by virtue of the cross (Rom 8:33-34), but the transformation of the penitent sinner into the image of the crucified and risen Christ. We will have to return to the issues here in #6 below.

A fuller exposition of NT soteriology would have to go on to treat the completion of the process of salvation by discussing the themes of final judgment, eternal life, and resurrection.[140] Here it will have to suffice to note that *only occasional images and fragmentary depictions* are available to us. Jesus responds to the Sadducean question about the resurrection of the dead by likening resurrection life to angelic existence in heaven (Mark 12:25). But he also promises the penitent thief: "Today you will be with me in Paradise" (Luke 23:43). Paul looks forward to being "with Christ" after death (Phil 1:23); but he also expects a transformed body when Christ returns (3:20-21). He thinks of those who have died as sleeping and looks for the dead in Christ to rise (from the dead) when Christ comes (1 Thess 4:13, 16). Revelation depicts the souls of martyrs sheltering under the heavenly altar (Rev 6:9-11) and talks of a first resurrection, with implication that there will be a second (20:5). Both the Jesus tradition and Revelation use very powerful imagery to describe the outcome of the final judgment,[141] but Paul is very unclear (or coy) as to how the process will work (1 Cor 3:15; 5:5). The hope for the restoration of Israel had a very earthly feel to it (Acts 1:6),[142] but there is also talk of the original glory of creation being restored, or of a future glorification,[143] and Revelation implies a restoration of the garden of Eden with access to the tree of life renewed (Rev 22:1-2) as part of a new heaven and a new earth and in the center of the new Jerusalem come down from heaven (21:1-2).

Such a kaleidoscope of imagery suggests that *any attempt to devise a single coherent picture of "the last things" is unlikely to be successful.* It would be like expecting to be able to translate a great painting or a musical masterpiece into propositioning prose. Here again we are in the language of metaphor and symbol, the only language open to us for talk of what we do not and cannot know, language that is more inspirational than informative.[144] To translate metaphor and poetry into prose is to lose the very thing that metaphor and poetry afford us—the possibility of speaking about that which is beyond human description.

Eschatology remains the most challenging and troublesome subject in NT theology and for NT theologizing.

4. CONCLUSION

The theme of salvation, then, cannot but be a major theme in any biblical theology of the NT.

1. It highlights the issues of continuity and discontinuity as sharply as any other. The recognition of utter dependence on the loving-kindness and grace of God is consistent throughout, and of God's amazing faithfulness and saving righteousness. That God makes provision for human salvation, for dealing with failure and transgression is a red thread that binds both Testaments together. The theme of hope, that there is a future salvation to look for, and that God's purpose is moving steadily towards its final goal, constantly re-emerges even after seemingly irrevocable disaster. At the same time, the focus as to the means of salvation shifts significantly, from repentance, priest, and sacrificial cult, to faith in Christ and trust in his death and resurrection. There is a similar hope for the future, for the completion of God's saving purpose decisively begun but not

yet complete; but for the NT, Christ again gives a new sharpness of focus, both for what has begun and for what is yet to be.

2.   On the issue of unity and diversity we have noted, for example, the tension with which the NT generally stands in relation both to its OT past and to its Christian future as to the role of temple and priest. The saving event of Christ's death and resurrection is imaged in various ways, of which cultic atonement is only one. The images of salvation are diverse and by no means always mutually compatible. The hopes and expectations for the future are similarly kaleidoscopic and virtually impossible to aggregate into a single narrative or picture. The delay of the *parousia* remains an unresolved enigma. Yet the centrality of Christ, to the beginning, to the process of salvation, and to its completion, remains constant.

3.   As to the role of Jesus' own mission in framing this theological theme, it should be clear enough that Christian eschatology began with Jesus. Jesus' mission as already fulfilling ancient hopes and expectations for the age to come was Jesus' own interpretation, his own theology of salvation. Correlatively it was the convictions that in Jesus' resurrection the resurrection of the dead had already begun, and that with the experience of the outpoured Spirit the last days had already arrived, which became determinative of the distinctive Christian understanding of salvation. The death of Jesus and the resurrection of Jesus marked not only events in time but could be understood as encapsulating the whole process of personal salvation from beginning to end—Jesus the alpha and omega of salvation.

4.   In all this the language of image and metaphor retains its tantalizing capacity both to indicate what is to be believed and to point to a reality beyond words. The reality being experienced and expressed, whether in terms of the kingdom of God, resurrection, the Spirit of God, or salvation itself, always escapes formal far less final definition. And yet the experience and the hope ever strive to express that reality afresh, drawing on tradition but ever finding it necessary to find fresh expression. Which is also to say that such language used in the NT is itself an invitation to continue the theologizing of which it is a canonical expression.

F I V E

THE CHURCH OF GOD

1. INTRODUCTION

Another defining theme of biblical theology has to be *Israel*.[1] For Israel is constitutive of the Jewish scriptures. Not only is the theme of God's choice of and expectation for the people of Israel an integrating motif running through the bulk of these scriptures, but, of course, they are primarily Israel's scriptures; it is only as Israel's scriptures and because they were acknowledged by Israel that they are scriptures in the first place. Christians did not attempt to decide their canonical status (even as OT) independently of the *de facto* prior decision of Israel on the subject. The fact that the Christian canon of the OT coincides so completely with that of the Hebrew Bible simply documents the point. The fuzziness of the Christian canon(s) of the Bible—the status of the OT apocrypha (in the Vulgate and Roman Catholic canon) or of writings like 1 Enoch (in the canon of the Ethiopian church)—simply reflects the degree of fuzziness that pertained in late Second Temple Judaism itself.

The fact that Israel remains a given for the NT is very striking, not least in view of the fact that by the end of the first century embryonic Christianity must already have been predominantly Gentile in composition. But fundamental it was. Jesus' message can be summed up in terms of a hope for the restoration of Israel.[2] The first believers were all Jews, and the great majority of the NT writings were composed by Jews. The Paul of Acts sums up his mission by reference to "the hope of Israel" (Acts 28:20), just as the Paul of Romans affirms the irrevocability of God's calling of Israel and purpose for Israel (Rom 11:25-32). The chief term for Christian congregations, "church" (ekklēsia), has been taken over from the LXX's translation of the qahal YHWH or the qahal Israēl (qahal = "assembly, congregation").[3] The assumption of the opening verses of James and 1 Peter is that the letters were addressed to (the twelve tribes[!] of) the Diaspora. And the seer of Revelation envisages salvation as embracing 144,000, 12,000 from each of the twelve tribes of Israel (Rev 7:4-8).

Given, once again, that Christianity soon became a predominantly Gentile religion and that its classic creedal formulations were to be the result of interaction with, not to say fusion into Greek philosophical categories, such an Israel-focused character of the NT writings is potentially a major problem for Christian theology. It certainly is for a NT biblical theology, bearing in mind not only the subsequent non-Jewish composition of Christianity but also the *adversus Judaeos* tradition within Christianity with its evil outworking in Christian anti-semitism.[4] So, what is the given in this case that the NT writers inherited as part of their biblical theology and therefore forms an integral element in biblical theologizing thereafter? Its elements can be summarized under the following heads:

A. The election of Israel
B. Separation, zeal and blessing
C. Jewish factionalism
D. Israel's eschatological hope

The NT contribution to the biblical theological debate about Israel once again can be attributed primarily to the impact of Jesus and the impact of the Spirit and may be presented under the following headings:

A. The restoration of Israel
B. Jesus, Gentiles, and "sinners"
C. "Even on the Gentiles"
D. The fulfillment of Israel's mission
E. The body of Christ
F. The supersession or (re)definition of Israel?
G. One covenant or two?

2. THE INHERITED THEOLOGY

A. The Election of Israel

Fundamental to Israel's self-understanding was the conviction that Israel had been specially chosen by Yahweh for himself. The conviction, of course, is part and parcel of Israel's understanding of God as the God of Israel (see chapter 3, section 2c above), as the God who has made his covenant with Israel and who is faithful to that covenant in exercising his saving righteousness on Israel's behalf (above #4.2c).

The motif is explicit already in the choice of Abraham and his seed (descendants) to be the recipients of the covenant promise.[5] Explicit too in the fact, made much of in Genesis, that the line of succession to the promised inheritance passes through Isaac and not Ishmael, through Jacob and not Esau (Gen 16–17, 21; 27); it is not without significance that Paul subsequently built much on both elements of the patriarchal narrative.[6] But the most explicit and indeed classic biblical formulation comes in the song of Moses in Deut 32:8-9:

> When the Most High gave each nation its heritage,
> when he divided humankind,
> he fixed the boundaries of the peoples
> according to the numbers of the sons of God;
> but the Lord's own portion was his people,
> Jacob his allotted share.[7]

The theme is a consistent element in the Jewish literature expressive of the Second Temple Judaism within which Christianity first emerged—for example, *Jub.* 15:31-32:

> He chose Israel that they might be a people for himself. And he sanctified them and gathered them from all the sons of man because (there are) many nations and many peoples, and they all belong to him, but over them he caused spirits to rule so that they might lead them astray from following him. But over Israel he did not cause any angel or spirit to rule because he alone is their ruler and he will protect them.

Similarly *Pss. Sol.* 9:8-9:

> And now, you are God and we are the people whom you have loved;
> look and be compassionate, O God of Israel, for we are yours, and do not

take away your mercy from us, lest they set upon us. For you chose the descendants of Abraham above all the nations, and you put your name upon us, Lord, and it will not cease forever.

The language of "election," Israel as "the elect of God," occurs regularly in the OT and Second Temple literature.[8] All the more striking, then, is the way in which the terminology is taken over in self-reference by the NT writers: the days of final tribulation will be shortened for the sake of the elect;[9] "who will bring any charge against God's elect?" asks Paul boldly and confidently (Rom 8:33); the Christian recipients of various NT letters are hailed as "the elect;"[10] Revelation envisages the Lamb conquering the hostile kings, accompanied by the "called, elect, and faithful" (Rev 17:14). And not only the terminology is taken over, but also, as we shall see below, the fundamental datum of Israel's election.[11]

Notable features of the original promise to Abraham, fraught with social and political consequences to this day, are the two strands of the promise to Abraham: the promise of seed, as numerous as the dust of the earth, as the stars in the sky, as the sand on the seashore;[12] and the promise of land, the land of Canaan, or even all the land from the Nile to the Euphrates.[13] One of the theological (and not just theological) dilemmas that stem from the first strand of promise is whether the covenant promise is made with all who may claim to be descendants of Abraham, even if only through the line of Isaac and Jacob. On the Christian side, the importance of the promise made to Abraham's seed is reaffirmed by Paul in his letters to the Galatians and Romans,[14] and the dilemma is posed by Paul's attempt to claim that the "seed" of Abraham can embrace all "in Christ," Gentile as well as Jew (particularly Gal 3:15-29). On the Jewish side, the dilemma is posed by the continuing question: *who is a Jew?* Whether the promise is to an ethnically identified nation, or to a people not defined by ethnicity; whether "Jew" is a national identifier or rather a religious identifier.[15]

The second strand, the promise of the land, has been equally fundamental to Israel's thought, with hope of restoration from exile ("next year in Jerusalem") ever a dream during the decades of exile and then the centuries of dispersion. The theme remains vital in the NT, whether with the Beatitude promise that "the meek will inherit the land" (Matt 5:5), or with Hebrews' play on the promise to the wandering people of God of a rest awaiting them in the land of promise (Heb 3:7–4:11).[16] Not least of importance, and especially in the ongoing tragedy of a land disputed and fought over by Israeli and Palestinian today, is whether the promise of the land, as the land of Israel/Palestine, is still integral to a contemporary biblical theology/theologizing. Or whether its more metaphorical extension as a promise that embraces the whole earth,[17] as reflected also in Paul's thinking (Rom 4:13), is as true or even truer to the intent of the original promise.

Here the stuff of biblical theology is the stuff of Jewish/Christian dialogue and has a contribution, possibly a decisive contribution, to make to the principles and policies that still inform Middle East politics.[18]

B. Separation, Zeal, and Blessing

The corollary of the axiom of Israel's election is, of course, the non-election of the other nations (Gentiles). This has been sometimes expressed in terms of Israel's "particularism," a convenient antithesis to a Christian apologetic for Christianity's "universalism,"[19] though, as already noted in chapter 3, Israel's theo-logy was of a universal God. Israel and early Judaism was quite as "universal" as Christianity—just as Christianity, by its insistence on faith in Christ was quite as "particular" as Judaism, by the latter's theology of the elect nation.[20] The one God is, more or less by definition, the God of all nations. As Paul argued, the unavoidable implication of the *Shema* is that God is God not just of the Jews, but of the Gentiles also (Rom 3:29-30).

Nonetheless, the corollary of God's choosing Israel to be his own was that Israel should keep itself apart for Yahweh alone. *Separation to God* (being holy) necessitated *separation from other peoples*. As Deuteronomy makes explicit, for Israel to be wholly Yahweh's, for the land of Canaan to be given wholly to Israel, necessitated the clearing of the land completely of the other nations already there, to prevent any entanglements, marital or religious, with them (Deut 7:1-7). It was precisely the failure of Israel to implement this strategy completely or consistently that resulted in the exile to Babylon, as Amos 5:25-27 pointed out forcefully, a passage drawn on with powerful effect in Stephen's speech in Acts 7:42-43. The lesson was well learned in the post-exilic period under the reforms of Ezra, with the enforced abandonment of mixed marriages to cleanse people and land of all such defiling entanglements (Ezra 9–10). Israel was to be a people separated to the Lord and for the Lord.

In turn, the strength of the Maccabean resistance to cultural and religious assimilation in the first half of the second century B.C.E. was motivated precisely by the same conviction that Israel, both land and people, was not simply one among so many others, but was the special choice of the one God for himself alone. The term "Judaism" in fact emerged from the Maccabean resistance to the hellenizing syncretism of Antiochus. The name first appears in 2 Maccabees[21] precisely as an expression of this resistance, as an expression of the fortitude and faithfulness of those who continued to prize the Torah, to practice circumcision and to observe the laws of clean and unclean despite the most brutal persecution. Here again, in the strongly and fiercely nationalistic self-assertion that the term "Judaism" expressed, we have an important insight into the matrix from which earliest Christianity emerged, an important factor in shaping the theological stance of the first Christians, and so an important contextual element in our understanding of a NT biblical theology.

The clearest and most poignant expression of Israel's sense of need to keep itself separate from the nations appears in the motif of "jealousy" or "zeal" (the same word). For at the heart of it was Yahweh's own jealousy, as one who demanded exclusive worship and loyalty from his people.[22] Not surprisingly, Israel's history is dotted with corresponding *heroes of zeal,* who exercised a zeal for exclusive commitment to God reflective of Yahweh's exclusive commitment to Israel. And not entirely surprising, these heroes of zeal were famous precisely for their actions that prevented Israel's set-apartness from being corrupted and polluted: Simeon and Levi, who expunged the defilement of Dinah;[23] Phinehas, who turned back Yahweh's jealous wrath from consuming a people who were yoking themselves to the Baal of Peor;[24] Elijah whose victory over and then slaughter of the priests of Baal likewise prevented the corruption of Israel's holiness;[25] and the Maccabees themselves, notably appealing to the past heroes of zeal and in their turn preventing the dilution of Israel's loyalty to God alone by force of arms.[26] A factor too little noticed in the shaping of NT theology, to the extent that Paul did so, is that Paul first appears on the scene as a persecutor motivated by the same zeal,[27] and that his theology-shaping conversion was in major part a reaction against such zeal to maintain Israel's separateness from the nations.[28]

At the same time, and despite this strong holiness strand to Israel's theology and praxis, there was another strand, less prominent but repeatedly revived and re-expressed in various ways. Apart from anything else, there was, it should be remembered, the strong tradition of *Israel's hospitality to the stranger* and provision within the community for the "resident alien."[29] The subsequent welcome for *proselytes* and recognition of *Gentile "God-fearers"* was a feature of the Second Temple Judaism from which Christianity emerged.[30] More to the point, there are repeated warnings, also within Israel's own canonical literature, that Israel's election should not be taken for granted or presumed upon: Amos gives the salutary reminder that as God brought Israel from the land of Egypt, so he brought the Philistines from Caphtor and the Arameans from Kir (Amos 9:7-8); the story of Jonah is a striking warning to all who might take offence at the thought of God caring for Ninevah; and John the Baptist, the last of Israel's prophets prior to Jesus, warns against the presumption that might arise among Abraham's descendants by pointing out abruptly that God is able to raise up children to Abraham from the stones lying around (Matt 3:9/Luke 3:8).

In some ways most salutary of all is the too often neglected fact that the promise to and covenant with Abraham had *a third strand*: not only seed and land, but that *in Abraham all the tribes/nations of the earth would be blessed*.[31] The original force of the promise is less than clear,[32] and this third strand does not seem to have been given so much prominence as the other two strands in the biblical theology of Israel. But we have several hints of such an outreaching or spilling-over concern in such passages as Jeremiah's commission to be "a prophet to the nations" (Jer 1:5) and the Servant's commission to be "a light to the nations" (Isa 42:6; 49:6). And we will note below the strong expectation within the prophets and early Judaism of an eschatological pilgrimage of the nations to Zion. More intriguing still is the way in which earliest Christianity was able to take up this third strand and use it in apology for their unprecedented mission to the Gentiles.

C. Jewish Factionalism

The counterpart of this degree of openness to non-Jews and righteous Gentiles is the troubled concern lest the whole of Israel would fail to remain faithful to the covenant and their covenant God, with the consequent response of *narrowing down the covenant and covenant people* to a faithful remnant or a faction within Israel. Hence the emphasis on "faithfulness" in Second Temple Judaism as the only appropriate response to the covenant offered by God, as exemplified by Abraham in particular and with particular reference to Abraham's obedient readiness to offer up his son Isaac in sacrifice,[33] a reading of Gen 15:6 that Paul seems to have been contesting in his famous exposition of that passage in Romans 4.

The *remnant* theme, both as a fear and a hope, is persistent in the OT. The stories of Noah and the flood and of Abraham and Sodom already provide warnings that God's larger saving purpose for humankind might have to narrow its focus to the righteous (Gen 6:9; 18:22-33). Joseph is an example of God's provision to sustain a remnant (Gen 45:7). Elijah has to be reassured that though Israel as a whole seems to have forsaken the Lord, yet there are seven thousand left who have refused to bow the knee to Baal (1 Kgs 19:18). Amos repeatedly agonizes that only a remnant will survive,[34] but Micah is more hopeful despite the same forebodings.[35] The catastrophe of the Assyrian destruction of the northern kingdom would leave but a remnant (Isa 17:1-6), but Isaiah faced with the same threat names his son Shearjashub ("a remnant will return");[36] and Jeremiah facing a similar catastrophe subsequently is similarly hopeful (Jer 31:7). In Haggai and Zechariah "the remnant of the people" becomes a way of referring to those who had returned from exile in Babylon.[37]

In the second Temple period the equivalent to the remnant theology came to expression as an often very bitter *factionalism* that set groups against one another. The shared concern was for an Israel that remained loyal to the covenant, but what that commitment involved in practice became more and more contested. Characteristic was the factional attitude of the Pharisees, whose very name ("separated ones")[38] itself makes the point. It manifested itself as a purity concern, a concern, that is, to extend the holiness of the Temple throughout the land (Exod 19:5-6), and probably included their regularly eating food separately. The Pharisees' primary concern was to keep the law with scrupulous accuracy (*akribeia*),[39] which also and inevitably implied a condemnation of those who did not keep it with the same accuracy, as law-breakers ("sinners"). As we shall see below, this background is vital for understanding Jesus' confrontation with the Pharisees. Paul's recollection of his days as a Pharisee probably gives a somewhat extreme but otherwise fair expression of the Pharisaic ideal and self-assessment.[40]

The Qumran Essenes seem to have been a more extreme purity sect, who saw their commitment to the law, or at least their interpretation of the law, as a proper reason for them to "separate," not just from Gentiles but also from the bulk of the people (4QMMT C7), and to take themselves down to their congregation beside the Dead Sea. They saw themselves as alone true to the covenant of the fathers, as "the sons of light," "the house of perfection and truth in Israel," the chosen ones, and so on.[41] The other side of the same coin of such self-affirmation was the dismissal of others, that is, *other Jews,* as "the men of the lot of Belial," "traitors," "the wicked," "the sons of Belial," who had departed from the paths of righteousness, transgressed the covenant, and the like.[42] They evidently counted the Pharisees among their opponents, dismissing them, it would appear, as "those who seek smooth things," "the deceivers."[43]

And besides Pharisee and Essene we should note the often vituperative criticism of other (fellow) Jews that we find in such documents from the period as *1 Enoch*, the *Testament of Moses, Jubilees,* and the *Psalms of Solomon*. For example, the *Enoch* corpus gives evidence of a bitter calendrical dispute that racked Judaism probably throughout the second century B.C.E. "The righteous," "who walk in the ways of righteousness," clearly distinguished themselves from those who "sin like the sinners" in wrongly computing the months and feasts and years (*1 Enoch* 82:4-7). Interestingly enough, a similar attitude of dismissive condemnation and disqualification is evident in the opposition to the Colossian church (Col 2:16-23), an opposition that probably stemmed from one or more of the synagogues in Colossae.[44] The accusation in *1 Enoch* 1–5 again draws a sharp line of separation between the "righteous/chosen" and the "sinners/impious" (1:1, 7-9; 5:6-7), evidently other Jews who practiced their Judaism differently. One other example is the intense polemic in the *Psalms of Solomon* on behalf of those who regarded themselves as "the righteous," "the devout," over against the "sinners." The latter included not only Gentile enemies and the blatantly wicked, but, it would appear, also the Hasmonean Sadducees who (in the eyes of the devout) had defiled the sanctuary.[45]

Here again is material vital to our understanding of the setting for many of the NT writings. We cannot and should not regard such as the Dead Sea Scrolls as part of biblical theology. But it is certainly the case that we will not begin to grasp the character of NT theology without an appreciation of the milieu in which Christianity began, and with which it interacted, since that interaction was a major factor in shaping the theological positions and arguments of several of the NT writers (and of Jesus).

D. Israel's Eschatological Hope

The OT documents cherished no illusions about Israel's faithfulness. Archetypally, Deuteronomy not only lays before the people the choice between life and death, between blessing and curse (Deut 27–29), but expects *both*, both blessing and curse, to be the experience of Israel. In particular, the dispersal of Israel from the land is entirely expected, and the hope that is held out is of a people who return to the Lord to be gathered in again from all the parts of the world to which they have been exiled (30:1-10). The fact that Paul seizes upon this same passage (30:11-14) to show how rooted his gospel is in the OT (Rom 10:6-10) indicates his awareness of how important this hope of restoration to the land of Israel was for his fellow Jews of the diaspora. Certainly we can easily see from a kaleidoscope of biblical and post-biblical Jewish writings that a widely cherished hope was for the outcasts of Israel, scattered among the nations, to be brought back to the promised land, for the unity of the twelve tribes to be re-established, and for the covenant relation of Israel as God's people to be fully restored. The hope is a repeated emphasis of Second Isaiah,[46] but is common elsewhere too.[47] The theme of sin-exile-return is particularly prominent in the Testaments of the Twelve Patriarchs.[48] And the tenth prayer of the Eighteen Benedictions (*Shemoneh 'Esreh*) well reflects the longings of Israel at the time of Jesus: "Proclaim the liberation with the great trumpet, and raise a banner to gather together our dispersed, and assemble us from the four corners of the earth. Blessed art thou, Lord, who gatherest the banished of thy people Israel." This hope, of course, was regularly linked with the hope of a royal messiah, a son of David, who would reverse the fortunes of Israel and restore the monarchy to its Davidic prosperity.[49]

How were the non-elect nations to fare within this hope for Israel? In fact, the future of the other nations (Gentiles) was a matter of some speculation and disagreement. For some there is an element of vengefulness in the hope that the former persecutors and oppressors of the scattered people will suffer the same fate and experience the curses that had fallen on Israel (notably Deut 30:7). Some could only envisage the Gentiles' destruction, as the inevitable precondition and complement to Israel's restoration and prosperity, a premonition echoed in Rev 19:17-21.[50] But the majority looked for the Gentiles to come in pilgrimage to Zion to pay tribute[51] or to worship God there[52]—often referred to as *eschatological proselytes*. This was often linked with the hope for the ingathering of the scattered tribes of Israel;[53] for Israel to be fully blessed it was not necessary for the others to be damned! It should also be noted, however, that factions within Second Temple Judaism counted other *Jews* among the practitioners of evil to be defeated and judged—notable examples being the fearful curses called down upon the men of Belial in 1QS 2:5-10, and the assumption of the *Psalms of Solomon* that God's judgment against "the righteous" was a matter of discipline but against "the sinners" was to destruction (for example *Pss. Sol.* 13:6-11). A factor that may also be relevant as we fill out the context within which embryonic Christianity began to grow, was that the major recruitment of proselytes to earliest Judaism was by force of arms, as a consequence of the conquest of Galilee and Idumea by the Hasmoneans (Josephus, *Ant.* 13:257-258, 318). It is difficult if not impossible to disentangle the heritage that came down to the first Christians from its national and political ramifications.

3. ISRAEL REDEFINED?

It is almost impossible to overemphasize the fact that Christianity began within and as a part of Second Temple Judaism. Jesus was a Jew, a Galilean. Although attempts have been made to soften his Jewishness,[54] it remains fundamental that Jesus was a Galilean Jew,[55] and that he functioned as a devout Jew.[56] This remains not only a historical fact, but a theological fact of undiminished significance: "Christ became servant of the circumcised for the sake of God's truth, to confirm the promises of the fathers..." (Rom 15:8). Likewise, as already observed, the first Christians were all Jews, including Paul, the most controversial figure for non-Christian Jews. And the NT documents are predominantly written by Jews. So the question of the relation of these first Christians to Israel and how they understood that relation is inescapable, though to pose the issue in terms of "the church and Israel," as though these were two quite distinct categories, is to prejudge the question in a way that is prejudicial to NT theology and may lead that theology down non-biblical paths.

A. The Restoration of Israel

It is important, once again, to start with Jesus—not least because he must have set the tone for much of the earliest Christian reflection on the subject, as is evident in the way the Jesus tradition was maintained and molded into its lasting shape in the Gospels.

At once we recall, as previously noted, that Jesus' mission can be summed up as aiming for the restoration of Israel.[57] This is evident in his call to repentance (Mark 1:15), with its echo of similar prophetic calls like that of Jeremiah: "return, apostate sons" (Jer 3:12, 14, 22).[58] It is even clearer in Jesus' evidently deliberate choice of twelve close disciples (Mark 3:16-19 pars.), which almost all recognize to have a powerful restoration symbolism: the twelve in some sense representing the twelve tribes of Israel in their eschatologically reconstituted state.[59] The symbolism of "the flock of Yahweh," including the thought of gathering in the sheep scattered abroad, appears also quite frequently in the Jesus tradition,[60] with its obvious allusion to the popular image of Israel as Yahweh's flock.[61] Consistent with this is the thought of "the meek inheriting the land" (Matt 5:5), of Jesus' death as the covenant sacrifice for a/the new covenant (Luke 22:30/1 Cor 11:25), and the suggestion that Jesus' talk of a rebuilt temple (Mark 14:58 pars.) had in view a new community as the new temple.[62] Also relevant is the fact that Jesus' concern for the poor[63] so strongly echoes the typically Jewish state concern for the poor in the community of Israel, so prominent in the Deuteronomic legislation.[64]

What Jesus may have intended for "the restoration of Israel" remains unclear, including the question of what he hoped to achieve by his final journey to Jerusalem and by his "cleansing of the Temple" (Mark 11:1-19 pars). Luke's account of the appearance of Jesus on the road to Emmaus includes the poignant lament of the two disciples: "we had hoped that he was the one to redeem Israel" (Luke 24:21). And it should not escape notice that according to the Acts of the Apostles the only question put to Jesus by his disciples during his resurrection appearances to them was the equally poignant, "Lord, is this the time when you will restore the kingdom to Israel?" (Acts 1:6)—a question Jesus does not rebuke but simply pushes to one side (1:7). The fact, already noted, that Luke ends his account of Christianity's beginnings by recalling Paul describe his mission as "for the sake of the hope of Israel" (28:20) and "proclaiming the kingdom of God…unhindered" (28:31), leaves the issue up in the air.

Here it is appropriate to note, somewhat by way of parenthesis, that the political dimension of Jesus' mission and subsequently of Paul's gospel has become a notable theme in recent discussion. In particular, that the proclamation of Jesus as Lord would inevitably be seen as in opposition to the claims made for Caesar, as also talk of "peace" and "salvation" would be set in contrast to the peace and prosperity introduced by Augustus.[65] Such claims have been overblown, since titles like "Lord" and "Savior" were used more widely, for such deities as Serapis and Asclepius, without their being seen to clash with or contend against the claims made by the imperial cult. More to the point is the marked playing down of titles like "Son of David" and "Messiah,"[66] and the explicit guidance given by Paul to the Roman Christians to avoid provocation and to be good citizens (Rom 12:9–13:7). The political and social overtones in the NT writings are a very relevant aspect of NT theology, just as the political and social implications are for NT theologizing. But the process of evaluating them is not helped by over-promotion of the overtones and implications.

B. Jesus, Gentiles, and "Sinners"

Even more striking is the relative lack of interest in the Jesus tradition in what might be called "the Gentile question." It is true that Jesus is remembered as encountering Gentiles and responding to them positively—notably the (presumably Gentile) centurion and the Syrophoenician woman.[67] In both cases it is recalled that Jesus was impressed by their faith. And in Matthew's version of the first episode is also included Jesus' talk of many coming from east and west to eat with Abraham, Isaac, and Jacob in the kingdom of heaven (Matt 8:11/Luke 13:29). So, did Jesus share the hope of an eschatological pilgrimage of the Gentiles?[68] In the material common to Matthew and Luke ("Q") there are also warnings to recalcitrant villages that in the day of judgment it would be more favorable for such as Ninevah and Tyre than for them.[69] And Mark includes the full quotation from Isa 56:7 in his account of the purging of the Temple—"my house shall be called a house of prayer for all nations" (Mark 11:17)—one of the classic texts in Jewish expectation of eschatological proselytes flooding in pilgrimage into Jerusalem.

At the same time, however, in the instructions remembered as given by Jesus when he sent out his disciples to extend his mission, Matthew has preserved the explicit injunction: "Do not go on the way of / towards the Gentiles, and do not enter a Samaritan town, but go rather to the lost sheep of the house of Israel" (Matt 10:5). And Matthew also includes in his telling of the encounter with the Syrophoenician woman Jesus' rather dismissive initial response: "I was sent only to the lost sheep of the house of Israel" (15:24). It is also worth noting that when Jesus extended the sweep of his own mission to the regions round Tyre and Sidon (Mark 7:24, 31) the inference may be that he was thinking in terms of greater Israel, territories that could be regarded as part of Israel's heritage, part of the land promised to Abraham. That is to say, it is quite possible that Jesus saw it as part of his task to extend his mission to the children of Israel still resident in these parts. Although the Evangelists, including Matthew, had no doubt that the gospel was to go to the nations,[70] Jesus himself, it would appear, was less bothered about pushing back or breaching the boundaries around Israel. To count Jesus' own intentions as part of NT theology is, of course, contentious. But by including such tradition within their Gospels, the Evangelists, or Matthew at least, acknowledges that these memories of Jesus' mission should be retained and therefore were grist to his/their own theologizing about Jesus, and therefore to NT theology also.

If Jesus did not see it as a primary part of his mission to push back or cross the boundaries *around* Israel, it can be stated with greater confidence that he was concerned to *challenge the boundaries within Israel*. The point relates to the factionalism so prevalent within Israel at the time of Jesus (#5.2c above), and comes to clearest expression in Jesus' attitude to "sinners." The basic meaning of "sinner" is "law-breaker," as, for example, the regular use of the term in the Psalms makes clear.[71] But it has already been observed how the term was used as a factional "boo-word" in the writings of Second Temple Judaism. Not only for Gentiles, who, by definition were outside the law, out-laws.[72] But also for other Jews, judged by one of the factions to be unfaithful to the covenant.[73] *The law-breaking in this case was primarily in the eye of the beholder*. The devout who interpreted the law in a particular way regarded those who did not follow their interpretation and practice as law-breakers, "sinners." So already with Daniel, "the sinners" who failed to understand the revelation given to Daniel were contrasted with "the wise" who did (Dan 12:10). In 1 Maccabees the "sinners and lawless men" certainly included other Judeans whom the Maccabeans regarded as apostates.[74] Similarly, the "sinners" in the early Enoch literature are opponents of the self-styled "righteous."[75] In the same way in the Dead Sea Scrolls "sinners" refers to the sect's opponents,[76] where again it was failure to accept the sect's interpretation of the law that numbered them among the wicked.[77] Most striking of all, as already noted, the *Psalms of Solomon* repeatedly speak for the "righteous" and berate the "sinners," who, it would appear, were the Sadducean guardians of the Jerusalem temple cult.[78]

The light that this feature of Second Temple Jewish factionalism sheds on the mission of Jesus, as it is remembered in the Synoptic Gospels, is considerable, though it has not been as fully appreciated as it should have been. For Jesus' mission was notable for Jesus' own summary of his mission, as for the sake of "sinners" and not for those who were (or claimed to be) "righteous" (Mark 2:17 pars.), a striking echo of a typical factionalist antithesis, as most clearly expressed in the *Psalms of Solomon*. Luke notes that Jesus told the parable of the lost sheep as a specific response to the criticism that he welcomed sinners and ate with them (Luke 15:1-7). The parable of the Pharisee and the toll-collector praying in the temple makes the same point, by portraying the Pharisee, confident of his Torah righteousness, dismissing the toll-collector sinner (Luke 18:9-14). And Jesus was evidently infamous for his consorting with those regarded as irreligious or beyond the pale of acceptable praxis—that is, beyond what the righteous deemed acceptable, that is, acceptable to God (Matt 11:19/Luke 7:34). Nor should we forget the parable of the Good Samaritan with its implicit rebuke to the typical hostility against and denigration of the Samaritans because of their factional interpretation of the Torah and claim to have the true site of the Temple at Mount Gerizim (Luke 10:30-37).

Although Jesus did not make mission to non-Jews a priority, then, it would appear that *he saw it as important to challenge the then current factional conceptions of Israel and of what it meant to be a member of the people of God*. This presumably was part of what we might call his "restoration of Israel program." That which constituted the restoration of Israel, and who belonged to the restored Israel, would not be determined by what he designated at one point as "the traditions of men" (Mark 7:8, with reference to Isa 29:13). It was *acceptance by God that determined membership of God's people*, and, as Jesus pointedly noted, God was more accepting of the penitent "sinner" than of the confident "righteous" (Luke 18:14). *There was no more forceful critic of a religious factionalism that excludes the other as not measuring up to the faction's yardstick than Jesus.* To lose this crucial theological stand taken by Jesus as not part of NT theology would be irresponsible.

C. "Even on the Gentiles"

If Jesus challenged the boundaries *within* Israel, the most striking feature of the earliest Jesus sect is that it challenged the boundaries *around* Israel. Indeed, it could be said, as an important point of theological continuity between Jesus and the earliest churches, that the leaders of the mission to the Gentiles were simply(!) following the theological logic that Jesus' own mission had so embodied and enacted.

A historical point of no little significance has to be highlighted here. For neither the religion of Israel nor early Judaism was a missionary religion. Of course not. Second Temple Judaism was the religion of the Jews; *Ioudaismos* was the religion of the inhabitants of *Ioudaia*, the *Ioudaioi*. It was the religion of a particular people, a religion more tightly identified with a particular people than any of the other major religions of the time. As already observed, Israel and Judaism were very hospitable to the stranger living in their midst, very tolerant of the many non-Jews who found themselves attracted by Judaism (the so-called "God-fearers"), and very welcoming of proselytes who converted to Judaism. It also was concerned through its various apologetic writings (4 Maccabees, Philo, and Josephus being the most obvious examples) to strengthen the self-confidence of the majority of Jews who lived among the nations (the Diaspora). And most Jews would welcome the eschatological proselytes when they came flooding to Mount Zion in the last days. But there is little or no evidence of Jews claiming a missionary or evangelistic commission to *go out* to convert non-Jews.[79]

In consequence, the emergence of a sect within Second Temple Judaism, which saw itself as having such a commission, was an astonishing development. Why should non-Jews be called to believe in a Jewish messiah figure? Why should non-*Ioudaioi* think to lay any claim to participate in the heritage from Abraham without taking the logical step of becoming proselytes? But this is what happened. And this development forms such a huge part of both the beginnings of Christianity and of the NT writings that it must be counted as one of the major factors and elements in any NT theology.

To trace why this extraordinary development took place is the task of a history of Christianity's beginnings[80] more than of a NT theology. But it is important to highlight the factors that made all the difference, already referred to in #2. The impulses into a new conception of what it meant to be the people of God can certainly be traced back to the realization that God had raised Jesus from the dead and to the experience of the Spirit, as well as those more implicit in Jesus' own mission examined above (#5.3b). It is precisely because these major factors produced within a generation or two such a different understanding of how the people of God is made up and how it should function that they are so crucial to NT theology. A NT theology that does not major on the resurrection of Jesus and the outpouring of the Spirit of Pentecost simply will not work, since it will be unable to explain how Christianity came to be.

As Luke clearly saw, the episode of Peter and Cornelius in Acts 10–11 was both pivotal and archetypal in its significance. Here Luke portrays Peter as the model of the devout Jew, loyal to the traditions that made his Judaism so distinctive—in this case, the laws of clean and unclean, which marked out the separation of Israel from the other peoples (Lev 20:22-26). Confronted with the heavenly command to kill and eat animals whether clean or unclean, Peter recoils in horror: "I have never eaten anything that is profane (*koinon*)[81] or unclean" (Acts 10:14). The response from heaven would shake the very foundations of that theological logic requiring Israel's separation from the (other) nations: "What God has made clean, you must not call profane (*koinou*)" (10:15). Implicit is the same antithesis as in Mark 7:8—between a scripture built on by human tradition, and God sweeping away hindrances (not least religious hindrances) to his will. And, as Luke unfolds the story, Peter learned the lesson. The first words he says to Gentile (unclean) Cornelius is, not that he (Peter) was free now to eat pork or to eat with him (Cornelius); but, more profoundly, *"God has shown me that I should not call anyone profane* (*koinon*) *or unclean"* (10:28, emphasis added)—any *person*, not any animal! And the story climaxes with Cornelius and his friends receiving the Spirit in an equally unexpected way, convincing even the more traditionalist believers who had accompanied Peter that God had indeed accepted Cornelius and his friends, and that therefore there could be no hindrance to the traditionalist believers also accepting them (10:44-48). In Luke's account of the Jerusalem council (Acts 15), it was Peter's testimony regarding Cornelius (15:7-11) that was decisive in the decision that Gentile believers in Jesus need not become proselytes (15:19-21, 28-29).

Paul gives a different account of the breakthrough to Gentile mission (Gal 2:7-9), but in both cases the striking feature was that *God* had made clear his acceptance of Gentiles who were responding to the gospel by manifest signs of grace (2:9). Presumably Paul had in mind the same sort of visible evidence of the Spirit's entering the lives of these Gentiles.[82] Were it not for such visible marks of God's intention and approval, it is doubtful whether Christianity would ever have pushed back the boundaries around Israel. Alternatively expressed, without such marks of divine acceptance, it is doubtful whether a Jewish movement thus opening itself to non-Jews would have proved acceptable to the more traditional of the first generation of Christians.[83] *This openness to the Spirit breaking through old and long-venerated tradition thus becomes one of the key markers of emerging Christianity.* As such it is clearly embedded in the NT and so must function as an integral and foundational factor in any NT theology.

D. The Fulfillment of Israel's Mission

What is also striking is the way the Gentile mission is defended: that it did not constitute a departure from Israel's election, but was actually a fulfillment of Israel's own mission. The case is made most effectively by Paul, the self-styled "apostle to the Gentiles" (Rom 11:13), and by common consent the person who did more than anyone else to push back the boundaries around Israel.

For one thing, Paul clearly saw his own mission as wholly in the prophetic tradition. This is indicated in one of his few references to his own conversion, in which he quite deliberately echoed two of the great prophetic callings. By speaking both of his having been set apart before his birth, and of being called to proclaim to the nations (Gal 1:15-16) he was obviously echoing the two passages referred to earlier—Jeremiah's commission as "a prophet to the nations" (Jer 1:5) and the Servant's commission as "a light to the nations" (Isa 49:1, 6). At least to some extent, then, Paul seems to have seen his mission as fulfilling or completing the Servant's role,[84] that is the Servant Israel (Isa 49:3). And Luke in his account of Paul's conversion echoes the same Isaianic passages,[85] reinforcing the point: Paul was not an *apostate from* Israel but an *apostle of* Israel.[86]

The other most striking feature in Paul's letters on this point is the way he picks up the third strand of the promise to Abraham: the promise not only of seed and land, but also that in Abraham all the tribes/nations of the earth would be blessed (#5.2b). This is the strand of the promise to Abraham on which Paul alights in his crucial exposition in Galatians 3. It is this promise that he describes as "the gospel" proclaimed beforehand to Abraham: "In you shall all the nations be blessed" (Gal 3:8). Here Paul makes it clear that *the gospel for him had in view not simply the justification of individual sinners, but also the outreaching beyond the bounds that had hitherto circumscribed the people of God.* To be sure the particularism of Israel's election was being replaced by the particularism of faith in Christ. But the outreach of evangelism and the ending of the separation between peoples was an important part of the gospel, in many ways the most important for Paul—and for any theologizing that tries to grapple with Paul's theology.[87]

Luke is also clear that the mission and early expansion of Christianity was an outworking of Israel's destiny. He picks up the same strand of the promise to Abraham in Acts 3:25, this time on the lips of Peter. And, as already noted, he depicts Paul as claiming that his mission was directed to fulfilling the hope of Israel (28:20). But the most striking aspect of the Lukan portrayal is the central role he gives to the other great first generation leader of Christianity, James the brother of Jesus, in Acts 15. There he portrays James as resolving the great conundrum of how mixed Jew and Gentile communities should live together—a conundrum that Paul also attempted to resolve,[88] probably less successfully. In addressing the question of what should be expected of Gentile believers as they become part of the new messianic sect of Christianity, James cites Amos 9:11-12—the prophetic hope for the restoration of Israel (the fallen booth of David) linked to hope that other peoples may seek the Lord, "all the Gentiles whom (God) has claimed for his own" (Acts 15:14-18). *The promise of blessing to the nations is part and parcel of Israel's own restoration.* But then James goes on to set out modest conditions for table fellowship between Jew and Gentile in the mixed churches—what has been called "the apostolic decree": "Gentiles who turn to God should abstain from things polluted by (contact with) idols, from fornication, from that which is strangled, and from blood" (15:20).[89] It is generally recognized that the principal source of "the apostolic decree" is the legislation regarding "the resident alien," that is, the non-Jews who were permanently resident in the land of Israel, "in the midst of" the people.[90] Here we can see an alternative but potentially complementary solution to the incoming of the Gentiles into Israel's heritage: that the legislation in relation to the *resident alien* provided the desired precedent—at any rate, a very different model from Gentiles taking over and usurping Israel's heritage. We need not pursue further the historical questions here posed: particularly whether either solution was viable in the long run. The point is that both Paul and James (in Acts) provide further grist for theologizing on the relation between church and Israel, and indeed between both and the nations of the world insofar as they seek to embrace the heritage of Israel and of Jesus.

One other issue not usually considered in NT theology is worth noting here. For Paul historically and theologically gave great weight to the collection he made among his predominantly Gentile churches for the poor Christians in the mother church in Jerusalem.[91] But the echo of Isa 66:20 in Rom 15:16 and the likely allusion to the collection in Acts 24:17 suggest that the collection could have been interpreted as some sort of fulfillment of the hope of an eschatological Gentile pilgrimage to Jerusalem bringing gifts and offerings. In other words, Paul may have allowed, or even encouraged the thought that his mission was not pressing out beyond the bounds of Israel, so much as drawing them into Israel. Which is also to say that theologically the collection should not be seen or reduced simply to a kindly act of shared resources. Rather its potential for some sort of resolution of the Jew/Gentile issue that has never left Christianity, and its hermeneutical ambivalence, mean that it has and continues to have a theological potential that has been too little explored.

E. The Body of Christ

Since the messianic renewal movement within Second Temple Judaism quickly expanded beyond the bounds of Israel, that is, beyond both Israel the land and Israel the ethnic identifier, it is obvious that "Israel" as such could no longer be the entity to which new Gentile converts to the movement belonged. The land and the temple that gave the bulk of Diaspora Jews/Judeans their identity could not function in the same way, if at all, for non-proselyte Gentile believers. Hebrews makes a fascinating attempt to transform both elements, land and temple, into viable theological motifs for believers with a felt need of both and access to neither. But for the most part the NT writers look elsewhere for Christian identity factors. "The church of God" was no longer understood as the gathered assembly of Israel in the promised land. What then did this new understanding of the *qahal Yahweh* involve? To what did the new churches belong?

The obvious answer is *Christ*. The notion that Christ was understood as in some sense a location by which all believers in Messiah Jesus could identify themselves is evident in the language of indwelling. Paul's predominant "in Christ" terminology has an inescapable locative sense for much of its usage.[92] Believers can be defined as being "in Christ," as "those who are in Christ Jesus."[93] Here we should note again Paul's argument in Galatians 3: that Christ is the defining "seed" of Abraham, and those who are "in Christ" are thereby Abraham's seed and heirs according to the promise given to Abraham.[94] More striking is Paul's image of churches as forming "the body of Christ,"[95] where it is clear that belongingness to Christ, as a limb or organ belongs to a body, is a defining image of the Christian assembly. Noticeably, the body of Christ becomes Paul's first theme following his exposition of what has happened to Israel and what that portends for its future (Rom 9–11), with perhaps the implication that it is the body of Christ that functions for Christians as Israel had functioned for the people of God hitherto.[96] Whether the point can be pressed quite so far, we can certainly say that for Paul it is by believers collectively functioning as the active members of Christ's body that both Christ still functions on earth and the members of his body know themselves. It is a more striking fact than is usually noticed, that Paul can identify both the bread of the Lord's Supper and the gathered congregation as "the body of Christ,"[97] in each case the shared experience of spiritual grace embodied in Christ being the bonding factor.[98]

In John's Gospel an equivalent image is believers as branches of the vine that is Christ (John 15:1-11). A nearer parallel is the understanding that Jesus' resurrected body fulfills the hope for a rebuilt temple (2:19-21)—the body of Jesus playing a similar role as in Paul as providing a reference point for the new believers similar to that which the temple had provided for Israel and Second Temple Judaism. And similarly to Paul's "in Christ" motif is Jesus' prayer that Christians may be in the Father and the Son (John 17:21).[99] A more sustained motif in John's Gospel is the presentation of Christ as the one who fulfills and replaces the characteristic and defining features of Israel's religious praxis. Not only does Jesus' resurrected body fulfill the hope for a rebuilt temple (2:19-21). Christ also provides the new best wine that is the transformed water of purification rites (2:6-11), and the living water that is so much more potent and thirst-quenching than water from the well of Jacob (4:10-14) or the water rites that marked the Feast of Booths (7:37-39). Not least, Christ is the living bread from heaven that far transcends the manna that Moses provided in the wilderness (6:25-58).

The same point is made elsewhere in the NT and forms a major theological theme that unites the diverse NT documents: that Jesus Christ fulfills or completes all that Israel represented in the eschatological purposes of God. Scriptures speaking of Israel find their fulfillment in him;[100] he transcends Moses as the one who has revealed God.[101] Jewish rituals and festivals "are only a shadow of what is to come, but the reality belongs to the Christ" (Col 2:17). Jesus' priestly order in succession from the mysterious Melchizedek far transcends that of the order of Aaron, as his sacrifice is the reality for which the Jerusalem cult only prepared (Heb 5–10). It was Christ that the prophets were struggling to express in their prophecies (1 Pet 1:10-12). The lamb that was slain alone has the power and authority to open the scroll that reveals God's purpose when no one else, even the greats of Israel's history, could do so (Rev 5).

This *transfer of the decisive identifier of the people of God*, of the church of God, from the ethnic seed of Abraham and the land promised to Abraham *to the Christ as the one to whom Israel's whole history and purpose aspired* is one of the most revolutionary features of the earliest Christian movement. It is this that cuts at the nerve of every and any attempt thereafter to identify Christianity with a particular nation or ethnicity or culture. *Christianity is defined by Christ and by reference to Christ*—period!

That is the gyroscope that alone holds the good ship Christianity steady and enables it to maintain forward momentum even in the most stormy of conditions.

F. The Supersession or (Re)definition of Israel?

The data just reviewed poses a major theological issue for Christianity. Has Christianity taken over from and replaced Israel in the purposes of God? This was a prominent conclusion drawn in Christian circles from the second century onwards. For example, Justin Martyr regarded Christians as "the true spiritual Israel," "the true Israelite race" (*Dial.* 11:5; 135:3, 6). And Melito of Sardis regarded Israel as the model, now made void and abolished, but the church as "the reality" (*Peri Pascha* 39- 45). It was this deduction that God had finished with Israel, wiped his hands of his ancient people, that produced the whole *adversus Judaeos* tradition within Christianity with its bitter fruit of Christian anti-semitism. Even well through the twentieth century, and even after the Shoah (Holocaust), theologians still referred to first-century Judaism as *Spätjudentum* ("late Judaism"), the theological rationale being the same assumption that Judaism's only purpose was to prepare for Christianity, and that Christianity had superseded Judaism, draining the substance from it and leaving it only the empty husk—the end of Judaism, therefore "late" Judaism!

The NT biblical theologian cannot ignore all this as going beyond the Bible, since it can be readily argued that the *adversus Judaeos* tradition began in the NT itself. And certainly it is not hard to make that case. Matt 27:25, the crowd at the Roman trial of Jesus shouting, "His blood be on us and on our children," became a scriptural justification for accusing later generations of Jews as "Christ-killers" and for the resultant pogroms. In Acts Luke makes no effort to correct the impression that the Jews crucified Jesus, even though crucifixion was a Roman penalty.[102] Neither does John have any scruples in having Jesus accuse "the Jews" of having the devil for their father (John 8:44). And Hebrews has no hesitation in concluding that God in making the new covenant (with believers in Jesus Messiah) "has made the first one obsolete. And what is obsolete and growing old will soon disappear" (Heb 8:13). The supersessionist tradition is rooted in Hebrews![103]

A NT theology must not ignore or cloak such disturbing material. It should be able to point out that much of this material can be softened by the reminder that such blunt condemnation and exaggeration always featured in intra-Israelite polemic and prophetic rebuke.[104] More important is to underline the historical character of NT theology, in its concern to hear the NT writers in their own situation and contexts. For example, an accusation of responsibility for the death of Jesus on the part of the citizens of Jerusalem is much more understandable in the months following that death, when feelings would still be raw among Jesus' disciples. And to preach on John 8:44 *simpliciter*, as promoting a dismissal of Jews in general as devil's spawn, would be highly irresponsible. Rather, set in a context in late first century (when most deduce John's Gospel to have been written), when there was evidently some acrid confrontation between the surviving and re-emerging synagogues and those who believed in Messiah Jesus, such vitriol is understandable if regrettable. When historical circumstance and the limited scope of particular texts are more fully appreciated, it becomes all but impossible credibly or morally to generalize from them to a universal condemnation of Jews of all generations and nations.

Equally, if not more important, is the fact that a NT theology can and should also take into account the other strand of NT theology noted at the beginning of this chapter—for example:

1. The fact that Jesus himself remained wholly within Second Temple Judaism;
2. The way in which James and 1 Peter address their letters to (the twelve tribes[!] of) the Diaspora; and particularly,
3. Paul's attempt to resolve the uncomfortable question of why the bulk of his fellow-Jews were rejecting the gospel of Messiah Jesus (Rom 9–11).

It is this last that provides the most substantive alternative to the *adversus Judaeos* tradition. For Paul as a Jew who was also a Christian could not separate the two. His treatment of Rom 9–11 is not, as often described, a treatment of "Israel and the church";[105] the theme of these chapters is Israel itself. Noticeably in these chapters he talks little of Jews and Gentiles/Greeks (his predominant formulation in the earlier chapters), but almost only of Israel.[106] It is no longer a matter of attempting to bridge the gap between two sets of ethnically identified peoples (Jews and other nations). It is now a matter of trying to make best sense of God's purpose for Israel. "Who is Israel?" Paul asks in effect (9:6).[107] His response is to attempt to *define Israel afresh*: Israel as defined not by physical descent

(Ishmael), nor by works (Esau), but defined by God's call (Rom 9:6-12), a call that now includes Gentiles as well as Jews (9:23-24). God has not uprooted the olive tree of Israel and replaced it with another. On the contrary, uncultivated branches of wild olives (Gentiles) have been grafted into the olive tree of Israel—the same original planting (11:17-24). But even while broadening the definition of Israel Paul cannot bring himself to doubt or deny God's faithfulness to his chosen people: the blessings of Israel are still Israel's (9:4-5); "the gifts and call of God are irrevocable" (11:29). His confident assurance is that when the full number of the Gentiles has been brought in, then "all Israel will be saved" (11:12, 25). For a NT theology, that is a challenging vision to interpret and to integrate with the other NT material relevant to the subject.

G. One Covenant or Two?

One way of resolving the conundrum of Paul's assurance regarding Israel is the proposal that Paul was thinking of two covenants and not just one. That is, on the basis of God's faithfulness to his covenant people, Paul deduced that God would save Israel by virtue of his prior election of Israel.

That is, he would save Israel on the terms of the original covenant, through the law rather than the gospel, through Israel's obedience to the law as laid down in the Pentateuch.[108] But Paul clearly thought of God's call, the same call, as embracing both Gentiles and Jews (Rom 9:11-12, 24), and of the gospel calling for faith in Christ as universal in its outreach (10:6-18; 11:28-32); why otherwise would he have been so troubled by Israel's rejection of the gospel (9:1-3)?[109] To be sure, it is not finally clear how Paul could affirm both the *irrevocability* of God's election of (ethnic) Israel and *Christ* as the *sine qua non* criterion for identifying the people of God. What is impressive in his penultimate paragraph of Romans 9–11 is the fact that his confidence is rooted most firmly in the mercy of God (11:30-32). This too, as noted above (#4.2b), is part of his heritage from Israel's most fundamental revelation of God's character (Exod 34:6-7). As an axiomatic principle of biblical theology, however, it provides if not a resolution to such conundrums at least a way of handling them: that in the final analysis "the love of God is broader than the measure of man's mind"; and that the breadth of God's mercy will always surprise the traditionalist and the dogmatist, the factionalist and the sectarian.

The same consideration probably can be applied to the other conundrum that the same passage in particular provokes: whether God's mercy is *universal*. "God has imprisoned all in disobedience so that he may be merciful to all" (Rom 11:32). That Paul's theology here can be simply classified as "universalistic" in fact is not as clear as it may seem; the "all," from the beginning of the letter, is directed particularly to the Jew/Gentile divide that his own mission set out to overcome—"all, Jew first but also Greek."[110] The theological point to be grasped may rather be that God has mercy on the disobedient; that the gospel is good news less for the righteous and more for the sinner. In any case, there is further grist for theologizing; for it is precisely the fact that no clear conclusions can be reached regarding the historical description of the theology of the NT writers (or NT theology generally) on particular theological issues of continuing importance that makes it imperative that the same NT material should be seen as a stimulus and resource for further theologizing on the same and similar issues today.

The same applies all the more to the specific issue that arises from this chapter for Jewish/Christian relations and dialogue. The NT material reviewed above should not be regarded as out of bounds for such dialogue. Rather it should stimulate that dialogue. In particular, Paul who is generally regarded as an apostate from Israel should be revisited on the subject. For, as we have seen, Paul regarded himself more as an apostle commissioned to help fulfill Israel's mission to be a blessing and a light to the Gentiles. Paul would not have written as he did had he not been wholly convinced that he was being faithful to Israel's scriptures and heritage (cf. again Rom 9:4-5). It is as *an authentically Jewish voice* from the final decades of Second Temple Judaism that Paul demands a hearing. All, be they Jews or Gentiles, who wish properly to respect the writings from that period and the character of Second Temple Judaism, should include Paul's among the voices to which they wish to listen afresh. And what applies to Jewish/Christian dialogue, applies *mutatis mutandis* to other inter-faith dialogues. NT theology as NT theologizing opens the way for the NT to be a voice (several voices) contributing to questions and issues of general religious and cultural concern.

4. CONCLUSION

The questions "What does it mean to be 'the people or church of God'?" or from a Christian perspective, "What does it mean to be the body of Christ?" are of first importance today, perhaps as never before.

That is, what are the implications for belief and worship, for relations within faith groups and among faith groups, for mission, outreach, and service, for community and society, for political involvement and moral stances, for daily living and conduct? These were the sorts of questions with which the prophets and sages of Israel wrestled, and the initial reflections of emerging Christianity on its relations with its Jewish forbears and with Israel within an antipathetic (when not hostile) Roman Empire had a pressing urgency that has left clear marks on the NT writings. Here not least NT theology cannot be content with its historical and descriptive task but should find in these scriptures resources for sustained theologizing on the equivalent questions today.

For a summary statement of what has emerged from this exploratory investigation of "the church of God" as it relates to the issues of a NT biblical theology, we should note the following:

1. The tension between the principle of an elect nation and belief in one God who is God of all and concerned for all peoples runs from the beginning of the Abrahamic story. It is as evident in the prophets (other nations defeated/destroyed or welcomed but only as proselytes?) as in the mission of Jesus: to what extent was the restoration of Israel central to Jesus' own conception of his mission, and how "exclusive" was that? How valid was Paul's attempt to re-identify the seed of Abraham? Can Gentile believers in Christ be classified as (belonging to) Israel without cost to or loss of the identity of "Israel"? The call to be a blessing to the nations is consistent, and the possibility of a universalism predicated on God's mercy is there throughout.

2. The diversity in NT presentation on the subject is clear enough. Matthew does not hide the fact that Jesus spoke of mission only as mission to Israel. The antagonism evoked by Paul's mission to the Gentiles is evident in passages like Acts 21:21 and Phil 3:2-16. The tension between Paul's affirmation of Israel and Hebrews' dismissal of the old covenant as "obsolete" is an integral part of NT theology. The evident hostility shown towards "the Jews" in John and Acts may be understandable in historical terms, but it still leaves a problem for the twenty-first-century reader and for liturgical use of these texts. The differing solutions to "the Gentile problem" indicated in Acts 15:14-21 and Gal 2:11-17, and the differing interpretations possible for Paul's col-

lection indicate festering sores that were never fully healed. And if Paul sought resolutions for the problem, which never proved acceptable theologically or realistic in practical terms, where does that leave the status of his resolutions within the canon?

3. If the other side of "the Gentile problem" is "the problem of Israel," then the biblical theology of "the church of God" speaks directly to the ongoing concerns of Jewish/Christian dialogue. It indicates to us not least that the question of the relationship between Judaism and Christianity, between Jew and Christian, is much more one of ecumenical dialogue than of evangelistic mission.[111] The NT consists of a sequence of Jewish voices speaking to Jewish concerns. "The church of God" is a subject not merely of NT theology but of biblical theology as a whole, and NT theologizing on the subject should never be allowed to stray far from that given.

4. I have said little about the usual issues that dominate ecclesial and ecumenical discussions—ministry and ordination, charisma and office, sacraments and church order[112]—not because they are unimportant, but simply because the issues reviewed above are so important from a biblical theology perspective and because these fundamental concerns of biblical theology have not been given the attention they deserve and demand.

S I X

THE ETHICAL
OUTWORKINGS

1. INTRODUCTION

T*he law* is a fourth fundamental issue for biblical theology. The centrality of the law for Israel and Judaism has posed a consistent
problem for a theology of the Christian Bible. For Jesus is popularly thought to have set his face against the law, or at least against a law-
regulated life, in his controversies with the Pharisees. And Paul has been
consistently characterized as the one who championed the gospel against
the law and who secured Christianity's liberty from the law (cf. Gal 5:1).
By making a fundamental distinction between gospel and law, Luther in
particular reinforced a sense of sharp discontinuity between Judaism and
Christianity that has haunted Christian theology more or less from the
first.[1] More to the point here, such a sharp distinction runs the danger of
undermining the whole project of biblical theology, precisely because the
law is so fundamental for the OT and Judaism.

It is essential, then, that the role of the law within the OT and Second
Temple Judaism be understood as fully as possible, so that the question of
the relevance of the law to conduct within earliest Christianity and the
role of the law within NT theology can be properly assessed. The Torah,
meaning the Pentateuch (the five books of Moses), is the center of Israel's
canon of sacred scripture. If a "canon within the canon" is a valid concept,
then the Torah is the canon within the canon of the Hebrew Bible, "the

norm that norms the norm." Of course the Torah, as the foundation and constitutional document of Israel and Judaism is more than rules for worship and living. Apart from anything else, it (the Pentateuch) includes the accounts of creation, the patriarchal narratives, and the stories of the exodus, the establishment of the covenant at Sinai, and various episodes from the period of the wilderness wanderings. And the dependence of the NT on the Torah in this broader sense is not in question, as we have already seen (#2.2). But the primary sense of Torah is "instruction," and the Torah as *law* is the dominant sense, both for Judaism and Christianity, the Torah as the law of Moses, as "the decrees, statutes and ordinances"[2] that make up the bulk of the Pentateuch, and that allow *Torah* to be translated in Greek simply as *nomos*, "law." It is Torah as law (*nomos*) that demands our focus here.

The question, How should the people of God live?, is not an addendum to NT theology. It is integral to it. The principles, values, and criteria that determine social relations and individual conduct are not simply to be addressed under the headings of "application," or of "religion" as something distinct from theology. For theology is not, or should not be seen simply as a cerebral activity or something carried out exclusively in the classroom or study or upper room of a sanctuary. And where theology meets the wider agendas of the wider society most effectively is in the attitudes and conduct it encourages and brings to expression. Ethics is the daily expression of theology, one of the tests or fruits by which the truth and value of theology can be witnessed and assessed.

As in the earlier chapters, therefore, we look first at the theological givens inherited from the religion of Israel and early Judaism and from the OT:

A. The priority of grace over law
B. The law of Israel
C. The wall of separation
D. The way of life and the way to life

Then we turn to examine the way Jesus and the earliest Christians responded to and drew upon this so valuable heritage:

A. Jesus and the *halakhoth*
B. Did Paul break with the law?
C. Do/(are) Christians (expected to) fulfill the law?
D. Judgment according to works

2. THE INHERITED THEOLOGY

A. The Priority of Grace over Law

I have already underlined the stress that Israel's scriptures lay on God's initiative, both in his election of Israel and in his saving righteousness.[3] It is important for biblical theology to appreciate that the same applies also to Israel's law.

The fact that the Torah is more than law, and that the law is set within the accounts of God's creation, of his dealings with the patriarchs, and of his initial dealings with "the children of Israel" is of crucial importance in any appreciation of the status and role of the law for Israel and for Second Temple Judaism. For the context makes the point that the giving of the law is rooted deeply in the narrative of Israel's history. The giving of the law at Sinai is, as it were, a second phase of God's saving purpose which presupposes as an essential antecedent the oath made to Abraham, Isaac, and Jacob, and which depends on that prevenient divine initiative for its rationale—a prevenient grace which is also part of and integral to the Torah.

Particularly striking is the way the whole sequence of law-giving is introduced in Exodus with the words: "I am the LORD your God, who brought you out of the land of Egypt, out of the house of bondage" (Exod 20:2); and then follows the most famous sequence of Israel's laws, the ten commandments. The sequence makes the point: "I am the Lord your God"—not, "Do this in order that I might become your God"; "I brought you out of the land of Egypt, out of the house of bondage"—redemption as prior to obligation, the presupposition of obedience, *the imperative of God's demand for obedience following from the indicative of God's saving action.*

This is a key point that E. P. Sanders made in his justified and effective protest against the popular caricature in Christian circles of Judaism as a religion that understood law-obedience ("works of the law") as the necessary means to attain God's acceptance in the first place.[4] The law was *not* presented as a means to become God's people. Rather it was given to show those who were *already* God's people, already recipients of his redemption, how they should live. Entry into covenant grace was not the end-point goal of the law; the covenant grace was the starting point for obedience. In Sanders's popularly phrased antithesis, the law was not a means of *getting into* the covenant people of God, it was rather a means of *staying in* the covenant people of God. He summed up Israel's soteriology in the neat phrase, "covenantal nomism": (1) as presupposing the freely covenanted grace of God ("covenantal"); and (2) as requiring a consequent obedience to the law (Greek *nomos*, hence "nomism").[5] The summary phrase has attracted a good deal of criticism,[6] and certainly it is true that the phrase itself does not specify how the symbiotic relation between divine grace and human response should work out or has worked out in practice. But the key points remain: that the phrase indicates that *both* elements are part of and integral to Israel's and Judaism's soteriology; and that it also reminds us of the priority of God's covenant choice and redemptive initiative.[7]

The most basic fact of all, which itself makes the point, is that the law was given to Israel, the law that showed the people of God how to live. The fact, of course, leaves biblical theology with the question: To what extent was/is Israel's law also law for the non-Israelite?

B. The Law of Israel

Discussion of Israel's law has often worked with the dichotomy between the ceremonial law and the moral law. This proved a convenient device in biblical theology (and Christian theology generally) to resolve the dilemma of how to hold together the more negative attitudes to the law within the NT and the fact that the law of Moses is still part of Christian scripture. The solution offered by the dichotomy was that early Christianity rejected the ceremonial law while holding firm to the moral law.[8] That such a distinction could encourage a suspicion of all ritual and ceremony became especially clear in the radical Reformation. But the distinction is a false one as usually worked out. The Torah did not work with such distinctions. The Pentateuch does not separate the two kinds of laws into separate categories. For example, the Ten Commandments include rules regarding the Sabbath as well as ethical demands; and the sequence of rules in Exod 21–23 runs unbroken from social legislation to what could appropriately be described as religious rulings.

Probably a more satisfactory way to describe the range covered by the law is to note that the law of Moses includes both laws governing relations between Israelites and God, and laws governing relations among Israelites.

(1) Laws Governing Relations Between Israelites

In his *Anchor Bible Dictionary* article on "Biblical and ANE Law" Samuel Greengus provides a convenient taxonomy:[9]

1. Laws protecting the family (sexual taboos, adultery, rape);
2. Personal injuries (the goring ox, miscarriage, battery, talion[10] and compensation);
3. Homicide (including the unsolved murder);
4. Theft;
5. Social welfare (debts and slavery, redemption and release).

This list makes clear what should be obvious but is sometimes forgotten: that the law of Moses was not simply a religious law, not simply a collection of religious rubrics that might be distinguished from civil law. *The law of Moses was the law of the nation Israel.* But it was a religiously inspired law. So of course it covered a wide range of social legislation, as one would expect when dealing with the law of the land, but it took its starting point and inspiration from the covenant that God had made with the people of Israel through Moses.

Worthy of particular note is the *strong sense of responsibility toward the disadvantaged of society* inculcated by the law, the obligation towards those less able to fend for themselves. Characteristically in view are the widow, the orphan, the stranger, and the poor.[11] A good example of the typical concern is Zech 7:9-10:

> Thus says the LORD of hosts, Render true judgments, show kindness and mercy each to one another; do not oppress the widow, the orphan, the alien, or the poor; and do not devise evil in your hearts against one another.

This concern for the disadvantaged should not be confused with a purely individualistic charity. It was enshrined in civil law, and thus formally recognized as a responsibility of society. Here Deut 24:10-22 should not be missed, with its requirement not to retain pledges of the poor overnight, not to withhold the wages of the poor but to pay them daily, not to take advantage of alien or orphan or widow, and always to leave some harvest for the alien, the widow, and the orphan to glean for themselves. It should also be noted that the concern for the poor shown in the NT is drawn entirely from the same OT heritage. This is evident not only in the priority given to the theme in Jesus' proclamation,[12] for James' tirade in Jas 5:1-6 is a prophetic denunciation of the ruthless rich wholly in the tradition of Amos; and, a fact often ignored, Paul's collection for the poor in Jerusalem had the same motivation (2 Cor 9:9-10), the almsgiving he urged on his Corinthian converts being presented as an act of "righteousness" as in Second Temple Judaism.[13]

In view of what has been said above about the exclusiveness of God's choice of Israel (#5.2b), and what will be said below about the law as what Ephesians calls "the dividing wall" between Israel and the other nations (#6.2c), it should be pointed out that the command to love the neighbor as oneself (Lev 19:18) was extended without demur to "the alien who resides among you": "The alien who resides with you shall be to you as the citizen among you; you shall love the alien as yourself, for you were aliens in the land of Egypt: I am the LORD your God" (19:34). Note the motivation: Israel's own experience of alienation and slavery should make Israelites more sensitive to and concerned for non-Israelites in their midst. The story of Ruth is included in the corpus of Israel's sacred history to highlight that very point; care for the stranger is a duty that follows from Yahweh being their God. Israel's "welfare state" had a deeply religious motivation, and underscores the moral and social implications that must follow if any biblical theology is to be true to itself.

(2) Laws Governing Relations Between Israelites and God

Inevitably a large proportion of Israel's laws relate to the ordering of the Temple, of the priesthood and the sacrificial cult, of tithes, the Sabbath, circumcision, and purity. I say *inevitably*, since the relation between Yahweh and his people was primary; it is what constituted them as a people and gave the motivation for their social law. Sufficient has probably been said already about the Temple and the sacrificial system (#4.2d). Here it is particularly important to focus on the issue of *purity*, since purity seems to have become an increasingly important issue for Jews by the time of Jesus—as attested archaeologically by the large number of *miqwaoth* (ritual baths) that have been discovered in the land of Israel.[14] Perhaps more to the point, it was division over purity issues that seems to have been a factor, if not the primary factor, in the factionalism that racked Second Temple Judaism: the Pharisees as the "separated ones"; the Essenes with their strong purity ritual as attested in 1QS 6-7 and at Qumran; the attacks on Sadducees for their defiling of the sacrifices in the *Psalms of Solomon*;[15] and the savage indictment of (probably) the Pharisees who "touch impure things" yet say "Do not touch me lest you pollute me" in *T. Mos.* 7:9-10.

The rationale in all this could be summed up in the word *holiness*. It was because the Lord God was holy that Israel had to be holy: "You shall be holy, for I the Lord your God am holy"—the repeated refrain of Leviticus.[16] Holiness meant set-apartness—set apart from the unavoidably defiling and corrupting character of human life and society, as represented most strikingly by death and the decaying corpse as the most seriously defiling agent. Purity was essential above all if one was to enter the sanctuary where God had put his name, the Temple in Jerusalem.[17] But the religious concern for purity extended more or less throughout the whole land (the holy land), as demonstrated by the presence of *miqwaoth* throughout the land of Israel.[18] It was to safeguard this extended holiness and their own holiness in particular, their own set-apartness to God, that Pharisees and Essenes literally separated themselves from the rest of the people.

This helps explain why purity legislation often has more the character of the *taboo* than of moral principle. The purification rituals, of course, exemplify the aspect of cleansing, but otherwise their rationale seems primarily aimed at highlighting the nature of the holy as something to be feared or held in awe. Why should a particular place or piece of clothing or person be regarded as "holy" and others not? Part of the point is presumably that the interaction between God and his people cannot be reduced to the straightforwardly rational; there is a fundamentally a-rational dimension to any encounter with the holy. And part of the rationale of the ritual, presumably, is to symbolize the absolute distinction between the divine and the human. It is precisely as reaching beyond the scope of every day rationality that the whole category of the holy has proved so powerful.

Part of the value of treating the relations between God and Israel and the relations between Israelites separately is that it helps us to see the difference between *impurity* and *sin*.[19] Impurity as such is not sin; it is simply a condition into which one inevitably comes in the course of everyday life, by normal interaction with the unclean. Sin, on the other hand, is transgression of the law; "sinner" means "law-breaker." So sin enters not with impurity as such, but only when and if the impure person fails to take the steps required to remove the uncleanness or end the state of impurity. The distinction, however, is easily lost, since "cleansing" as a metaphor so readily lends itself to the process for removing sin, as Christian spirituality and hymnody so frequently attest. *Cleansed* becomes synonymous with *forgiven*. That is deeply unfortunate since it identifies distance from God with *guilt*, whereas Israel's impurity legislation teaches us that one can be impure and distant from God without being guilty of sin.

Here again is a major theme for any biblical theologizing: How to give the theme of purity its appropriate weight, especially when the Jerusalem Temple is no more? Does it all simply carry over to any other cult center, as so often Christianity has simply transferred Sabbath legislation to the Christian Sunday? Is Christian baptism a kind of ritual washing, or does its once-only character preclude the idea of the renewed cleansings that worshipers presumably need when they approach the Holy One (cf. Heb 10:22)? And more broadly, how to assess the a-rationality of so much purity symbolism and to integrate it with different patterns of worship as well as with the moral and social obligations of the people of God? And how to retain the sense of *awe* that the holiness legislation promoted and safeguarded?

C. The Wall of Separation

A third aspect of the law of Moses has often been disregarded or played down. This is the fact that the law served as a boundary marker, separating Israel from the other nations round about.[20] I have already drawn attention (#5.2b) to the stringent requirements that the land (Canaan) must be cleared completely of the other nations already there, to prevent any entanglements, marital or religious (Deut 7:1-7). Ezra is remembered as the one who brought the returned exiles back to the law by insisting that all mixed marriages (Judeans with "foreign wives") must be ended and the foreign wives be "sent away"; Judea must separate itself from the people of the land (Ezra 9–10). The attitude is most harshly expressed in the second century B.C.E. *Jubilees*:

> Separate yourself from the Gentiles, and do not eat with them, and do not perform deeds like theirs. And do not become associates of theirs. Because their deeds are defiled, and all their ways are contaminated, and despicable, and abominable. (*Jub.* 22:16)

The role of the law as protecting Israel from such corrupting influences is well illustrated by the Letter of Aristeas:

> In his wisdom the legislator [i.e. Moses] . . . surrounded us with unbroken palisades and iron walls to prevent our mixing with any of the peoples in any matter. . . . So, to prevent our being perverted by contact with others or by mixing with bad influences, he hedged us in on all sides

with strict observances connected with meat and drink and touch and hearing and sight, after the manner of the law. (*Let. Aris.* 139, 142)

Philo, the Alexandrian Jewish philosopher and elder contemporary of Paul, draws on the prophecy of Balaam (Num 23:9) to describe Israel similarly as a people "which shall dwell alone, not reckoned among other nations... because in virtue of the distinction of their peculiar customs they do not mix with others to depart from the ways of their fathers" (*Mos.* 1:278). And the Roman historian Tacitus shows that such attitudes of the Jews were well known to others in the Roman Empire: "They sit apart at meals and they sleep apart.... They adopted circumcision to distinguish themselves from other peoples by this difference" (*Hist.* 5.5.2).

The purity concern behind both attitudes and rules is obvious and the link between cleanness (purity) and separation is clear already in Lev 20:24-26:

> I have said to you: You shall inherit their land, and I will give it to you to possess... I am the LORD your God; I have separated you from the peoples. You shall therefore make a distinction between the clean animal and the unclean, between the unclean bird and the clean; you shall not bring abomination on yourselves by animal or by bird or by anything... which I have set apart for you to hold unclean. You shall be holy to me; for I the LORD am holy, and I have separated you from the other peoples to be mine.

The passage makes clear that the theological rationale behind the laws of clean and unclean, sealed by the blood of the Maccabean martyrs (1 Macc 1:62-63), and so fundamental to (orthodox) Jewish identity to the present day, is not the issue of hygiene or health but the felt need of the law-makers of Israel and early Judaism to hold the chosen people *separate from the other nations,* holy to God alone. Alternatively expressed, there was an excluding aspect of the law of Moses that has been too much neglected—not just the fact that the law excluded the sinner or the impure from the presence of God, but the fact that peoples other than Israel were excluded from the covenant mercies of God by virtue of being other than Israel, outside the law, out-laws, and as such (regarded as) impure and sinners.

The tension that this function of the law set up within Second Temple Judaism and the messianic missionary sect of Jesus that sprang up within

Second Temple Judaism we have already looked at in some detail (#5). Here it is the importance of the law of Moses as underlining and enforcing that separation that needs to be brought out more clearly than has traditionally been the case.

D. The Way of Life and the Way to Life[21]

The most obvious function of the law was to show Israel the way of life they should live as God's people. It was the corollary to and consequence of the covenant that God made with Israel in fulfillment of the oath previously made to the patriarchs—God saying in effect: Since you are my people, this is how you should live as my people, both to honor me and to demonstrate to the other nations that you are my people.[22]

The theological rationale is set out most clearly in Deuteronomy—Moses laying down the law on how the people of Israel should live in the land they were about to possess. The carrot and stick are clear particularly in the opening chapters: if Israel observed these laws its people would prosper in the land; but if they failed to obey the laws of Moses they would perish and be expelled from the land, like the other nations.[23] I illustrate by citing the initial statement of the repeated theme and the climax to the opposing list of blessings and curses set before the people in chs. 28–30.

> So now, Israel, give heed to the statutes and ordinances that I am teaching you to observe, so that you may live to enter and occupy the land that the LORD, the God of your ancestors, is giving you.... You must observe them diligently, for this will show your wisdom and discernment to the peoples, who, when they hear all these statutes, will say, "Surely this great nation is a wise and discerning people!" (Deut 4:1, 6)

> See, I have set before you today life and prosperity, death and adversity. If you obey the commandments of the LORD your God ... by loving the LORD your God, walking in his ways, and observing his commandments, decrees, and ordinances, then you shall live and become numerous, and the LORD your God will bless you in the land that you are entering to possess. But if your heart turns away and you do not hear, but are led astray to bow down to other gods and serve them, I declare to you today that you shall perish; you shall not live long in the land that you are crossing the Jordan to enter and possess. I call heaven and earth to witness against you today that I have set before you life and death, blessings and curses. Choose life so that you and your descendants may live,

loving the LORD your God, obeying him, and holding fast to him; for that means life to you and length of days, so that you may live in the land that the LORD swore to give to your ancestors, to Abraham, Isaac, and to Jacob. (30:15-20)

To be noted in this normative formulation of the law of Moses, the law of the covenant—Deuteronomy is the classic formulation of covenantal nomism—are three features of importance for biblical theology.

1. One is the point I am making here: that the law was given to show the people *how they should live* in the promised land.
2. A second is the *conditional* character of the commandments: obey, and you will prosper and live long in the land; disobey, and you will not prosper but rather perish and be driven from the land.
3. A third is that the promise is to the *people* not to individuals; obedience is necessary if the descendants of those who go into the land are to prosper in the land, live long and possess it.

A text that expressed the theological rationale well in summary form, and one of special note for a NT biblical theology, since Paul quotes it twice,[24] is Lev. 18:5: "You shall keep my statutes and my ordinances and shall live by them."[25] The obvious sense of the text is "that one should live his life in accordance with God's laws and commandments and that he should obey them all his life or while he is still alive."[26] And the fact that it was so understood by subsequent generations is confirmed by what may be regarded as the earliest commentary on the text in Ezek 20:5-26: "I gave them my statutes and showed them my ordinances, by whose observance everyone shall live" (20:11, 13, 21); balanced later by 20:25—"I gave them statutes that were not good and ordinances by which they could not live." The same understanding is reflected elsewhere in Jewish literature,[27] and, I would argue, is reflected also in Paul's recognition that the role of the law is not to establish the basic relation between God and humans, but to indicate the way of life, life to be lived by doing what the law requires (Gal 3:12). The role of the law was not to *give* life, but to *direct* life (3:21).[28]

However, as the thought of the salvation of the *individual*, and not simply the prosperity of the people in the land, grew stronger, the thought of *long* life evolved into the idea of *eternal* life in the age to come. The clauses of Lev 18:5 lent themselves to the text being understood as a conditional promise: Keep my statutes and by doing so you will acquire life. The transition is evident in the Qumran texts: 1QS 4:6-8—"plentiful peace in a long life...eternal enjoyment with endless life"; CD 3:20—he "will acquire eternal life"; 7:6—"they shall live a thousand generations." And again in the *Psalms of Solomon*—here 14:1-10:

> The Lord is faithful to those who truly love him...
> To those who live in the righteousness of his commandments,
> In the Law, which he has commanded for our life.
> The Lord's devout shall live by it forever
> The devout of the Lord will inherit life in happiness. (14:1-3, 10)[29]

The understanding of the conditional character of law-obedience at the time of Jesus is well illustrated by the question of the rich man to Jesus, "What must I do to inherit eternal life?" (Mark 10:17 pars). And the same understanding also lies behind so much of the factionalism of Second Temple Judaism: the desire of Pharisees and Essenes not merely to safeguard Israel's heritage of law but also to ensure their own participation in the inheritance of the world to come.

It is this conditional character of the life held out by the law—Do this and you shall live—which came to dominate the understanding of the law particularly in Protestant perception of Second Temple Judaism and which gave substance to the Christian criticism of Jewish "legalism": salvation/ eternal life as having to be acquired by deeds. And there is certainly an emphasis in much teaching in Second Temple Judaism that reinforces that critique. Simon Gathercole, for example, has drawn attention to a consistent motif in the literature of Second Temple Judaism in which "the images of final judgment and reward or punishment for individuals after death are prominent," where it is clear that "obedience is a vital basis for receiving eternal life."[30] The point should not be surprising for those who have taken the full force of Deuteronomy's "covenantal nomism."[31] For the nomism part of the formulation underlines the importance always laid, from Sinai onwards, on Israel's obedience to the law if the covenant was to be maintained, if length of life and then eternal life was to be attained and enjoyed. The only point that needs to be reiterated, in order to ensure that the balance of the "covenantal nomism" formulation is itself properly maintained, is that the promise was held out to Israel, to the elect nation. The call to obedience assumed that it was *addressed to the people already chosen by God's gracious initiative.* The balance is by no means always maintained in individual texts; exhortations and warnings use a different vocabulary from statements of theological premise. But the covenant context is always assumed, and for any biblical theology of Jewish soteriology it can certainly be taken as the antecedent of calls to obedience and promises of life.[32]

It is important for biblical theology that these several aspects or dimensions of Israel's law (#6.2b-d) be fully appreciated and taken into account when assessing the role of the law in NT theology.

3. THE LAW AND THE NT

A. Jesus and the *Halakhoth*

The interpretation of the law was a major preoccupation among the various factions in Israel at the time of Jesus. The Jewish historian Josephus (from the generation following Jesus) characterized the difference between the Pharisees and the Sadducees thus:

> The Pharisees had passed on to the people certain regulations handed down by former generations and not recorded by the Sadducean group, who hold that only those regulations should be considered valid which were written down [that is, in scripture], and that those which have been handed down by former generations need not be observed. And concerning these matters the two parties came to have controversies and serious differences. (*Ant.* 13:297-298)

The point of difference is clear: the Sadducees were more conservative, content with the law in its traditional, centuries-old language and terms; whereas the Pharisees recognized that the passing of the years and changing circumstances threw up issues and questions not dealt with in the Torah, issues and questions to which the law's application had to be drawn out. *Halakhah* (plural *halakhoth*), from the Hebrew root *hlk*, "to walk," refers to the rulings that the Pharisees (and others) derived from the written Torah to determine how they ought to conduct themselves (to walk) in particular situations—in effect, case law. These rulings were passed down orally and grew in number until they were written down in the Mishnah about 200 C.E.[33] One of the chief fascinations about the Qumran document 4QMMT, only published in 1994, is that it contains a catalogue of the *halakhoth* that were distinctive of the Essene group and on the basis of which they separated from the rest of the people, in order to live in accordance with these rulings.[34]

Jesus is recalled as referring to the Pharisaic *halakhoth* as "the tradition of the elders" (Mark 7:5), and the general perception is that, like the Sadducees(!), he rejected the oral traditions of the Pharisees. More challengingly, many would press the point further to argue that Jesus abrogated the law, abolishing some or many of its precepts.[35] Certainly the Jesus tradition is clear that he disputed several of the practices developed by the Pharisees on the basis of their *halakhoth*. The obvious cases are the Sabbath and some of the purity *halakhoth*.[36] But it would be more accurate to say that Jesus did not deny the necessity to interpret the law. Rather he interpreted it more radically. In regard to the Sabbath, he pressed beyond the issues of doing work on the Sabbath, to the more fundamental issue of whether it could be unlawful to do good or to save life even on the Sabbath (Mark 3:4). And in regard to purity, he pressed beyond the issue of cleansing hands to the more fundamental issue of purity of heart (7:1-8, 14-23). Similarly, the Jesus tradition recalls that he pressed below the surface of the laws prohibiting murder and adultery to the more fundamental issues of unjustified anger or insult, and of uncontrolled lustful desire (Matt 5:21-30). There is a consistency here that treats the law as indicative of or a window into the divine intention for human relationships and that presses the theological rationale of the commandment to bring out its full force. *He criticized the Pharisees not because they interpreted the law, but because their interpretations were obscuring what he claimed to be the true intent of the law.*[37]

Whether Jesus disputed with the Essenes, of Qumran or anywhere else, is less clear. The one point in the Jesus tradition where our knowledge of the historical context may indicate a critical allusion to Qumran is to be found in Luke 14. There Jesus twice exhorts that table-fellowship and hospitality should be open to "the poor, the maimed, the lame, and the blind" (14:13, 21). But that list strongly echoes the categories excluded from the priesthood (Lev 21:17-24), a list that the Qumran community drew on to indicate who should be excluded from their assemblies; the lame, the blind, and those smitten in the flesh were among those debarred because the angels of holiness were present in the congregation.[38] In complete contrast, Jesus inculcated the spirit of open fellowship, his own table-fellowship welcoming the irreligious (according to such excluding *halakhoth*) and the despised, toll-collectors, and sinners. As already observed, he did not see holiness as achieved or safeguarded by multiplying *halakhoth*, by building up the protective boundaries. Unlike John the Baptist, he did not even call for would-be disciples to be baptized during his mission. Such openness is not to be set over against the law as such, but in the spirit of the Jesus tradition, is to be seen rather as expressing what Jesus saw to be the intent of the law.[39]

The clearest expression of Jesus' attitude to the law is probably given in the tradition of his response to the question, "Which commandment is first of all?" (Mark 12:28); "Which commandment in the law is the greatest?" (Matt 22:36). Jesus' answer is remarkable. He points first to the *Shema*: "You shall love the Lord your God with all your heart, and with all your soul, and with all your mind, and with all your strength" (Mark 12:30 pars.). But then he adds, "The second is this, 'You shall love your neighbor as yourself.' There is no other commandment greater than these" (12:31). Matthew has Jesus concluding differently: "On these two commandments hang all the law and the prophets" (Matt 22:40). The remarkable thing is that in citing the second (greatest) commandment from Lev 19:18, Jesus abstracted it from a list of varied commandments (Lev 19) and *exalted that part-verse to be the headline commandment that governed all the rest*. We know of no other reference to Lev 19:18 in Jewish literature prior to Jesus, so almost certainly it was Jesus who first pressed home the injunction to "love your neighbor as yourself" as summing up the heart of the law.[40] The fact that the same text is highlighted in the same way and to the same intent in early Christian literature confirms that "the love command" became a distinctive feature of Christian paraenesis, almost certainly in conscious dependence on the Jesus tradition.[41] Such continuity between Jesus and Paul, and between Jesus and Paul on the one hand and between Jesus and the law on the other is of first importance for a NT biblical theology—again not as showing how the law was dispensed with, but rather how the law was interpreted in a much more demanding way.

Two other points should be noted here. One is the question whether Jesus' teaching was intended to provide guidance for only a limited period, that is, the period before the coming of God's kingdom—what Albert Schweitzer famously described as an "interim ethic."[42] In one sense at least he was right. Whatever we make of the tension in Jesus' preaching between the kingdom as already actively present and the kingdom's coming as something still to be prayed for (#4.3a), it is not unjustified to describe his ethical teaching as teaching for living between the two manifestations or comings of the kingdom. The fact that the prayer for God's kingdom is still to be prayed is a major theological problem, as we have already noted (#4.3e). But the more important point is that *Jesus evidently himself lived by the light of the kingdom*, whether present or still to come, and taught his disciples to do so also.[43] He ministered to people's needs in ways seen as characteristic of the age to come (Matt 11:5/Luke 7:22). The poor were already experiencing the blessings of God's kingdom through his preaching.[44] His table-fellowship was already an enactment of the open hospitality of the heavenly banquet.[45] His last meal with his disciples was indicative of the covenant renewed.[46] In short, his disciples were to live *now* as they would live when under God's rule alone, to forgive others as they had been and were being forgiven, to live in the light of the future they hoped and prayed for. The fact that so much of Jesus' own teaching is simply absorbed into early Christian paraenesis, as indicated by the many allusions to and indications of the influence of the Jesus tradition in the NT epistles,[47] is indication also that the same attitude (eschatological ethics) was inherited by the first Christians.

The other point that should be noted here is that the NT reflects *different attitudes to the law and to Jesus' teaching*. The Jesus tradition regarding the Sabbath still presupposes the importance of observing the Sabbath, whereas Rom 14:5 (and Col 2:16) reflect a Christian view that the Sabbath was no different from other days. Matthew's rendering of Jesus' teaching on purity (Matt 15:17) is less antithetical to continued observance of purity laws than Mark's (Mark 7:18-19), just as Matthew goes out of his way to deny that Jesus abolished the law or called for less obedience to the law than the Pharisees (5:17-20). And James' commendation of the Jesus tradition of the love command (Lev 19:18) is set in the context of a generally much more positive attitude to the law than Paul's.[48] Of course, what lies behind such differences is the reality of the different kinds of Christianity that emerged during the first two generations of Christianity—a more traditionally-minded Jewish Christianity, and a Gentile Christianity that sat loose to many more of the commandments of Moses than most of the Christian Jews felt comfortable with (to put it no more strongly).[49] For a NT biblical theology such evidence that the tradition of Jesus' own teaching was recalled differently and used differently to validate different patterns of conduct is an important aspect of the NT witness worthy of considerable reflection.

B. Did Paul Break with the Law?

It is Paul who really poses the problem of the law within Christianity and within any Christian biblical theology. So we will concentrate on Paul for most of what follows.

The historical conclusion is inescapable that Paul was regarded by almost all his fellow Jews, including (probably) the majority of Jews who had come to faith in Messiah Jesus, as in effect an apostate from the law.[50] This is evident from Paul's own letters, that he was confronted by, and strongly resisted, the insistence of many fellow Jewish believers that the law should be enforced in its traditional terms on Gentile converts, or at least should govern Jewish and Gentile association in the new churches.[51] The evidence of Galatians and Philippians 3 in particular would be hard to account for otherwise. And the bleak report attributed to James the brother of Jesus in Acts 21 simply confirms what Paul's letters imply: many thousands of Jews who had come to believe (in Jesus) were "all zealous for the law," and had been told that Paul instructed Diaspora Jews to forsake Moses, and not to circumcise their children or to observe the (traditional Jewish) customs (21:20-21). The point for biblical theology, however, is, as just noted, that these extreme tensions are reflected in milder terms in the NT documents themselves—in the more conservative and traditionalist view that Matthew and James (and probably we should add, Revelation)[52] maintain within the diversity of the NT.

There is no doubt that Paul's theology contains a strongly negative streak with regard to the law.[53] It is indicated by such texts as Galatians, 2 Corinthians 3, and Romans 5:20 and 7:5.

In *Galatians* Paul speaks of having died to the law, so that he might live to God (2:19). That is, the law had ceased to be the primary motivator and determinant of his life, his conduct, and his relationships. Evidently he had in mind the sharp contrast with his pre-conversion "over the top" zeal for the law, which he now regarded as obsessive and misconceived (1:13-14). He looked back on his previous way of life with the somewhat jaundiced perspective of the convert; that former way of life was finished for him; he had died to it. Similarly when he likens life under the law as slavery (5:1). The thought ties into his description of Israel as heirs but minors, "no better than slaves."[54] His claim is that the gift of the Spirit, the first installment of the promised inheritance,[55] had brought believers beyond that phase, to mature sonship, no longer "under the law" (4:4-7). This passage in turn carries forward Paul's exposition of why the law was given in the first place (3:19-25). His main answer to the question, "Why then the law?" (3:19), is that the law "was ordered through angels"[56] to guard and protect Israel, to provide a kind of protective custody (3:23),[57] or, alternatively imaged, to serve in the role of the *paidagōgos*, the slave who was charged with the responsibility of looking after the child, disciplining and correcting the youth when necessary (3:24).[58] With the coming of faith that role had been rendered unnecessary (3:25). This line of thought, it should be noted, ties in with the function of the law as also perceived within early Judaism—*the law as a protective wall surrounding Israel.*[59] Paul now saw that as too constrictive, a custodial rather than a liberating regime. Paul, we may say then, broke with the law to the extent that he claimed that this function of the law had ended. The coming of faith and the Spirit, to Gentile as well as Jew, had changed the situation completely.[60]

This line of interpretation is consistent with what is also evident in the still earlier accounts of the Jerusalem council (Gal 2:1-10) and the incident at Antioch (2:11-14). For the law as it was being demanded on these occasions was the law that defined Israel (circumcision) and the law that required separation (on the issue of shared meals) between Israel and the nations (Lev 20:22-26). In the Antioch incident Paul's fierce indictment against Cephas/Peter was to the effect that he (Cephas) was "compelling the Gentile believers to live Jewishly, to live like Jews" (2:14). It was that distinctively Jewish character of the law that Paul insisted was neither appropriate nor necessary for Gentile believers to observe; to insist on it was to put "the truth of the gospel" in jeopardy (2:5, 14). Then, in one of his most famous statements, Paul goes on to draw the more general principle from the particular issue in Antioch, to insist that *no works of the law* should be required of any believers in addition to faith in Christ (2:16).[61] It was the whole attitude that Paul now rejected completely—his own attitude before his conversion, that the law was (in the imagery of Ephesians 2) a wall dividing Jew from Gentile (Eph 2:14), and that the law required those who did not observe it with the necessary accuracy[62] to be labeled as "sinners" and "transgressors" and regarded as excluded from covenant grace (Gal 2:15, 17-18).

In *2 Corinthians 3* Paul develops a contrast between his own ministry and that of (or which appealed to) Moses. "The ministry of death" and "condemnation" (3:7, 9) is characterized by the old covenant with its commandments engraved in stone. The life-giving ministry of the Spirit, Paul claims, operates rather on the heart and produces transformed lives (3:3, 6, 18). However, the contrast, it should be noted, is between the external and superficial (the glory reflected on Moses' face fades—3:7) and the internal and enduring. The contrast is with an aspect of the law, its outward appearance; he does not use the term *law* at all, only *gramma*, "letter," the visible documentation (cf. Rom 2:28-29). The allusions in

2 Cor 3:3 and 6 to Jer 31:31 ("new covenant") and Ezek 11:19 and 36:26 (the promise to replace Israel's "heart of stone" with "a heart of flesh") clearly imply that Paul was claiming the fulfillment of what the prophets had longed for.[63] What is too easily forgotten, however, is that these prophets saw this new covenant and heart of flesh, the circumcision of the heart, as providing *a more effective way of knowing and doing God's will*.[64] It is presumably this immediacy of knowledge of God's will (as in Rom 12:2), rather than by having to depend on the written text (*gramma*), as in Rom 2:18,[65] that Paul contrasts so sharply here. Nevertheless, the fact that Paul could refer to his own past in terms of death and condemnation remains striking.

In *Romans* Paul writes of the law in stark terms as multiplying sin: "the law came in to increase the trespass" (5:20); "the sinful passions operate through the law" (7:5). Indeed, Paul "lays it on" against the law so thickly as to invite the corollary that "the law is itself sin" (7:7)! What needs to be noted here, however, is that *Paul sets up a case against the law precisely in order to clarify the position regarding the law*. The rest of Romans 7 is in effect a *defense* of or apology for the law.[66] Paul explains how it is that the law "increases the trespass": it is really sin taking advantage of the law and stirring up the sin that the law condemns (7:7-12); in so doing it brings sin to consciousness as sin and as something to be condemned (7:13).[67] And failure to do the law is not the fault of the law as such; the blame is sin's, and human weakness (the weakness of the flesh).[68] So when Paul talks of "the law of sin and death,"[69] he evidently had in mind the law as manipulated and abused by sin (7:8-11).[70]

In short, then, it would appear that Paul's antipathy to the law was much more specific and targeted than has regularly been maintained, particularly within Protestant exposition.[71] It was the law as it marked off Jew from Greek/Gentile and required their separation, the law to the extent that it encouraged a superficiality in observance, the law as it was manipulated and abused by the power of sin. These were the targets of his anti-law polemic.

The other side of the same coin is *the positive attitude that Paul also displays to the law*. For example, he insisted that faith did not invalidate the law; on the contrary, the law was established through faith (Rom 3:31). He introduces the claim by speaking of "the law of faith" (3:27). For Paul, the way to live obediently to the will of God expressed in the law was to live "from faith."[72] Similarly, he contrasts "the law of sin and death" with "the law of the Spirit of life" (8:2).[73] The logic is clear from the preceding chapter: the law is so incapacitated because of the weakness of the flesh and power of sin; but under the power of the Spirit and the new life of the Spirit, fulfilment of the law is not only reaffirmed as a goal to be aimed at, but as a goal that can be achieved (8:4). Of a piece with this is Paul's insistence elsewhere, taking up the teaching of Jesus, that the love generated by the Spirit[74] is the summation and fulfillment of the law,[75] "the law of Christ" (Gal 6:2).[76] Paul is fighting a different battle from James, and James almost certainly found it necessary to qualify or correct what he knew of Paul's teaching,[77] but when Paul insists that the only thing that matters is "faith working (operating effectively) through love" (Gal 5:6), he and James are "singing from the same sheet."[78]

The tension that Paul's teaching on the law sets up and leaves us with is nowhere more clearly indicated than in 1 Cor 7:19: "Circumcision is nothing, and uncircumcision is nothing; but (what is really important is) keeping the commandments of God." For any Jew in the congregation listening to this letter being read out, the statement must have appeared astonishing. How could Paul say that circumcision was a matter of indifference while in the same breath insist that what mattered was keeping God's commandments? For, of course, the obligation to circumcise all Jewish males was one of these commandments (Gen 17:9-14)! The only way to make sense of the verse is to recognize that in speaking like this *Paul must have been differentiating between requirements of the law.* First Cor 7:19, in other words, demonstrates both the negative and the positive in Paul's attitude to the law, and confirms that *the negative attitude was focused on only certain aspects or commandments of the law.*[79] In this case (and he speaks similarly in Gal 5:6 and 6:15) we are forced to deduce that it was the role of (and importance attributed to) *circumcision* that reduced it (for Paul) to the level of something indifferent (*adiapheron*) among the commandments of scripture. Paul's attitude to the law was much more nuanced than he has characteristically been given credit for.

C. Do (Are) Christians (Expected to) Fulfill the Law?

The fact that Paul talks positively of "the law of righteousness" as something to be pursued and attained (Rom 9:30-31), of faith as establishing the law (3:31), and love as the fulfilment of the law (13:8-10), raises the obvious corollary question: Did Paul expect his converts to fulfil the law? I continue to focus the issue on Paul, since it is he who so sharply poses the question, though it is worth noting again that Matthew and James had an overall more positive attitude to the law and to doing it.

The answer that Rom 8:4 invites is that Paul believed that "those who live in accordance with the Spirit" "fulfil the just requirement of the law." And this answer has been sufficient for many: the Spirit enables an obedience previously impossible. For example, Tom Schreiner: "Those who have the Spirit actually keep the law."[80] Also Simon Gathercole: "The Spirit does offer power to fulfill the Torah under the new covenant."[81] And certainly Paul's emphasis on "walking by the Spirit" and "being led by the Spirit"[82] is not to be denied or ignored. Paul implies that such conduct is different from observing the letter of the law, from walking according to the flesh.[83] He evidently distinguished "faith working through love" as of a different order from doing "all that the law requires" (Gal 5:3, 6). Clearly, then, Paul saw a fundamental role for the Spirit in Christian ethics.

What does it mean to "live in accordance with the Spirit"? What did it mean in practice? The answer is not as clear as it might be. But presumably the thought ties into Paul's talk of the renewal of the mind that enables discernment (*dokimazein*) as to the will of God (Rom 12:2), with his characterization of those who have received the Spirit as thus enabled to "judge or discern (*anakrinein*) all things" and "having the mind of Christ" (1 Cor 2:15-16); also with his prayer for the Philippians that they might have knowledge and "all insight to discern the things that matter (*dokimazein ta diapheronta*)" (Phil 1:9-10). Tied in too would be the thought that Christians have experienced in the Spirit the circumcision of the heart,[84] the law written in the heart as promised in the new covenant,[85] the heart of flesh in place of the heart of stone implying a greater sensitivity to the will of God. Tied in also would be the conviction that to let love for God and love of neighbor motivate and direct conduct would result in the law being fulfilled.[86] In short, what Paul seems to have envisaged could be described as a form of "charismatic ethics."

Of course, this does not mean that Paul envisaged ethical conduct always being devised in the moment of existential decision. "The commandments of God" were still there as a norm, a guide and yardstick; his hostility both to idolatry and to *porneia* (sexual license) is the clearest indication of the givenness of the law for Paul. His dependence on the Jesus tradition for direction on various issues is likewise clear from the references and allusions that pepper his paraenesis; Col 2:6 catches the point well—"As you have received the tradition of Christ Jesus as Lord, walk in him."[87] Nor did Paul think of discernment as a gift given to all as individuals; the gift was to be exercised in the gathered assembly, where testing and evaluating (*diakrinein, dokimazein*) could take place.[88] In 1 Corinthians 12–14 Paul himself offers clear tests by which an inspired revelation or exhortation could be evaluated: that it is in accord with the Lordship of Christ (12:3), is genuinely expressive of love (ch. 13), and is effective for the edification (*oikodomē*, "upbuilding") of the congregation.[89] The careful advice he gives in passages like 1 Corinthians 7 (on marriage) and 10:23-30 (on maintaining social relations with nonbelievers)[90] presumably illustrates the kind of sensitivity he encouraged. And presumably Paul would have understood his own discernment between commandments of the law—circumcision and laws of clean and unclean as irrelevant to Gentile believers, but commandments against idolatry and *porneia* as applicable to Gentile believers as much as to Jews—as further examples of the realignment in relation to the code of written law that the gift of the Spirit entailed.

The point not to be ignored, however, is that Paul saw the fulfillment of the law, the keeping of God's commandments, as *still an obligation on the part of Christians*. Faith and obedience were in no way mutual alternatives; on the contrary, Paul saw his mission as to bring his converts to "the obedience of faith" (Rom 1:5). The extent to which Paul's converts did in the event "walk according to the Spirit," did in fact "keep the commandments," is far from clear. Were they any more successful in their fulfilling the law than earlier generations of Israelites, than the more devout of their Jewish contemporaries?—an intriguing question that a biblical theology should not ignore, even if it cannot be answered! The fact that the typical second half of Paul's letters is devoted to ethical exhortation—and warnings!—clearly implies that such conduct was by no means assured or a given in the earliest churches. Justification by grace through faith in no way exempted believers from the religious and ethical obligation of the law. Paul expected his converts to "lead a life worthy of God" (1 Thess 2:12), to produce "good works" (Col 1:10). Such exhortations and warnings in Paul as Rom 8:13 ("If you live in accordance with the flesh, you will certainly die; but if by the Spirit you put to death the deeds of the body, you will live") and Gal 6:8 ("Those who sow to their own flesh shall from the flesh reap corruption; but those who sow to the Spirit shall from the Spirit reap eternal life") need to be given as much stress as the indicatives of salvation.[91] That brings us to the final point.

D. Judgment According to Works

On too many occasions in both the distant and recent past, the contrast between gospel and law, and between Judaism and Christianity, has
resulted in a downplaying of Paul's exhortations to moral focus and
effort.[92] The line of reasoning has been in effect: Paul's gospel must be so
different from the Jewish emphasis on the Torah, that any thought of
human effort being part of the process of salvation and its final outworking is to be regarded as anathema. Only as a sinner, as ungodly, could the
human individual hope for justification, for final acquittal at the judgment seat.[93] And certainly, in Paul's terms, justification is by faith alone,
by the pure grace of God.[94] Yet there is a further dimension to the issue
and at least two clarifications are called for.

One is the point made in #6.2 above, that the conditionality of Israel's
soteriology (#6.2d) should not obscure the priority of grace over law
(#6.2a) that is the starting point of Israel's soteriology. Sanders may have
overstated the covenant aspect of his "covenantal nomism" characterisa-
tion of the understanding of salvation in Second Temple Judaism.[95]
However, the proper response to any such imbalance is not to deny the
first element (covenant), but to flesh out the proper balance implied by
both words in the two-word phrase (covenantal nomism).

The second is that it is difficult to avoid the conclusion that *Paul's soteriology has itself a similar tension between grace given and obedience called for.*
For Paul, as elsewhere in the NT, final judgment will be "according to
works."[96] Paul, like Jesus, holds out the prospect of reward for achieve-
ment or good works.[97] Paul's warnings against the perils of moral failure
assuredly imply that he did not assume that Christians would live blameless lives.[98] As Morna Hooker observed in her review of Sanders: "In
many ways, the pattern which Sanders insists is the basis of Palestinian
Judaism fits exactly the Pauline pattern of Christian experience: God's
saving grace evokes man's answering obedience."[99]

What seems to have been often forgotten in all this is that salvation
was never conceived of by Paul as a single event, either in terms of the
cross and resurrection of Jesus, or in the pronouncement of the believer
as "justified" (Rom 5:1), a single event that required nothing further for
that event to achieve its full effect. As already observed (#4.3e), Paul also
envisaged salvation as a *process* of "being saved,"[100] a process with a clear-
cut beginning, but also an end yet to be achieved,[101] a process of the wast-
ing away of the "outward person" and renewal of the "inward" person
(2 Cor 4:16).[102] He expected the process to produce a tested, approved

character (*dokimē*),[103] a metamorphosis into the image of the Creator[104] as the end result. He wanted to be able to present his converts and the recipients of his letters "pure," "blameless," "faultless," "irreproachable," and "mature/perfect" at the coming of Christ.[105] The inevitable corollary is that *Paul's soteriology had a conditional character not unlike the conditionality in the soteriology attested in Second Temple Judaism.*[106] Salvation (eternal life) for Paul too was in some degree conditional on obedience or perseverance;[107] believers could be disqualified in the race and be "cut off."[108] To make this point is not to question the centrality and *sine qua non* of divine grace or that the believer is totally dependent on it as a pure gift and on its enabling, which are consistent features of Paul's teaching on the subject elsewhere.[109] But by the same token, the outcome at the final judgment for which Paul looked was clearly not simply to be expressed as the acquittal of individual sinners, no different than when they first believed; rather, in Paul's perspective the resurrection of the body would be the completion of *a process of personal transformation* already well under way during a life of discipleship.

What also seems to have been too quickly forgotten is that the legal imagery of justification/acquittal is by no means the only language and imagery used by Paul in expounding his theology and its outworking.[110] More prominent in his letters is the thought of believers as being "in Christ," a phrase that occurs eighty-three times in the Pauline corpus. It is the "in Christ" character of Paul's soteriology that correlates most readily with his talk of transformation, including moral transformation— transformation as the process of becoming like Christ, of being conformed to his death in the hope of being conformed also to his resurrection.[111] Also more prominent than the forensic imagery is Paul's talk of the gift of the Spirit and its outworking in a Christian pattern of conduct, of walking in accordance with the Spirit, of faith operating through love, as already indicated.

The straightforward fact is that Paul's theology of salvation and its outworking uses *all these motifs* (legal imagery, "in Christ," Spirit). Not only so, though this is difficult for those who want to understand images as logistical data to be processed into a neat and consistent schema, Paul uses all three without any sense (so far as we can tell) that they rubbed uncomfortably far less irreconcilably together.[112] These were all ways of expressing the reality of God's saving righteousness, of Christ's transforming presence, of the Spirit's motivating and energizing power—the same reality, not different realities. Paul, I strongly suspect, would have been amazed—and deeply disappointed—by the insistence of some that one motif should be played off against another, or that one motif should be given dominance over the others and the others made to fit with it, and where they did not fit they should be ignored or discarded.[113] A *biblical theology of the NT must deal with the whole Paul* and not with just those passages that fit a grid formed from a selection of Pauline texts.

It is as well that this treatment is rounded off by such an intense focus on Paul. For Paul is the one who poses the problems of biblical theology most profoundly. The dominant tendency in the past has been to take Paul as the beginning of a trajectory that leads unfailingly into anti-Judaism or even anti-semitism, a rejection of Judaism or even a rejection of the OT (Marcion). But if the above exposition is on the right lines, the more justified conclusion is that such a trajectory points in a quite wrong direction. The starting point, as located in Paul's own letters, has been mislocated and misaligned. There *is* in Paul *contrast and discontinuity* with what came before in the history and theology of Second Temple Judaism: in particular, the "in Christ" replaced "within the law" as the starting point for obedience. But there is also *confirmation and continuity*: the gift of the Spirit, Paul would have claimed, enabled the more sensitive discernment of God's will for which the prophets had longed.[114] And there is a similar or equivalent attempt to marry the experience of prevenient grace with the response of grateful obedience. One of the principal challenges for a biblical theology of the NT is to explore the ramifications and corollaries, the consistencies and inconsistencies, the fulcrum points and paradoxes, of these attempts to speak coherently of "the obedience of faith."

4. CONCLUSION

I have in effect been insisting that theology is not to be restricted to statements of and discussions about belief. Nor is theologizing to be limited to the process of thought and reflection. This is a mistake into which Christians can often fall: theology and theologizing as what one does with the mind and in an ecclesial context. But the religion of the OT and of Judaism is better understood in terms of *praxis*, of doing rather than of (simply) believing. And the religion inculcated in OT and NT embraces the whole of life—not life separated from others, not life in the holy place shut off from the outside world, not private as distinct from public life. So ethics is part of theology. And theology provides the principles and the motivation for ethics. To adapt the language of #3, theology is the *logos* of thought, ethics is the *logos* of speech, thought coming to expression in action. Without the two together, the former becomes a kind of narcissism, the latter a kind of blundering in the dark.

So, once again by way of summary, several of these points should be highlighted.

1. The continuity is clear between, on the one hand, a religion of Israel that began with election and demanded a consequent obedience, and on the other, a faith in Jesus Christ that begins with grace and expects the obedience of faith in consequence. The call for love of neighbor that summed up the law for both Jesus and his first followers is drawn directly from the Torah. The concern for the poor is assumed as an obligation in the NT for no other reason than that the God to whom scripture bears witness is God of the poor. Fulfillment of the law (however differently) is expected of Christians as much as it is expected of Jews. The disagreements among the earliest believers (and to a lesser extent the NT writers) as to how the law applies are somewhat of a piece with the disputes between the factions of Second Temple Judaism. And there is even a similar conditionality in the hope of eternal life and of a prize at the final reckoning.

2. It is in the matter of praxis and ethics that the continuing importance of Jesus' own teaching in determining conduct, and so the role of Jesus' teaching within NT theology, is clearest. His eschatological ethic (better than interim ethic) embodied a living in the light of God's (coming) kingdom as a model of how life should be lived now. That model was evidently cherished in the Jesus tradition as it functioned in the early Christian congregations; the fact that it forms the bulk of the Gospel material, for the most part much as he had first given it, assuredly attests the continuing effect of Jesus' teaching in shaping the lives of the first Christians. And the way that tradition has influenced and been absorbed into the paraenesis of the NT letters confirms the strong line of continuity running from Jesus to Paul and beyond. A NT ethic is no more imaginable without the input of Jesus as it is without the heritage of the OT.

3. As to the diversity within NT ethics, the picture is no less clear. The disagreements within earliest Christianity are an extension

150

of the disagreements between Jesus and the religious leaders of his time, which in turn are an extension of the disagreements between the factions of Second Temple Judaism. The centrality of Jesus for the Christians, and the opening to the Gentiles introduced determinative new factors. But the diversity around the new unifying factors was no less intense. Paul was clear that the elements of the law that could be characterized as "living like Jews" should not be enforced on Gentile believers. But his more traditionalist fellow Jewish believers did not agree. At least some of that disagreement is reflected in the differences between the portrayals of Mark and Matthew and between Paul and James. A life lived under the banner of Jesus the Christ and drawing on his teaching was the common starting point. But on particular issues, not least on social involvement in the wider society, disagreement flourished. That it has been thus for most of Christianity's existence should not blind us to the fact that it was so from the beginning.

4. This emphasis on the love command as the agreed fundamental principle in Christian ethics serves to tie together the major themes of NT theology examined above: God as characterized by steadfast love and mercy—"God is love" (1 John 4:8); God demonstrating his love to us "in that Christ died for us" (Rom 5:8); Israel's *Shema* as calling for love of God with the whole of one's being (Deut 6:4-5); and Jesus' complementing this by commanding his followers to love their neighbor as themselves (Mark 12:29-31). *Ubi caritas, ibi deus est.* What tensions would be resolved, what factional disputes put in their proper perspective, what recognition and respect would we learn to have for views and practices different from our own, what coming together and working harmoniously as one, might be possible if we simply lived by that most fundamental of insights![115]

CONCLUSION

In this volume I have attempted to set out some of the key problems, the determining factors, and the main themes of a New Testament biblical theology. As an introductory volume to a series, the intention was not to provide a full-scale Theology of the New Testament,[1] only to bring to sharper focus the main issues and the relevant material for the treatment of these issues in a biblical theology of the NT.

1. THE MAIN FINDINGS

(A) I hope that it has become apparent that to write a biblical theology of the NT is an entirely viable venture. Not only so, it should have become clear that a *New Testament* theology cannot but be a *biblical* theology of the NT. I have studied only four themes, it is true. But these themes are bound to be at the heart of any NT theology. And in each case it has been obvious (and not simply from the way the discussion was set out) that *the NT themes could not begin to be grasped and understood without a full awareness of the givens that the NT writers had evidently taken over from their heritage in the scriptures,* that is, Israel's scripture—the Hebrew Bible and the LXX. It is precisely in the way the NT writers drew upon and developed the language and themes of their scriptures that the fascination (and the problems) of a biblical theology of the NT lies. It also follows that, whether or not Jewish scholars wish to talk in terms of a biblical theology, a biblical theology of the NT will inevitably include at least some dialogue with such scholars as to the legitimacy of the ways in which the NT writers have handled the givens that they inherited. Whether and to what extent the NT writings form a continuum with the OT writings is a question that the NT writers themselves would have wanted to answer positively.

(B) *The canonical texts of OT and NT show themselves to be the natural providers of the subject matter for such a NT theology.* This is not because the canon of the OT was finalized in the first century C.E., far less the canon of the NT! The variableness of the textual tradition of the OT drawn upon by the NT writers is itself a reminder of the point. To speak of an OT canon for the first century includes recognition both of a degree of ambiguity in the full range of what was accounted scripture and of a certain fluidity in the wording of the OT texts themselves. Nor does recognition of the dependence of the NT writers on what became the OT canon exclude the use of post-biblical literature of the Second Temple period. On the contrary, it soon became evident in the above chapters that many aspects of the theological claims and assertions of the NT writers could not be appreciated without our being aware that they were interacting with issues in Second Temple Judaism of which we are aware only through the post-biblical (intertestamental) literature. Even so, the canonical point remains firm, since there is a difference between *dependence* on scripture and *interaction* with issues and themes of Second Temple Judaism.

As to the issue of limiting a NT theology to the NT canon, two points should be restated. One is that the question of the authenticity of apocryphal works, like the Gospel of Thomas, certainly has to be discussed in a full NT theology, since these gospels raise the question of how adaptable was the Jesus tradition to diverse and divergent interpretations—as does John's Gospel, of course. At the same time, however, the point bears repetition that the canonical documents proved themselves worthy to be the principal, if not the sole contributors to a NT theology, by the fact that their widening acceptance and use (as demonstrated finally in their canonization) proved their authority as the documentary basis for Christian theology. The NT canon was the outcome of theologizing with the writings that became the NT.

(C) That *a NT theology must adopt a historical critical approach to the material* it presents has also become clearer. A straightforward description of what the NT writers say on most subjects will simply not suffice. A historical critical approach that enquires into how these texts would have been heard by those for whom they were written and into why they were framed in the way they were (which is itself a definition of such an approach) is essential for an obvious reason. The texts themselves have an inescapable *historical particularity*. They were written in and for particular situations. These situations inevitably determined the language and themes that make up these writings. The point has long been recognized that the language of the NT is the language of first-century eastern Mediterranean Greek. It cannot be understood without a knowledge of the vocabulary, grammar, and idiom of first-century Greek. But it also follows that without some appreciation of the historical situations which called forth these writings and to which they were addressed, we cannot begin to appreciate the rhetoric of the writings, why narratives and teaching, arguments and exhortations were framed as they were. Without such an appreciation the NT theologian may be tempted to generalize from what was directed only to a particular situation and applicable only to that situation. *The canonizing of these documents does not generalize all the particularities into universals.* The point is nowhere clearer than in the various antagonistic references to "the Jews," which in the following centuries were allowed to justify Christian anti-Judaism and anti-semitism. Only when one appreciates the prophetic denunciations of Israel's failures, the vitriolic polemic of Second Temple Judaism's factionalism (including the faction/sect of Christians), the suspicions and hostility between the different factions of earliest Christianity itself, and the antagonisms between embryonic Christianity and embryonic rabbinic Judaism, can such language be historically understood and appropriately handled.

The issue here for a NT theology that wishes to have relevance for the present day is *whether what once was heard as the word of God is therefore the word of God for all times and generations.* Students of the NT are (for the most part) quite comfortable with the recognition that many OT scriptures no longer have force for Christians (circumcision, animal sacrifice, and many features of purity legislation, for example). The logic would be that of historical particularity—conventions and regulations appropriate to particular historical circumstances and periods no longer deemed appropriate to the different circumstances and conditions of later generations. Many fewer are comfortable with the application of the same logic to particular conventions and rulings in the NT: the NT's acceptability of slavery would be regarded as unacceptable by all; the attitudes of a patriarchal society (reflected in the NT) would be unacceptable to most; the Bible's (including the NT's) hostility to a homosexual lifestyle remains a divisive issue. A biblical theology of the NT cannot ignore or avoid such testing hermeneutical issues. Even if NT theology is conceived only as historically descriptive, *it remains incumbent on it that it should spell out the historical particularities of the different aspects of theoretical and applied theology that it examines.*

(D) To highlight the issues of unity and diversity in NT theology was not a priority for this volume; I had already said sufficient on the subject in my earlier *Unity and Diversity in the New Testament*. The low priority given to the issue here, however, should not be taken as questioning the importance of the issue for NT theology. It is again the outworking of a historical critical approach, which takes as full account as possible of the *distinctive* features of *each* of the NT writings, to bring out the diversity that goes to make up the very small collection of writings that we call the New Testament. For the unity of the NT—which is the NT itself!—cannot be appreciated without its character as *unity in diversity* being fully appreciated. In the preceding chapters I have given various instances of the *diversity*: the different presentations of Jesus in four Gospels, including the more nuanced variations between the Synoptic Gospels, and the major differences between the Synoptic Gospels and John's Gospel; the different titles and ways of expressing the significance of Jesus and of his death; the different metaphors of salvation not capable of being squeezed into a single metaphor without substantial loss; the different attitudes to Gentile believers among the earliest churches; and the different attitudes to the Torah and different codes of conduct for believers engaging with non-believers. At the same time, the fact that *Jesus Christ provides the unique focus and bond for all the NT documents* (including such as James and 3 John) ensures the *unity* that allows these documents to stand together as the New Testament.

(E) On the question *whether the mission and message of Jesus himself is part of NT theology*, the answer has had to be *an unequivocal Yes*. The eschatological perspective of the NT began with Jesus. The already/not yet tension of Christian soteriology is rooted in Jesus' teaching on the kingdom of God, already active through his mission but its coming still having to be prayed for. The tension of Jew/Gentile, the identity of Israel, is rooted in Jesus' own mission to Israel and openness to non-Jews who sought his help. The disputes as to the continuing applicability of the law began with Jesus' disputes with Pharisees on Sabbath and purity ritual. And even the claims made for Jesus and the significance of what he had done can be substantially rooted in Jesus' own attitudes and the authority with which he acted in his mission. The resurrection of Jesus and its immediate aftermath (exaltation, outpouring of the Spirit) of course involved a major heightening and transformation of his disciples' apprehension of him. But the fact that the great bulk of the Synoptic tradition retains the teaching he gave (without significant modification) and bears the clear impression of the impact he made assuredly confirms *the substantial continuum from Jesus' own implicit christology to the explicit christologies of the NT writers*. The fact is that no case of major substance can be made for the thesis that the significance claimed for Jesus by the NT writers in image and metaphor would have been denied by Jesus in whole or in large part. *Jesus' own teaching, both spoken and lived out, is the beginning of NT theology*.

2. THEOLOGY AS THEOLOGIZING

The most distinctive feature of the present volume is *my attempt to draw together both historical critical description and theological reflection*, both entering into the situations out of which the theology of the NT grew and continuing the process by highlighting the questions still posed by what is in the NT—the attempt to define NT theology more in terms of theologizing, theology as a stream of reflection that has flowed more or less unbroken from the earliest apprehensions of God as revealing his will to Moses and Israel's prophets. The hermeneutical corollaries of this perspective on NT theology are worth a final word.[2]

So to see the flow of NT theologizing as an unbroken stream running through and beyond the NT means, of course, that we have to reformulate the classic Reformed antithesis between scripture and tradition. For the ongoing tradition of the Church/churches is in effect the continuation of the same stream of theologizing that came to definitive expression in the NT, the frozen moment(s) of canonicity. Even though church tradition is to be seen, entirely properly, as in effect interpretation of scripture, the contrast is not between fixity and fluidity, the one finally authoritative and the other misleading and always liable to corruption (in Protestant perspective). Rather, if my argument thus far carries any weight, the NT itself is best seen as *theology in motion*, as theologizing, as itself expression of and interaction with tradition, as *itself living tradition*, as ongoing revelation of God's Spirit. In consequence, the tradition of the Church/churches is best seen more as a continuation of that process. As the *Sache* of the OT comes to us variously in the various renderings of it in the NT—as the Jesus tradition comes to us in the diversity of the various canonical Gospels—as the text of the NT comes to us in the different forms and versions that functioned as scripture for different groups and churches—so *the NT that is effective in each denomination is the NT as appropriated in and understood by the tradition of that denomination,* and not some ideal of the NT untouched by denominational diversity.

The point can be put thus: the old clear-cut dichotomy between scripture and tradition was possible because of the equally clear-cut dichotomy between text and interpretation of the text. But it is precisely that latter dichotomy that contemporary hermeneutics breaks down. As the historical "fact" is not the historical data themselves, but the *interpretation* of the data, so the text actually in view is the *interpreted* text. An earlier phase of Qumran studies coined the phrase "pesher text" to indicate texts that already had the interpretation incorporated within the textual form being commented on. And many of the OT passages cited in the NT are like that, with the textual form already embodying the interpretation being given.[3] *What are the different versions of items of Jesus tradition but the tradition itself as it was variously appropriated and functioned as normatively authoritative?* The often multitudinous text forms confronting the textual critic are the scriptures as received and understood and used in different churches and communities. The ancient versions are not simply more or less valuable witnesses to a primordial original text of the NT; they *were* the NT for those concerned. In short, the text is not fixed and is not static; the phenomena with which we are confronted in the interpretation of scripture is what my former colleague David Brown characterizes as the "moving text,"[4] or in my own terms, the text as "living tradition."

Perhaps nothing exemplifies this at everyday level more than *the amazing range of translations of the Bible* (or parts thereof) that currently compete for attention and for church/individual usage. Simply to compare a handful of these translations is or should be sufficient to bring home the point, as we see how *differently* the *same* Hebrew or Greek text (including variants) can be rendered—at times so diversely that the reader must wonder whether it is the same text. Of course, the NT scholar deals primarily if not exclusively with the Greek text. But its degree of fluidity (textual variants) is vastly compounded by the diverse understandings of the text with which the NT commentators actually work. The translations often provided within commentaries simply add to the already overwhelming range of translations "in the market."

The point should not be overdone, of course. For the relative stability of the text still functions as a norm for the way it is appropriated and understood and interpreted. As there can be bad and even plainly wrong translations of the Hebrew or Greek, so there can and should be unacceptable appropriations, interpretations, and use made of the scriptures entexted. The canonical scripture can and should still function as the *norma normans* within the unbroken flow of living tradition. But not as something fixed and final, whose meaning is in principle self-evident and beyond reasonable dispute, only as a reference point to which recourse is made again and again in the course of our own engagement in the theological process.

So, *NT theologizing*, rather than *NT theology*, seems to be the more appropriate term. And NT theology/theologizing is not to be seen as simply something we observe and describe, but rather as something we do. Students of the NT and NT scholars theologize *newtestamently* (probably better expressed in German!). We produce not simply New Testament Theologies, but New Testament theology. It is not Paul and John who write NT theology, but we do! We theologize in, with, and through the writings of the NT—a much more engaging and exciting pursuit than simply describing the thought processes of some early Christians in antiquity.

SELECT BIBLIOGRAPHY

Adam, A. K. M., *Making Sense of New Testament Theology: "Modern" Problems and Prospects*. Macon, Ga.: Mercer University, 1995.

Alexander , T. D. & B. S. Rosner, eds. *New Dictionary of Biblical Theology*. Downers Grove: Ill.: InterVarsity Press, 2000.

Balla, P. *Challenges to New Testament Theology: An Attempt to Justify the Enterprise*. WUNT 2.95. Tübingen: Mohr Siebeck, 1997.

Barr, J. *The Concept of Biblical Theology: An Old Testament Perspective*. Minneapolis: Fortress Press, 1999.

Bartholomew, C. et al., eds. *Out of Egypt: Biblical Theology and Biblical Interpretation*. Milton Keynes, England: Paternoster Press, 2004.

Barton, J., and M. Wolter, hrsg. *Die Einheit der Schrift und die Vielfalt des Kanons/ The Unity of Scripture and the Diversity of the Canon*. BZNW 118. Berlin: de Gruyter, 2003.

Berger, K. *Theologiegeschichte des Urchristentums: Theologie des Neuen Testaments*, Tübingen, Germany: Francke, 1994.

Boers, H. *What Is New Testament Theology?* Philadelphia: Fortress Press, 1979.

Braun, H. "The Problem of a Theology of the New Testament" in *Journal for Theology and Church* 1 (1965): 169–83.

Bultmann, R. *The Theology of the New Testament*. 2 vols. London: SCM, 1952, 1955.

Caird, G. B. *New Testament Theology*. Oxford, England: Clarendon Press, 1994.

Childs, B. S. *Biblical Theology in Crisis*. Philadelphia: Westminster Press, 1970.

———. *Biblical Theology of the Old and New Testaments*. London: SCM/ Minneapolis: Fortress Press, 1992.

Collins, J. J. *The Bible after Babel: Historical Criticism in a Postmodern Age*. Grand Rapids, Mich.: Eerdmans, 2005.

Conzelmann, H. *An Outline of the Theology of the New Testament.* London: SCM, 1969.

Dohmen, C., and T. Söding, hrsg. *Eine Bibel—zwei Testamente: Positionen Biblischer Theologie.* Paderborn, Germany: Ferdinand Schöningh, 1995.

Dunn, J. D. G. *Unity and Diversity in the New Testament: An Inquiry into the Character of Earliest Christianity.* London: SCM, 1977, 1990, 2006.

Dunn, J. D. G., and J. P. Mackey. "The Task of New Testament Theology" in *New Testament Theology in Dialogue.* London: SPCK, 1987: 1–26.

Ebeling, G. "The Meaning of 'Biblical Theology'" in *JTS* 6 (1955): 210–25.

Esler, P. F. *New Testament Theology: Communion and Community.* Minneapolis: Fortress Press, 2005.

Fuller, R. H. "New Testament Theology" in *The New Testament and its Modern Interpreters.* E. J. Epp and G. W. MacRae, eds. Atlanta: Scholars Press, 1989: 565–84.

Gnilka, J. *Theologie des Neuen Testaments.* Freiburg, Germany: Herder, 1994.

Grässer, E. "Offene Fragen im Umkreis einer Biblischen Theologie" in *ZTK* 77 (1980): 200–221.

Guthrie, D. *New Testament Theology.* Leicester, England: InterVarsity Press, 1981.

Hahn, F. *Theologie des Neuen Testaments: Band. I. Die Vielfalt des Neuen Testaments; Theologiegeschichte des Urchristentums; Band II. Die Einheit des Neuen Testaments; Thematische Darstellung.* Tübingen, Germany: Mohr Siebeck, 2002.

Harrington, W. J. *The Path of Biblical Theology.* Dublin: Gill & Macmillan, 1973.

Hasel, G. *New Testament Theology: Basic Issues in the Current Debate.* Grand Rapids, Mich.: Eerdmans, 1978.

Hübner, H. *Biblische Theologie des Neuen Testaments.* 3 vols. Göttingen: Vandenhoeck & Ruprecht, 1990, 1993, 1995.

Janowski, B. "The One God of the Two Testaments: Basic Questions of a Biblical Theology" in *Theology Today* 57 (2000): 291–324.

Jeremias, J. *New Testament Theology. Vol. One: The Proclamation of Jesus.* London: SCM, 1971.

Käsemann, E. "The Problem of a New Testament Theology" in *NTS* 19 (1972–73): 235–45.

Kraftchick, S. J., et al., eds., *Biblical Theology: Problems and Perspectives: In Honor of J. Christiaan Beker.* Nashville: Abingdon Press, 1995.

Kraus, H.-J. *Die biblische Theologie: Ihre Geschichte und Problematik.* Neukirchen-Vluyn, Germany: Neukirchener, 1970.

Kümmel, W. G. *The Theology of the New Testament.* London: SCM, 1974.

Ladd, G. E. *A Theology of the New Testament.* Grand Rapids, Mich.: Eerdmans, 1974, 1993.

Lohse, E. *Grundriss der neutestamentlichen Theologie.* Stuttgart, Germany: Kohlhammer, 1974.

Marshall, I. H. *New Testament Theology: Many Witnesses, One Gospel.* Downers Grove. Ill.: InterVarsity Press, 2004.

Matera, F. J. *New Testament Theology: Exploring Diversity and Unity.* Louisville: Westminster John Knox Press, 2007.

Mead, J. K. *Biblical Theology: Issues, Methods, and Themes.* Louisville: Westminster John Knox Press, 2007.

Merk, O. *Biblische Theologie des Neuen Testaments in ihrer Anfangszeit.* Marburg, Germany: N. G. Elwert, 1972.

———. "Biblische Theologie II" in *TRE* 6 (1980): 455–77.

———. "Gesamtbiblische Theologie: Zum Fortgang der Diskussion in den 80er Jahren" in *VF* 33 (1988): 19–40.

Morgan, R. *The Nature of New Testament Theology.* London: SCM, 1973.

———. "Theology (NT)" in *ABD* 6 (1992): 473–83.

Müller, M. "Neutestamentliche Theologie als biblische Theologie: Einige grundsätzliche Überlegungen" in *NTS* 43 (1997): 475–90.

Olson, D. T. "Biblical Theology" in *NIDB* 1 (2006): 461–65.

Penner, T., and C. Vander Stichele, eds. *Moving Beyond New Testament Theology? Essays in Conversation with Heikki Räisänen.* Helsinki: Finnish Exegetical Society; Göttingen, Germany: Vandenhoeck & Ruprecht, 2005.

Pokorny, P. "The Problem of Biblical Theology" in *HBT* 15 (1993): 83–94.

Räisänen, H. *Beyond New Testament Theology.* London: SCM, 1990.

Reventlow, H. G. *Problems of Biblical Theology in the Twentieth Century.* London: SCM, 1986.

———. "Theology (Biblical), History of" in *ABD* 6 (1992): 483–505.

Richardson, A. *An Introduction to the Theology of the New Testament.* London: SCM, 1958.

Rowland, C., and C. Tuckett, eds. *The Nature of New Testament Theology: Essays in Honour of Robert Morgan.* Oxford, England: Blackwell, 2006.

Schelkle, K. H. *Theology of the New Testament.* 4 vols. Collegeville, Minn.: Liturgical Press, 1971, 1973, 1976, 1978.

Schmithals, W. *The Theology of the First Christians.* Louisville: Westminster John Knox Press, 1997.

Schnelle, U. *Theologie des Neuen Testaments.* Göttingen, Germany: Vandenhoeck & Ruprecht, 2007.

Scobie, C. H. H. *The Ways of Our God: An Approach to Biblical Theology.* Grand Rapids, Mich.: Eerdmans, 2003.

Stendahl, K. "Biblical Theology: Contemporary" in *IDB* (1962): 1.418–32.

Strecker, G., hrsg., *Das Problem der Theologie des Neuen Testaments.* Darmstadt, Germany: Wissenschaftliche Buchgesellschaft, 1975.

―――. *Theology of the New Testament.* Berlin: de Gruyter, 2000.

Stuhlmacher, P. *Biblische Theologie des Neuen Testaments.* 2 vols. Göttingen: Vandenhoeck & Ruprecht, 1992, 1999.

―――. *How to Do Biblical Theology.* Allison Park, Pa.: Pickwick Press, 1995.

―――. *Biblische Theologie und Evangelium: Gesammelte Aufsätze.* WUNT 146. Tübingen, Germany: Mohr Siebeck, 2002.

Thielman, F. *Theology of the New Testament: A Canonical and Synthetic Approach.* Grand Rapids, Mich.: Zondervan, 2005.

Vanhoozer, K. J. ed., *Dictionary for Theological Interpretation of the Bible.* Grand Rapids, Mich.: Baker; London: SPCK, 2005.

Via, D. O. *What Is New Testament Theology?* Minneapolis: Fortress Press, 2002.

Watson, F. *Text and Truth: Redefining Biblical Theology.* Edinburgh, Scotland: T & T Clark, 1997.

Wilckens, U. *Theologie des Neuen Testaments: Band 1. Geschichte der urchristlichen Theologie.* 4 vols. Neukirchen-Vluyn, Germany: Neukirchener, 2005.

Wrede, W. "Über Aufgabe und Methode der sogenannten Neutestamentlichen Theologie" (1897) in G. Strecker, *Theology of the New Testament.* Berlin: de Gruyter, 2000: 81–154; ET "The Task and Methods of 'New Testament Theology'" in R. Morgan, *The Nature of New Testament Theology.* London: SCM, 1973: 68–116.

NOTES

Introduction

1. See below, chapter 1 note 5.

2. For bibliographical details see below, chapter 1 notes 1, 27, 54.

3. For example in the present decade, F. Hahn, *Theologie des Neuen Testaments: Band. I* (Tübingen, Germany: Mohr Siebeck, 2002); I. H. Marshall, *New Testament Theology: Many Witnesses, One Gospel* (Downers Grove, Ill.: InterVarsity, 2004); U. Wilckens, *Theologie des Neuen Testaments: Band 1. Geschichte der urchristlichen Theologie,* 4 vols. (Neukirchen-Vluyn, Germany: Neukirchener, 2005), vols. 3-4; F. Thielman, *Theology of the New Testament: A Canonical and Synthetic Approach* (Grand Rapids, Mich.: Zondervan, 2005); F. J. Matera, *New Testament Theology: Exploring Diversity and Unity* (Louisville: Westminster John Knox Press, 2007). Both Marshall and Thielman proceed document by document, though with synthesizing chapters.

4. For example, A. Richardson, *An Introduction to the Theology of the New Testament* (London: SCM, 1958); K. H. Schelkle, *Theology of the New Testament,* 4 vols. (Collegeville, Minn.: Liturgical, 1971, 1973, 1976, 1978); D. Guthrie, *New Testament Theology* (Leicester, England: InterVarsity Press, 1981); G. B. Caird, *New Testament Theology* (Oxford, England: Clarendon, 1994); F. Vouga, *Une théologie du Nouveau Testament* (Geneva: Labor et Fides, 2001). The thematic approaches of Richardson and Schelkle were earlier described by G. Hasel, *New Testament Theology: Basic Issues in the Current Debate* (Grand Rapids, Mich.: Eerdmans, 1978), 73–82.

5. Having reviewed four other types of NT theology (the Dogmatic Approach, the Chronological Approach, the Kerygmatic Approach, and the Author-by-Author Approach), Caird takes the Conference Table Approach, with the apostolic conference (Gal. 2:1-10) as his model, and the different participants (the NT writers) contributing to each theme discussed (*New Testament Theology,* 5–26). Marshall critiques the model: "For Caird it is not really possible to offer more than position papers from each of the speakers without any indication of how, say, John would have responded to Paul" (*New Testament Theology,* 25).

6. Cf. particularly C. H. H. Scobie, *The Ways of Our God: An Approach to Biblical Theology* (Grand Rapids, Mich.: Eerdmans, 2003), whose "sketch" (over eight hundred pages!) is divided into "God's Order," "God's Servant," "God's People," and "God's Way."

1. What Is New Testament Theology?

1. J. P. Gabler, "Von der richtigen Unterscheidung der biblischen und der dogmatischen Theologie und der rechten Bestimmung ihrer beider Ziele" (1787) in O. Merk, *Biblische Theologie des Neuen Testaments in ihrer Anfangszeit* (Marburg, Germany: N. G. Elwert, 1972), 273–84; also in G. Strecker, hrsg., *Das Problem der Theologie des Neuen Testaments* (Darmstadt, Germany: Wissenschaftliche Buchgesellschaft, 1975), 32–44; ET by J. Sandys-Wunsch and L. Eldredge, "J. P. Gabler and the Distinction between Biblical and Dogmatic Theology: Translation, Commentary and Discussion of his Originality" in *SJT* 33 (1980): 133–58. G. Ebeling, "The Meaning of 'Biblical Theology'" in *JTS* 6 (1955): 210–25, traces the earliest use of the phrase "biblical theology" to a funeral oration delivered at Tübingen in 1669 (214). But Scobie, *Ways of Our God* 3, notes a now lost book by W. J. Christmann, *Teutsche biblische Theologie* (1629), and also H. A. Diest, *Theologia Biblica* (1643).

2. B. S. Childs, *Biblical Theology of the Old and New Testaments* (London: SCM/Minneapolis: Fortress, 1992), 30–33.

3. "There is truly a biblical theology, of historical origin, conveying what the holy writers felt about divine matters; on the one hand there is a dogmatic theology of didactic origin, teaching what each theologian philosophises rationally about divine things..." (Sandys-Wunsch and Eldredge, 137).

4. Gabler saw the task of biblical theology as the careful collection of the opinions of the biblical writers "suitably digested, carefully referred to the universal notions, and cautiously compared among themselves," thus providing the *dicta classica*, "as the fundamental basis for a more subtle dogmatic scrutiny," "those certain and undoubted universal ideas...which alone are useful in dogmatic theology" (Sandys-Wunsch and Eldredge, 142–43). In his "Theology (NT)" in *ABD* 6 (1992), R. Morgan comments: "Gabler's proposals for biblical theology as a historical, not a dogmatic, discipline were confused, because his final step was more theological and less historical than he recognized" (476). See also J. Frey, "Zum Problem der Aufgabe und Durchführung einer Theologie des Neuen Testaments" in C. Breytenbach and J. Frey, hrsg., *Aufgabe und Durchführung einer Theologie des Neuen Testaments*, WUNT 205 (Tübingen, Germany: Mohr Siebeck, 2007), 21–24.

5. There are several reviews of the history of the project of biblical theology. See especially Merk, *Biblische Theologie*; "Biblische Theologie II" in *TRE* 6 (1980): 455–77; "Gesamtbiblische Theologie: Zur Fortgang der Diskussion in den 80er Jahren" in *VF* 33 (1988): 19–40; H. Räisänen, *Beyond New Testament Theology* (London: SCM, 1990), Parts I and II; and H. G. Reventlow, "Theology (Biblical), History of" in *ABD* 6 (1992): 483–505. See also Hasel, *New Testament Theology*; D. O. Via's wide-ranging *What Is New Testament Theology?* (Minneapolis: Fortress Press, 2002); Scobie, *Ways of Our God*, 9–45; and most recently J. K. Mead, *Biblical Theology: Issues, Methods, and Themes* (Louisville: Westminster John Knox Press, 2007), though he fails to engage with the German contributions of the 1990s (see note 6 below).

6. H. Hübner, *Biblische Theologie des Neuen Testaments*, 3 vols. (Göttingen, Germany: Vandenhoeck & Ruprecht, 1990, 1993, 1995); Childs, *Biblical Theology of the Old and New Testaments*; P. Stuhlmacher, *Biblische Theologie des Neuen Testaments*, 2 vols. (Göttingen, Germany: Vandenhoeck & Ruprecht, 1992, 1999).

7. As most notably in G. L. Bauer, *Biblische Theologie des Neuen Testaments*, 4 vols. (Leipzig, 1800–1802) and B. Weiss, *Biblical Theology of the New Testament* (1868); ET in 2 vols. (Edinburgh, Scotland: T & T Clark, 1882, 1883).

8. R. Morgan, "New Testament Theology" in S. J. Kraftchick, et al., eds., *Biblical Theology: Problem and Perspectives* (Nashville: Abingdon Press, 1995), 129.

9. R. H. Fuller, "New Testament Theology" in E. J. Epp and G. W. MacRae, eds., *The New Testament and its Modern Interpreters* (Atlanta: Scholars Press, 1989), 565–84 (here 567). For other formulations of isues see e.g. E. Grässer, "Offene Fragen im Umkreis einer Biblischen Theologie" in *ZTK* 77 (1980) 200–221; T. Söding, "Probleme und Chancen Biblischer Theologie aus neutestamentlicher Sicht" in C. Dohmen and T. Söding, hrsg., *Eine Bibel—zwei Testamente* (Paderborn, Germany: Ferdinand Schöningh, 1995), 159–77; P. Balla, "Challenges to Biblical Theology" in T. D. Alexander and B. S. Rosner, eds., *New Dictionary of Biblical Theology* (Downers Grove, Ill.: InterVarsity Press, 2000) 20–27; B. Janowski, "Biblical Theology" in J. W. Rogerson and J. M. Lieu, eds., *The Oxford Handbook of Biblical Studies* (Oxford, England: Oxford University, 2006) 716–31; Frey, "Problem."

10. I draw on two earlier essays—"Das Problem 'Biblische Theologie'" in Dohmen and Söding, hrsg., *Eine Bibel* 179–93, more or less = "The Problem of 'Biblical Theology'" in C. Bartholomew et al., eds., *Out of Egypt: Biblical Theology and Biblical Interpretation* (Milton Keynes, England: Paternoster Press/ Grand Rapids, Mich.: Zondervan, 2004) 172–84; and "Not so Much 'New Testament Theology' as 'New Testament Theologizing'" in Breytenbach and Frey, hrsg., *Aufgabe* 225–46. My "New Testament Theology" in Rogerson and Lieu, eds., *Oxford Handbook* 698–715 is a summary treatment of this volume.

11. So particularly Hübner, *Biblische Theologie*: "working out the theological relationship of the NT authors with the OT is the primary and basic task of a biblical theology" (1.28); see also chapter 2 note 9 below.

12. See also R. Rendtorff, "Die Bibel Israels als Buch der Christen" in Dohmen and Söding, hrsg. *Eine Bibel*: "The Old Testament is an integral and indispensable part of our Christian Bible; but it is also first and foremost the Jewish Bible" (103).

13. Cf., for example, S. Fish, *Is There a Text in This Class? The Authority of Interpretive Communities* (Cambridge, Mass.: Harvard University, 1980); J. A. Sanders, *Canon and Community: A Guide to Canonical Criticism* (Philadelphia: Fortress Press, 1984); Scobie, *Ways of Our God*, 40–42.

14. Childs, *Biblical Theology*, 77–78, 91, 444–45.

15. Ibid., 85–88.

16. Hence what Peter Stuhlmacher regards as a fundamental feature of his *Biblische Theologie*: "The theology of the New Testament must be designed as a biblical theology of the New Testament originating from the Old Testament and open to it, and must be comprehended as part of a biblical theology of Old and New Testaments considered as a whole" (1.5). Scobie (*Ways of Our God*, 58–60) and Marshall (*Theology*, 38–39) agree.

17. But see J. Levenson, "Why Jews Are Not Interested in Biblical Theology" in J. Neusner, et al., eds., *Judaic Perspectives on Ancient Israel* (Philadelphia: Fortress Press, 1987) 281–307. "Jews have a basically different understanding of how the Hebrew Scriptures are appropriated religiously without the need of Biblical Theology" (Childs, *Biblical Theology*, 25).

18. I would maintain that the same is true for Paul—see my "Paul: Apostate or Apostle

of Israel?" in *ZNW* 89 (1998): 256–71; also "The Jew Paul and his Meaning for Israel" in T. Linafelt, ed., *A Shadow of Glory: Reading the New Testament after the Holocaust* (New York: Routledge, 2002), 201–15—but the claim is more controversial than with Jesus. See also below #1.6.

19. Dunn, "Problem," 183.

20. Söding ("Probleme und Chancen Biblischer Theologie," 164) asks a similar range of questions.

21. In the Hebrew Bible, Daniel is included in the Writings. See, for example, the summary treatments in Stuhlmacher, *Biblische Theologie*, 1.6–7.

22. Discussion in Hübner, *Biblische Theologie*, 1.44–70.

23. See particularly M. Hengel, "Die Septuaginta als 'christliche Schriftensammlung,' ihre Vorgeschichte und das Problem ihres Kanons" in M. Hengel and A. M. Schwemer, hrsg., *Die Septuaginta zwischen Judentum und Christentum* (Tübingen, Germany: Mohr Siebeck, 1994), 182–284.

24. The most disputed were Hebrews, James, Jude, and Revelation.

25. Luther's negative estimates of James and Calvin's failure to deal with Revelation in his NT commentaries are well known illustrations. On the range of issues relating to the canons of OT and NT see L. M. McDonald and J. A. Sanders, eds., *The Canon Debate* (Peabody, Mass.: Hendrickson, 2002). The classic treatment of the emergence of the Christian canon is H. von Campenhausen, *The Formation of the Christian Bible* (London: Black, 1972).

26. See my *The Unity and Diversity of the New Testament* (London: SCM, 1977, 1990, 2006), ##54–55.

27. It was W. Wrede who first brought this issue home with force in his "Über Aufgabe und Methode der sogenannten Neutestamentlichen Theology" (1897) in Strecker, hrsg., *Das Problem*, 81–154, translated by R. Morgan in his *Nature of New Testament Theology* (London: SCM, 1974), 68–116. The texts include what are usually described as the OT apocrypha and pseudepigrapha; see J. H. Charlesworth, ed., *The Old Testament Pseudepigrapha*, 2 vols. (London: Darton, Longman & Todd, 1983, 1985).

28. W. Schneemelcher and R. McL. Wilson, eds., *New Testament Apocrypha*, 2 vols. (Cambridge, England: James Clarke, 1991); J. K. Elliott, *The Apocryphal New Testament* (Oxford, England: Clarendon, 1993).

29. See for example R. W. Funk, et al., *The Five Gospels* (New York: Macmillan, 1993).

30. See also Hahn, *Theologie*, 1.734–42. L. T. Johnson, "Does a Theology of the Canonical Gospels Make Sense?" in C. Rowland and C. Tuckett, eds., *The Nature of New Testament Theology*; R. Morgan FS (Oxford, England: Blackwell, 2006), 93–108, offers a concise but effective comparison of the canonical and apocryphal Gospels (102–5).

31. See also J. Schröter, "Die Bedeutung des Kanons für eine Theologie des Neuen Testaments" in Breytenbach and Frey, hrsg., *Aufgabe*, 149–54.

32. Galatians 3:10—"the book of the law," that is, Deuteronomy; "the book of the covenant"—Hebrews 9:19; cf. Hebrews 10:7, quoting Psalm 40:7; the Jewish Scriptures as "the books" (2 Clem 14:2). See also Hahn, *Theologie*, 2.38–9.

33. Revelation 1:11; 5:1-9; 10:8; 22:7, 9-10, 18-19; also "the book of life" (Rev 13:8; 17:8; 20:12; 21:27).

34. Matthew, Mark, the unknown author of Hebrews, James, Jude, and probably the seer of Revelation.

35. Ephesians and the Pastoral Epistles are regarded as pseudonymous by the great

majority in current scholarship, with opinion more equally divided on Colossians and 2 Thessalonians.

36. I address the issue in *The Theology of Paul the Apostle* (Grand Rapids, Mich./Edinburgh, Scotland: Eerdmans/T & T Clark, 1998), #1.

37. The main criticism of my *Theology of Paul* was to this effect. Writing a theology of Paul helps focus many of the problem issues confronting those who want to write a NT theology, so we will return to the subject below (#1.6).

38. In his presidential address to the Society of New Testament Studies, "The Problem of a New Testament Theology," *NTS* 19 (1972–73), Ernst Käsemann puts forward as his first thesis, that "the New Testament as we have it is a fragmentary collection of documents from the earliest period.... By and large there is no internal coherence. The tensions everywhere evident amount at times to contradictions" (242).

39. As maintained, for example, by P. Pokorny, "The Problem of Biblical Theology," *HBT* 15 (1993): 87–88.

40. "The Kingdom of God is the theological centre of the synoptic gospels, but not elsewhere; Paul and John have much to say about God's love in sending His Son, while on this the synoptics, Hebrews, and 1 Peter are silent; Paul, who believes in the theological significance of the earthly life of Jesus, betrays singularly little acquaintance with its details; John the Seer does not, like John the Evangelist, portray Jesus as the Saviour of the World. It would appear then that there never was a time when anybody's belief consisted of the highest common factor of New Testament teaching" (Caird, *New Teastament Theology*, 17).

41. This was one of my principal findings in *Unity and Diversity in the New Testament*, #76.

42. The theme of unity and diversity has become prominent in recent theologies; note particularly Hahn's *Theologie des Neuen Testaments: Band I—Die Vielfalt des Neuen Testaments; Band II—Die Einheit des Neuen Testaments*—"The unity can only be unity in the diversity" (1.770); Eduard Lohse's two volumes of collected studies on the theology of the NT took the titles *Die Einheit des Neuen Testaments* (Göttingen, Germany: Vandenhoeck & Ruprecht, 1973) and *Die Vielfalt des Neuen Testaments* (Göttingen, Germany: Vandenhoeck & Ruprecht, 1982); the subtitle of the second volume of L. Goppelt's posthumous *Theology of the New Testament* is *The Variety and Unity of the Apostolic Witness to Christ* (1976; ET Grand Rapids, Mich.: Eerdmans, 1982); see also Marshall, *New Testament Theology: Many Witnesses, One Gospel*; Matera, *New Testament Theology*, xxviii–xxx and ch. 31. G. Strecker, *Theology of the New Testament* (Berlin: de Gruyter, 2000) and Vouga, *Une théologie* give more weight to the diversity; "in the writings of the New Testament we are met with a multiplicity of theological conceptions" (Strecker, *Theology*, 2–3). See also J. Barton, "Unity and Diversity in the Biblical Canon" in J. Barton and M. Wolter, hrsg., *Die Einheit der Schrift und die Vielfalt des Kanons/ The Unity of Scripture and the Diversity of the Canon*, BZNW 118 (Berlin: de Gruyter, 2003), 11–26.

43. Review of earlier discussion in Hasel, *New Testament Theology*, ch. 3; more recently see for example Hahn, *Theologie*, 2.9–12.

44. H. G. Reventlow, *Problems of Old Testament Theology in the Twentieth Century* (London: SCM, 1985), ch. 4; idem "Theology," 493–94; and see again Levenson, "Why Jews...," 283–84, 292–93, 296–97.

45. For example, G. F. Hasel, "The Problem of the Center in the OT Theology

Debate," *ZAW* 86 (1974): 65–82; Reventlow, *Problems*, 131–33; Hübner, *Biblische Theologie* 1.149–50, and further 149–72; "Theology begins with the revealing God; theology 'ends' with the revealing God. *Principium et finis theologiae est Deus se relevans*" (3.277); B. Janowski, "The One God of the Two Testaments: Basic Questions of a Biblical Theology," *Theology Today* 57 (2000): 316–21.

46. For example, P. Stuhlmacher, *How to Do Biblical Theology* (Allison Park, Pa.: Pickwick Press, 1995) ch. 2; R. Morgan, "Can the Critical Study of Scripture Provide a Doctrinal Norm?" *JR* 76 (1996): 206–32; M. Müller, "Neutestamentliche Theologie als Biblische Theologie: Einige grundsätzliche Überlegungen," *NTS* 43 (1997): "Faith in Jesus as the risen one and the Christ is the creative and constitutive factor in the composition of the different NT writings" (481); U. Schnelle, in *Theologie des Neuen Testaments* (Göttingen, Germany: Vandenhoeck & Ruprecht, 2007), cites Luther's famous formulation, that whatever preaches Christ is apostolic (38); "There is diversity in the NT only on a clear basis: the experiences of God's eschatological saving actions in Jesus Christ in the cross and resurrection" (40–41).

47. Childs has no doubt that the "subject matter" of biblical theology is Jesus Christ. The "fundamental goal" of biblical theology is "to understand the various voices within the whole Christian Bible, New and Old Testament alike, as a witness to the one Lord Jesus Christ, the selfsame divine reality." "The heart of the enterprise is christological" (*Biblical Theology*, 78–79, 85–86, 480). Similarly F. Watson, *Text and Truth: Redefining Biblical Theology* (Edinburgh, Scotland: T & T Clark, 1997), 13–14; "From the standpoint of Christian faith, it must be said that the Old Testament comes to us with Jesus and from Jesus, and can never be understood in abstraction from him" (182). Schnelle responds bluntly: "A biblical theology is not possible, because the Old Testament is silent on Jesus Christ" (*Theologie*, 40).

48. See for example my *Unity and Diversity*, ch. 10; though I also conclude that "the different unifying factors in first-century Christianity focus again and again on Christ, on the unity between Jesus the man and Jesus the exalted one" ([2006] 405; see more fully 403–13). Similarly W. Thüsing, as cited by Frey, "Problem," 37.

49. Bultmann's demythologizing project focused on the kerygma; see also, for example, the final sections of W. G. Kümmel, *The Theology of the New Testament* (London: SCM, 1974); E. Lohse, *Grundriss der neutestamentlichen Theologie* (Stuttgart, Germany: Kohlhammer, 1974) 161; G. Strecker, *Theology of the New Testament* (Berlin: de Gruyter, 2000), 8.

50. *Unity and Diversity*, chap. 2. The common elements in the diversity of kerygmata I identified as proclamation of the risen, exalted Jesus; the call for faith, for acceptance of the proclamation and commitment to the Jesus proclaimed; and the promise held out to faith (the Spirit, forgiveness, salvation, union with Christ) (#7.1). Cf. Marshall's critique of my rather sparse characterization of the unifying theme (note 48)—*Theology*, 712–15.

51. Stuhlmacher's "Mitte der Schrift" is in effect a mini-NT theology (*Biblische Theologie*, 2.320).

52. See also M. Wolter, "Die Vielfalt der Schrift und die Einheit des Kanons," and R. Morgan, "The New Testament Canon of Scripture and Christian Identity," in Barton and Wolter, hrsg., *Einheit der Schrift*, 45–68 and 151–93 respectively.

53. I have already noted that Paul's image of the church as the body of Christ is the best model of unity in diversity—many members, and all different, yet one body; and itself a bounded entity.

54. R. Bultmann, *Theology of the New Testament*, 2 vols. (London: SCM, 1952, 1955) 1.191, 2.251. More strongly by H. Braun, "The Problem of a Theology of the New Testament," *Journal for Theology and the Church* 1 (1965): 169–83; cf. Vouga, *Une théologie*, 19.

55. "Bultmann's interpretive program depends so heavily on specifically Western existential philosophical premises that it cannot possibly be considered as the only appropriate way to interpret the New Testament kerygma about Jesus Christ" (Stuhlmacher, *Biblische Theologie*, 1.17).

56. I echo the classic Lutheran evaluation of justification by faith (*articulus stantis et cadentis ecclesiae*). E. Käsemann, ed., *Das Neue Testament als Kanon* (Göttingen, Germany: Vandenhoeck & Ruprecht, 1970) regarded justification by faith as the "canon within the canon" (405); see further Hasel, *New Testament Theology*, 160–62. Scott Hafemann sees "the righteousness of God in Paul's thought as the theological foundation for Stuhlmacher's *Biblical Theology*" (in Stuhlmacher, *How to Do Biblical Theology*, xv–xli).

57. This has been part of the concern voiced in "the new perspective on Paul"; see my *New Perspective on Paul: Collected Essays*, WUNT 185 (Tübingen, Germany: Mohr Siebeck, 2005; revised edition, Grand Rapids, Mich.: Eerdmans, 2008).

58. As Matera, *New Testament Theology*, xxvii–xxviii. Influential here has been R. B. Hays, *The Faith of Jesus Christ: The Narrative Substructure of Galatians 3:1–4:11* (Grand Rapids, Mich.: Eerdmans, 1983, 2002). See also N. T. Wright, *The New Testament and the People of God* (London: SPCK, 1992) 69–80, 139–43, 215–23; B. W. Longenecker, ed., *Narrative Dynamics in Paul: A Critical Assessment* (Louisville: Westminster John Knox Press, 2002); C. G. Bartholomew and M. W. Goheen, "Story and Biblical Theology" in Bartholomew et al., eds., *Out of Egypt* 144–71. This approach could be described as a modern version of the attempt to locate the unifying centre in "salvation history," usually associated with O. Cullmann, *Christ and Time*, revised ed. (London: SCM, 1962); also *Salvation in History* (London: SCM, 1967) (see also Reventlow, "Theology," 497–98).

59. See for example Merk, "Gesamtbiblische Theologie," 19–40. On the historical critical method see my *Christianity in the Making: Vol. 1. Jesus Remembered* (Grand Rapids, Mich.: Eerdmans, 2003) 27–29, 68–70, 101–11; and see also Schnelle, *Theologie*, 17–29.

60. Wrede, "Aufgabe/Task"; "'New Testament theology' ought to be replaced . . . with two different projects: first, the 'history of early Christian thought' (or theology, if you like), evolving in the context of early Judaism; second, critical philosophical and/or theological 'reflection on the New Testament'" (Räisänen, *Beyond New Testament Theology*, xviii). Caird for example agrees: "New Testament theology is a historical discipline. . . . Its purpose is descriptive" (*Theology*, 1).

61. K. Stendahl, "Biblical Theology, Contemporary," *IDB* 1 (1962): 418–32.

62. The "historical-descriptive" role of biblical theology has been the dominant feature of the enterprise since Gabler; so for example Reventlow finds a classic example in Weiss's *Biblical Theology*, 10n3 ("Theology," 487); Via's review in his *What Is New Testament Theology?* ch. 4 ("New Testament Theology as a Historical Project"). A. K. M. Adam, *Making Sense of New Testament Theology: "Modern" Problems and Prospects* (Macon, Ga.: Mercer University, 1995) regards Wrede and Stendahl, together with Gabler, as typical exemplifiers of "modernity," all emphasizing the chronological gap and "the distance that separates the modern reader from the New Testament text" (ch. 2), and he goes on to cite the critique of Richardson's *Introduction* by L. E. Keck, "Problems of New Testament Theology," *NovT* 7 (1964–65): 217–41, as an example of a modernist

critique (91–93). Adam's thesis is that the modernist, historical critical agenda has been deeply damaging to NT theology and is the cause of the decline of biblical theology as a subject.

63. P. Balla, *Challenges to New Testament Theology: An Attempt to Justify the Enterprise*, WUNT 2.95 (Tübingen, Germany: Mohr Siebeck, 1997), though he still sees the task in historical and descriptive terms. Hahn begins his *Theologie* with the assertion: "Theology of the New Testament concentrates on the faith testimony of early Christianity, which as such is the foundation of all Christian proclamation and theology" (1.1).

64. Notably K. Berger, *Theologiegeschichte des Urchristentums: Theologie des Neuen Testaments* (Tübingen, Germany: Francke, 1994); see also J. Becker, "Theologiegeschichte des Urchristentums—Theologie des Neuen Testaments— Frühchristliche Religionsgeschichte" in Breytenbach and Frey, hrsg., *Aufgabe*, 115–33. Strecker sees his task as "to investigate the theological conceptions advocated by the New Testament authors on the basis of the theological (church) traditions they had received"; but he also stresses "the critical function of the New Testament" and that the church today must allow itself to be measured by the foundational claim and demand made by the New Testament (*Theology*, 3–4).

65. The tension is classically discussed by R. Morgan in a series of contributions beginning with his *The Nature of New Testament Theology*, in which he compares and contrasts the approaches of Wrede and of Adolf Schlatter; see also his "Theology (NT)"; and several comments in "New Testament Theology"—"'NTT' implies not merely that it speaks of God, but that it claims to tell the truth, and not only the historical truth of what the texts are saying, but a religious truth valid today" (105; similarly 108, 109–10, 126). See also Watson, *Text and Truth*; and Wilckens, who does not hesitate to begin his massive *Theologie* project by confessing, "The reality of the resurrection of Jesus from the dead has become *the* theme of my life" (1.1.v), and who, in agreement with Stuhlmacher, argues for "the necessity of *historical* exegesis of the biblical texts above all on *theological* grounds" (1.1.23); and P. F. Esler, who in his prolegomenon to the subject, *New Testament Theology: Communion and Identity* (Minneapolis: Fortress Press, 2005), wants to use "the results of historical research into the New Testament to strengthen and enrich the beliefs, experience, and identity of Christians in the present," "in the belief that the results of such historical investigation are, *in and of themselves*, the bearers of theological truth" (20, 36), though I am not convinced that his appeal to "communion with the saints" (chs. 8–10) helps forward the hermeneutical task.

66. See the larger discussions indicated by K. J. Vanhoozer, "Exegesis and Hermeneutics," and D. A. Carson, "Systematic Theology and Biblical Theology" in Alexander and Rosner, *New Dictionary of Biblical Theology*, 52–64 and 89–104 respectively.

67. Bultmann was the great exponent of *Sachkritik*; see Morgan, *Nature*, 42–52. Morgan concludes: "the risk involved in *Sachkritik* is a necessary element in historical research," though he adds that such a critical interpretation will always be open to criticism from fellow-historians (52). Morgan's concern is to elucidate "the legitimate activity of *theological interpretation* of the New Testament, or doing one's own theology through a theologically motivated historical interpretation of certain texts" (52), but he allows that the theological interpretation can be ruled out by the historical findings—"theology done through interpretation of the tradition must meet the condition that it does not contravene what historians can say about the tradition" (57). Similarly in his *ABD* article: "History and exegesis retain critical controls over what is said in NTT, even though

theological interpretation and criticism (*Sachexegese* and *Sachkritik*) go outside the realm of historical discourse" ("Theology [NT]," 483). In this he echoes Ebeling: that "'biblical theology' as an historical discipline exercises a normative function over against dogmatics in all matters concerning the relation to the Bible. Dogmatics must render account of its use of scripture before the judgement seat of historical study of the Bible" ("The Meaning of 'Biblical Theology,'" 218).

68. H.-G. Gadamer, *Truth and Method* (New York: Crossroad, 1989). On his concept of the *Wirkungsgeschichte* ("history of effect") of a text, and his more elaborate phrase *wirkungsgeschichtliches Bewusstsein* ("historically effected consciousness") see my *Jesus Remembered*, 122–23; and on the relevance and importance of the *Wirkungsgeschichte* or reception history of the NT see particularly U. Luz, "The Contribution of Reception History to a Theology of the New Testament," in Rowland and Tuckett, eds., *The Nature of New Testament Theology*, 123–34.

69. Stuhlmacher calls for "a hermeneutic of 'good will' (B. F. Meyer) or 'critical sympathy' (W. G. Kümmel) toward the texts'" (*Biblische Theologie*, 1.11); his own term is "a hermeneutic of consent"—*Historical Criticism and Theological Interpretation of Scripture: Towards a Hermeneutic of Consent* (Philadelphia: Fortress Press, 1977).

70. See my "Not so much 'New Testament Theology,'" 225–46. In an earlier essay, "The Task of New Testament Theology" in J. D. G. Dunn and J. P. Mackey, *New Testament Theology in Dialogue* (London: SPCK, 1987), 1–26, I defined "the task of New Testament theology" as "to hear what the New Testament author intended his readers to hear, and so to hear that the message of the text helps shape our own theology" (20). My concern is similar to that of Esler, as articulated in his *New Testament Theology* Introduction and chapter 1. Note also Morgan's insistence "against some current English usage," "that the phrase NTT [NT Theology] should refer to the activity of doing (thinking, writing, speaking) *theology,* or to the results of that activity, not simply to the linguistic, historical, or philosophical analysis of theological concepts or texts" ("Made in Germany: Towards an Anglican Appropriation of an Originally Lutheran *Genre*" in Breytenbach and Frey, hrsg., *Aufgabe*, 86.

71. What is in view is more than the *religionsgeschichtlich* protest (as in Wrede, "Aufgabe"/ "Task") against theology too narrowly defined.

72. See particularly B. D. Ehrman, *The Orthodox Corruption of Scripture: The Effect of Early Christological Controversies on the Text of the New Testament* (Oxford, England: Oxford University, 1993); D. C. Parker, *The Living Text of the Gospels* (Cambridge, England: Cambridge University, 1997); E. J. Epp, "The Multivalence of the Term 'Original Text' in New Testament Textual Criticism," *HTR* 92 (1999): 245–81.

73. I have developed the point in "What Makes a Good Exposition?" (*The Expository Times* Lecture, June 2002), *Expository Times* 114 (2002–2003): 147–57.

74. For Räisänen, "the actualizing efforts of the exegete can only result in theologizing *about* the sources" (*Beyond New Testament Theology*, 137); I would prefer to say "theologizing *with* the sources." C. Kavin Rowe begins his review of recent contributions to the field of NT theology, "New Testament Theology: The Revival of a Discipline," *JBL* 125 (2006): 393–410, with a quotation from Ebeling's "The Meaning of 'Biblical Theology,'" *Word and Faith* (Philadelphia: Fortress Press, 1963): "*The* New Testament theology will never be written. It can never be written, because in principle the discipline...New Testament theology is never a finally closed book but constitutes a task that continues with us all our days" (94). See also C. Rowland and Z. Bennett, "'Action Is the Life of

All': New Testament Theology and Practical Theology" in Rowland and Tuckett, eds., *The Nature of New Testament Theology*, 186–206.

75. I have debated with Robert Morgan on the issues here in response to his review of my *Jesus Remembered*—"On Faith and History, and Living Tradition (In Response to Robert Morgan and Andrew Gregory)", and "A Letter to Robert Morgan," *ExpT* 116 (2004–2005): 13–19 and 286–87.

76. J. Barton, *The Nature of Biblical Criticism* (Louisville/London: Westminster John Knox Press, 2007). Barton also protests against the suggestion of Stendahl's famous distinction that "what the text meant" is now passé; "what the text meant is what it still means. The fact that it can be used as a vehicle for many other meanings does not undermine this. . . . A given meaning in the text persists over time even when its significance is differently perceived" (citing E. D. Hirsch) (86–88).

77. Räisänen also emphasizes the importance of the concerns of NT theology being heard beyond the church (*Beyond New Testament Theology*, 93–100).

78. One of the attractions of the "descriptive task" for Stendahl was that it "can be carried out by believer and agnostic alike" ("Biblical Theology," 422).

79. The last with reference to Adam, *Making Sense*, ch. 6.

80. "Paul's key position for the historical study of Christianity, together with his theological profundity, gives him undue weight in a historically oriented NTT" (Morgan, "New Testament Theology," 125).

81. My argument here does not depend on whether and how many of the Pauline letters we can label as "authentic."

82. H. Räisänen's *Paul and the Law*, WUNT 29 (Tübingen, Germany: Mohr Siebeck, 1983) is a notable example of a critique which fails because he treats texts individually and atomistically, without seeking to hear them within the flow of particular arguments and context of particular situations.

83. The proceedings of the Seminar are recorded in a sequence of volumes entitled *Pauline Theology*—Vol. 1 (ed. J. M. Bassler), Vol. 2 (ed. D. M. Hay) and Vol. 3 (ed. D. M. Hay and E. E. Johnson) published by Fortress Press, Minneapolis (1991, 1993, 1995) and Vol. 4 (ed. E. E. Johnson and D. M. Hay) by Scholars Press, Atlanta (1997). Calvin Roetzel entitles chapter 4 of his *Paul: The Man and the Myth* (Columbia: University of South Carolina, 1997) "The Theologizer."

84. At notes 36 and 37 above.

85. *Theology of Paul*, #1.

86. Part of the greatness of J. L. Martyn's work on *Galatians*, AB 33A (New York: Doubleday, 1997) is that he enters into the dialogic nature of Paul's writing, even if (in my view) he attributes too much of the theology of the letter to the other side of the dialogue!

87. *Christology in the Making* (London: SCM, 1980, 1989; Grand Rapids, Mich.: Eerdmans, 1996), xii–xvi.

88. See chapter 3 note 78.

89. I am indebted at this point to D. G. Meade, *Pseudonymity and Canon*, WUNT 39 (Tübingen, Germany: Mohr Siebeck, 1986).

2. The Determining Factors

1. C. H. Dodd, *According to the Scriptures: The Substructure of New Testament Theology* (London: Nisbet, 1952). "The reception of OT content belongs so constitutively to the

theology of the respective NT authors, that it would lose its identity without the OT traditions which they received" (Hübner, *Bibliache Theologie*, 1.31–32).

2. A detailed sequence can be found in the indexes at the end of most Greek New Testaments.

3. For example, Mark 1:2; John 12:14; Acts 15:15; Rom 1:17; 4:17; 15:19; 1 Cor 1:31; 2 Cor 8:15; 2 Pet 3:15.

4. Matt 1:22; 2:15, 17, 23; 4:14; 8:17; etc.; also for example Mark 14:49; Luke 24:25-27, 44; John 13:18; 15:25; Acts 1:16; Rom 13:8; Jas 2:23.

5. Details in my *Jesus Remembered* (Grand Rapids, Mich.: Eerdmans, 2003) 777–81.

6. A. T. Lincoln, "Hebrews and Biblical Theology", in Bartholomew, et al., eds., *Out of Egypt*, 313–38: "The writer to the Hebrews does his theology by reading Scripture" (330).

7. I am thinking of passages such as Gal 3:16-18, 4:22-31, and Heb 8.

8. See Hahn, *Theologie* II Teil I, "The Old Testament as the Bible of early Christianity"; also Childs, *Biblical Theology*, 225–29; Frey, "Problem," 48–49. When Morgan says, "What for Judaism is the decisive revelation of God (Torah) is relativized and relegated to religious tradition for Christians by the coming of the Messiah" ("New Testament Theology," 129), he overstates his point; "relativized" no doubt, but "relegated to religious tradition" hardly does justice to the importance of the Jewish scriptures for the first Christians.

9. Of the three authors referred to in the introduction to chapter 1 (note 6), Hübner regards this as the primary and foundational task of his *Biblische Theologie des Neuen Testaments* (see above chapter 1 note 11); but he is interested in the OT only as taken up by the New—*Vetus Testamentum in Novo receptum* (1.18, 62–70); idem, "Eine hermeneutisch unverzichtbare Unterscheidung: Vetus Testamentum und Vetus Testamentum in Novo receptum," in T. Fornberg and D. Hellholm, eds., *Texts and Contexts: Biblical Texts in Their Textual and Situational Contexts*; L. Hartman FS (Oslo: Scandinavian University Press, 1995), 901–10. Childs protests: "The significance of emphasizing the continuing canonical integrity of the Old Testament lies in resisting the Christian temptation to identify Biblical Theology with the New Testament's interpretation of the Old, as if the Old Testament's witness were limited to how it was once heard and appropriated by the early church" (*Biblical Theology*, 77), though he is too constrained by the canonical forms of both Testaments. Stuhlmacher, *Biblische Theologie*, pays more heed to the movement of thought involved. Caird is much less concerned with this aspect of NT theology.

10. H. Hübner, *Vetus Testamentum in Novo*, 2 vols (Göttingen, Germany: Vandenhoeck & Ruprecht, 1996). For other bibliography on the NT use of the OT see for example D. A. Carson and H. G. M. Williamson, eds., *It Is Written: Scripture Citing Scripture*; B. Lindars FS (Cambridge, England: Cambridge University, 1988).

11. Marshall still uses this imagery (*New Testament Theology*, 39).

12. In indexes of Greek Testaments the list of echoes and allusions is much longer than the list of actual citations.

13. The challenges and potential of the task are well represented by R. B. Hays, *Echoes of Scripture in the Letters of Paul* (New Haven, Conn.: Yale University, 1989); also *The Conversion of the Imagination: Paul as Interpreter of Israel's Scripture* (Grand Rapids, Mich.: Eerdmans, 2005); F. Watson, *Paul and the Hermeneutics of Faith* (London: T & T Clark International, 2004).

14. Here I follow Morgan's observation that a NT theology "should . . . include far more OT content than is customary . . . in order to underline the importance of what is taken for granted in the NT and Christianity" ("New Testament Theology," 129).

15. See below #4.2c and chapter 3 note 90.

16. The old argument of E. Haenchen, "Das alte 'Neue Testament' und das neue 'Alte Testament,'" *Das Bibel und Wir: Gesammelte Aufsätze. Zweiter Band* (Tübingen, Germany: Mohr Siebeck, 1968), 13–27, "that the OT understood in its *original* sense has never belonged to the Christian canon" (18), misses the point that the "original sense" was never the determinative factor in the understanding of these texts during the process up to and beyond the *de facto* canonization of the Torah, the Prophets, and the Writings.

17. The first round of the debate was B. S. Childs, *Biblical Theology in Crisis* (Philadelphia: Westminster Press, 1970), and J. A. Sanders, *Torah and Canon* (Philadelphia: Fortress Press, 1972); see Scobie, *Ways of Our God*, 38–39, also 73–75 in agreement with Childs. See also my earlier reflections on the subject in "Levels of Canonical Authority," *Horizons in Biblical Theology* 4 (1982), 13–60, reprinted in Part II of my *The Living Word* (Philadelphia: Fortress Press, 1987, 2008).

18. I think, for example, of the Song of Moses (Exodus 15), "the Book of the Covenant" (Exodus 21–23), and the credo of Deuteronomy 26:5-9, as well as individual prophetic oracles, and refer particularly to the classic treatment of G. von Rad, *Old Testament Theology*, 2 vols. (Edinburgh, Scotland: Oliver & Boyd, 1962) especially 1.105–28 and 2.319–35. Influential also has been H. Gese, *Essays on Biblical Theology* (Minneapolis: Augsburg, 1981)—note particularly the opening essay, "The Biblical View of Scripture"; idem, "Über die biblische Einheit" in Dohmen and Söding, hrsg. *Eine Bibel*, 35–44.

19. The controversy stories of Mark 2:23–3:5 show awareness not simply of the Sabbath laws of Exodus and Deuteronomy but also of the developed tradition attested in *Jub.* 2:17-33, 50:8-12 and CD 10:14–11:18.

20. See my "Jesus, Table-Fellowship, and Qumran," *Jesus and the Dead Sea Scrolls*, ed. J. H. Charlesworth (New York: Doubleday, 1992) 254–72.

21. See for example my *The Theology of Paul the Apostle* (Grand Rapids, Mich.: Eerdmans/Edinburgh: T & T Clark 1998) 357–60.

22. For example, Rom 10:6-8 (Deut 30:12-14) and Eph 4:8 (Ps 68:18); see M. McNamara, *The New Testament and the Palestinian Targum to the Pentateuch*, AB 27A (Rome: Biblical Institute, 1978), 70–81.

23. Cf. Müller, "Neutestamentliche Theologie," 488–89. It will be appreciated that what is in view here is more than simply taking seriously the tradition-history of motifs, a perspective which runs the danger of treating the process too simply as a (merely) literary phenomenon.

24. Contrast Hübner, *Biblische Theologie*, 1.17–18.

25. I do not resile from or ignore what I said earlier about the importance of the non-canonical ("intertestamental" literature) in determining many of the terms and attitudes struck in the NT. The point is that the influence in these cases is mostly in terms of *inter-action* with or *reaction* to, rather than dependence on and continuity with, as is generally the case with the NT's relation to the OT.

26. Cf. P. Stuhlmacher, *How to Do Biblical Theology* (Allison Park, Pa.: Pickwick Press, 1995): "one must speak of one canonical process from which the Hebrew Bible, the Septuagint, and the New Testament all proceed and which, although multi-layered, represents a continuum" (78); see also his *Biblische Theologie* 1.5.

27. Janowski reminds us that no attempt was made to "Christianize" the Old Testament by introducing redactional intrusions. "What must be acknowledged is precisely the lack of a Christian redaction of the Old Testament. The Old Testament is not 'Christianized' internally, but externally; a further collection of writings is placed alongside it, which together form the Christian Bible" ("The One God," 303).

28. See further #3.3b below.

29. The study of earliest Christian traditions has clearly established the centrality of earliest Christian belief in the cross and resurrection; the data is summarized, with bibliography, in my *Theology of Paul*, 174–77, particularly W. Kramer, *Christ, Lord, Son of God* (London: SCM, 1996); also Hahn, *Theologie*, 1.134–40; Schnelle, *Theologie*, 166–70.

30. Discussion in my *Jesus Remembered*, 866–79.

31. Rom 1:4; 1 Cor 15:20, 23; cf. Matt 27:53.

32. Räisänen sees his phenomenology of early Christian religious thought as beginning with eschatology (*Beyond New Testament Theology*, 118–19), echoing E. Käsemann's famous characterization: "Apocalyptic was the mother of all Christian theology"—"The Beginnings of Christian Theology" (1960), *New Testament Questions of Today* (London: SCM, 1969), 101–2). An indication of his proposed "Wredean" account of early Christianity is given in his contribution to the Morgan Festschrift—"Towards an Alternative to New Testament Theology: 'Individual Eschatology' as an Example" in Rowland and Tuckett, eds., *The Nature of New Testament Theology*, 167–85.

33. See for example L. E. Keck, "Paul in New Testament Theology: Some Preliminary Remarks" in Rowland and Tuckett, eds., *The Nature of New Testament Theology*, 109–22: "When Jesus' resurrection is construed as his resuscitation or as the disciples' awareness of Jesus' on-going impact, it becomes impossible to think with Paul" (112–16). See further below #4.3a.

34. "The message of Jesus is a presupposition for the theology of the New Testament rather than a part of that theology itself....The theology of the New Testament begins with the *kerygma* of the earliest Church and not before" (*Theology*, 1.3); H. Conzelmann, *An Outline of the Theology of the New Testament* (London: SCM, 1969) agrees but criticizes Bultmann for taking too little notice of the Synoptic tradition (7–8); as also J. Gnilka, *Theologie des Neuen Testaments* (Freiburg, Germany: Herder, 1994), 11. Contrast J. Jeremias, *New Testament Theology. Vol. One: The Proclamation of Jesus* (London: SCM, 1971).

35. Most famously by W. Wrede, *Paul* (London: Philip Green, 1907): "This second founder of Christianity has even, compared with the first, exercised beyond all doubt the stronger—not the better—influence" (180).

36. One of the most effective responses to Bultmann was that of N. A. Dahl, "The Problem of the Historical Jesus," *Jesus the Christ: The Historical Origins of Christological Doctrine*, ed. D. H. Juel (Minneapolis: Fortress Press, 1991), 81–111: "Though the Gospels may be proclamation and witness, it would be contrary to the intention of the evangelists to declare inquiry into the historicity of the narratives as irrelevant" (103). Christopher Tuckett gives a strongly affirmative answer to his question, "Does the 'Historical Jesus' belong within a 'New Testament Theology?'" in Rowland & Tuckett, eds., *The Nature of New Testament Theology*, 231–47; "The historical Jesus belongs inextricably within any attempt to engage in a 'theological' interpretation of the New Testament, i.e. to produce a 'New Testament theology'" (244).

37. Hahn, *Theologie*, 1.30–32, 40–43.

38. Given a decisive boost by D. F. Strauss, *The Christ of Faith and the Jesus of History* (1865; ET Philadelphia: Fortress Press, 1977).

39. "Every verse of the Gospels shows that their authors saw the origin of Christianity not in the kerygma but in the appearance of Jesus of Nazareth" (Schnelle, *Theologie* 32; see further 30–34).

40. I recall Vincent Taylor's comment from my student days: "If the Form-Critics are right, the disciples must have been translated to heaven immediately after the Resurrection"—*The Formation of the Gospel Tradition* (London: Macmillan, 1935), 41.

41. As evidenced by the various echoes of Jesus' teaching in the letters of Paul, James, and 1 Peter (see for example Stuhlmacher, *Biblische Theologie*, 1.301–4; and my *Jesus Remembered*, 181–84) and by the quite appropriate early form-critical deduction that the shape of the Jesus tradition reflects, at least in some measure, the forms in which the Jesus tradition was used and drawn on by the earliest Christian communities in their own catechesis and exhortation.

42. I focus more closely on the two points in *A New Perspective on Jesus: What the Quest for the Historical Jesus Missed* (Grand Rapids, Mich.: Baker Academic/London: SPCK, 2005). See again my debate with Robert Morgan (chapter 1 note 75 above).

43. Watson makes the point strongly: "In the customary opposition between the Jesus of history and the Christ of faith, 'history' is taken to be synonymous with reality, whereas 'faith' is identified either with illusion or, at best, with an ungrounded non-rational conviction" (*Text and Truth*, 38).

44. Contrast the comment of Strecker, typical of those influenced by Bultmann on this point: "Christian faith occurs only under the material presupposition of the cross and resurrection" (*Theology*, 242).

45. I have been much influences by H. Schürmann's important article—"Die vorösterlichen Anfänge der Logientradition: Versuch eines formgeschichtlichen Zugangs zum Leben Jesu" in H. Ristow and K. Matthiae, eds., *Der historische Jesus und der kerygmatische Christus* (Berlin: Evangelische, 1961), 342–70.

46. It is important to note that I am not advocating a historical reconstruction of what Jesus said and did as part of NT theology (such as Morgan warns against—"New Testament Theology," 114). I am rather attempting to undermine the dichotomy of "historical Jesus" versus "Christ of faith," on the grounds that the theologizing evident in the Jesus tradition itself provides a continuum from the historical impact of Jesus' mission to the full blown gospel of the first Christians.

47. See also my "Altering the Default Setting: Re-envisaging the Early Transmission of the Jesus Tradition," *NTS* 49 (2003): 139–75, reprinted (using English translation of the Greek texts) as an appendix to *A New Perspective on Jesus*. Esler also stresses the importance of the oral dimension for the task of *New Testament Theology*, especially chapters 4, 6, and 7.

48. But see above chapter 1 note 72.

49. Most influential has been the finding of A. B. Lord, *The Singer of Tales* (Cambridge, Mass.: Harvard University, 1978): "In a sense each performance is 'an' original, if not 'the' original. The truth of the matter is that our concept of 'the original,' of 'the song,' simply makes no sense in oral tradition" (100–101). R. Finnegan, *Oral Poetry: Its Nature, Significance and Social Context* (Cambridge, England: Cambridge University, 1977) also glosses Lord—"There is no correct text, no idea that one version is more 'authentic' than another: each performance is a unique and original creation with its own

validity" (65)—and credits Lord with bringing this point home most convincingly (79). W. H. Kelber, *The Oral and the Written Gospel* (Philadelphia: Fortress Press, 1983) already took up the point: "each oral performance is an irreducibly unique creation"; if Jesus said something more than once there is no "original" (29; also 59, 62).

50. See above note 41.

51. See my *Theology of Paul*, 189–95.

52. Cf. Scobie, *Ways of Our God*, ch. 5; contrast Stuhlmacher, who headlines the Spirit only in #22, "Sacrament, Spirit and Church" (*Biblische Theologie*, #22); and Hahn, who considers "the work of the Holy Spirit" within the Part headed "The Revelation Act of God in Jesus Christ" (*Theologie* 2.Teil II), though he recognizes the crucial importance of both Easter ("the 'Urdatum' of a genuine Christian proclamation") and Pentecost (*Theologie*, 1.131–32).

53. For discussion, see my *Christianity in the Making. Vol. 2: Beginning from Jerusalem* (Grand Rapids, Mich.: Eerdmans, 2008), #22.3.

54. John 20:22; also 19:30 (literally "handed over the Spirit").

55. Rom 8:11; Gal 3:3.

56. Rom 8:23; 2 Cor 1:22; 5:5; Eph 1:13-14.

57. Luke adds a repetition to Joel's prediction that "they shall (all) prophesy" in Acts 2:18.

58. Acts 8:14-17; 19:1-7.

59. 1 John 3:24; 4:13.

60. The rather neglected centrality of the Spirit to the beginnings of Christianity was brought home to me by my early research—*Baptism in the Holy Spirit* (London: SCM, 1970), and *Jesus and the Spirit* (London: SCM, 1975).

61. Acts 10:44-48; 11:15-18; 15:7-11, 14; Gal 2:7-9; 3:2-5.

62. See again my *Beginning from Jerusalem*, #27.

63. Acts 2:16-17; Joel 2:28.

64. Acts 2:33; 10:45; Rom 5:5; Titus 3:6.

65. Ezek 11:19; 36:26; 37:6, 14.

66. Gen 2:7 and Ezek 37:9 are the only two occasions in the LXX when *emphusaō* is used to translate the Hebrew *napach* (A also has Ezek 22:20); these two passages together with Wis 15:11 are the only ones to link *emphusaō* with the divine creative breath.

67. The reference is not simply to Luke 4:17-21 and Acts 10:38; Isa 61:1-2 is evidently in mind also in Matt 5:3-4/Luke 6:20-22 and Matt 11:5/Luke 7:22 (see *Jesus and the Spirit*, ch. 3).

68. 1 Cor 2:13, 15; cf. Rom 12:2; Phil 1:9-11.

69. "Long before the Spirit was a theme of doctrine, he was a fact in the experience of the community" (E. Schweizer, *TDNT*, 6.396).

70. For example Exod 10:13, 19; 14:21; 1 Kgs 19:11; Isa 7:2; Ezek 27:26; Hos 13:15.

71. Judg 3:10; 6:34; 11:29; 14:6, 19; 15:14-15; 1 Sam 10:6.

72. See further #3.2d below.

73. John 6:63; Rom 8:11; 1 Cor 15:45; 2 Cor 3:6; 1 Pet 3:18.

74. Hence the subtitle of my *Jesus and the Spirit: A Study of the Religious and Charismatic Experience of Jesus and the First Christians as Reflected in the New Testament*. I welcome the renewed attention given to the subject by L. T. Johnson, *Religious Experience in Earliest Christianity: A Missing Dimension in New Testament Studies* (Minneapolis: Fortress, 1998).

75. Mark 1:12; cf. Matt 4:1; Luke 4:1, 14; John 3:34.

76. Acts 2:4; 4:31; 10:44-48; 19:6; a physically manifest effect is implicit in 8:17-19.

77. Heb 2:4; 1 John 3:24; 4:13.

78. 1 Cor 2:4; 1 Thess 1:5.

79. Rom 7:6; 8:2-4; 15:19; 1 Cor 1:4-7; 12:4-14; etc. See further my *Theology of Paul*, #16.

80. Rom 8:15-16; Gal 4:6—both using the loud or intense verb *krazein*, "cry."

81. For example Isa 44:3; Joel 2:28.

82. It should not be forgotten that the early History of Religions School was interested in experience as a factor in shaping religion.

83. Cf. especially R. A. Knox, *Enthusiasm* (Oxford: Oxford University, 1950).

84. *Unity and Diversity in the New Testament*, chapter 9.

85. 1 Cor 12:1-3; 14:12, 23.

86. See further my *Jesus and the Spirit*, #49.2. On the danger of "false prophecy" in the biblical tradition see particularly R. W. L. Moberly, *Prophecy and Discernment* (Cambridge: Cambridge University, 2006).

87. "The books of the New Testament do not simply record teaching but also tell the story of the religious experience of the Christians, and understanding the experience is part of the task, not least because the teaching arises out of the experience" (Marshall, *New Testament Theology*, 28).

88. See my *Theology of Paul*, ##7.1 and 13.2.

89. Historically, the experience of renewal within Christianity has characteristically found expression in new hymnody, the experience seeking fresh expression beyond the more traditional forms. In the NT we may think particularly of Col 3:16.

90. See above Introduction, note 3.

91. *The Partings of the Ways Between Christianity and Judaism* (London: SCM, 1991, 2006), chapter 2, where I note that such an analysis of early Judaism seems to resonate well with other treatments on the subject, by both Jewish and Christian scholarship. Cf. Hahn's *Theologie* Band II, on "the Unity of the New Testament," which focuses on "God's act of revelation in Jesus Christ," "the soteriological dimension of God's act of revelation," "the ecclesiological dimension of God's act of revelation" (including two chapters on ethics), and "the eschatological dimension of God's act of revelation"; and those mentioned above in the Introduction, note 4.

3. The Theology of God

1. Typically, "Grace to you and peace from God our Father..." (Rom 1:1; 1 Cor 1:1; 2 Cor 1:2; etc.); doxologies—for example Rom 1:25; 2 Cor 1:3; Eph 1:3; 1 Pet 1:3.

2. Hence the title of the essay by N. A. Dahl, "The Neglected Factor in New Testament Theology," *Jesus the Christ: The Historical Origins of Christological Doctrine*, ed. D. H. Juel (Minneapolis: Fortress Press, 1991) 153–63, which is "*theo*-logy in the strict sense of the word" (153). "The basic presupposition of every theology of the NT is that in Old as in New Testament one and the same God is borne witness to" (Wilckens, *Theologie*, 1.1.2).

3. Paul did not hesitate to speak of Abraham as "our forefather" when writing to churches which were predominantly Gentile in membership (Rom 4:1); so also 9:10; 1 Cor 10:1.

4. Note the interesting contrast of the two sermons to audiences quite outside the

bounds of the synagogue, in Acts 14:15-17 and 17:22-31, where the primary concern is to give a better understanding of God.

5. Hahn heads the second part of his second volume: "The revelation act of God in Jesus Christ," with the chapter headings, "The God who reveals himself" and "Jesus Christ as revealer of God" (*Einheit* Teil II: #6 and #8). "What consequences has the revelation event in Jesus Christ for the picture of God? How is God to be conceived, who has made known in Jesus Christ his will in continuity and discontinuity with the first covenant?" (Schnelle, *Theologie*, 45).

6. See also H. Kleinknecht, *TDNT*, 3.73–74; H. Sasse, *TDNT*, 3.874–80.

7. See J. Dillon, *The Middle Platonists* (London: Duckworth, 1977), 155–78.

8. Pseudo-Aristotle, *De Mundo* 6; Seneca, *Ep.* 65.8; Marcus Aurelius, *Medit.* 4.23; see further my *Romans*, WBC 38; (Dallas: Word, 1988), 701–2.

9. Note also Rom 1:19-20; Rev 3:14; 4:11; 10:6. See further Childs, *Biblical Theology*, 384–402.

10. Jer 18:1-6; but the image was common in Jewish thought of the creator God; see my *Romans*, 556–57.

11. As in John 20:22; 1 Cor 15:45; 2 Cor 3:6.

12. See also chapter 2 note 66 above.

13. See W. Foerster, *TDNT*, 3.1000–35; J. Bergman, et al., *TDOT*, 2.242–49.

14. LSJ, 1002–3.

15. Cited by E. Schweizer, *TDNT*, 7.1026–27.

16. Gen 1:10, 12, 18, 21, 25, 31.

17. In Greek thought the two words, *sōma* and *sarx*, were much closer synonyms.

18. See further my *Theology of Paul*, 55–73.

19. As, again, pre-eminently in Paul, and specifically in his letter to the Romans (Rom 1:19-25; 5:12-21; 7:7-14; 8:19-22).

20. See for example Childs, *Biblical Theology*, 396–412.

21. See for example the data assembled in my *Romans*, 678.

22. Rom 11:25-27; Eph 3:3-6; Col 1:26-27. Also for example Acts 2:23; Eph 1:4-5; 1 Pet 1:20, and the heavenly scroll in Rev 5–6.

23. For example Isa 13:6-16; 34:8; Dan 7:9-11; Joel 2:1-2; Zeph 1:14-23; 3:8; Mal 4:1; *Jub.* 5:10-16; *1 Enoch* 90:20-27; see further F. Büchsel, *TDNT*, 3.933–35.

24. Prov 6:34; Jdg 16:17; Pss Sol 15:12.

25. A particular emphasis of Zephaniah—Zeph 1:15, 18; 2:2-3; cf. 3:8.

26. For example Matt 10:15; 11:22, 24; 12:36; Rom 2:5, 16; 1 Cor 5:5; Phil 1:6, 10; 2:16; Rev 6:17; 16:14.

27. Quoting Ps 62:12 and Prov 24:12; but see also Job 34:11; Jer 17:10; Hos 12:2; Sir 16:12-14; *1 Enoch* 100:7; *Jos. Asen.* 28:3; Ps-Philo, *Lib. Ant.* 3:10.

28. In Jewish thought God is presented consistently as the model of impartiality (Deut 10:17; 2 Chr 19:7; Sir 35:12-13; *1 Enoch* 63:8; *Jub.* 5:16; 21:4; 30:16; 33:18; *Pss. Sol.* 2:18; *2 Bar.* 13:8; 44:4; Ps-Philo, *Lib. Ant.* 20:4). See also E. Lohse, *TDNT*, 6.779–80; J. M. Bassler, *Divine Impartiality: Paul and a Theological Maxim*, SBLDS 59 (Chico, Calif.: Scholars, 1982); K. Berger, *EDNT*, 3.179–80.

29. R. Bauckham, "Biblical Theology and the Problems of Monotheism" in Bartholomew, et al., eds., *Out of Egypt*, 187–232, reads the Shema as "YHWH our God, YHWH is one," as indicated by the subsequent references to it (219).

30. See for example Bauckham on "The Quest of the Historical Monotheism" ("Biblical Theology," 196–206).

31. "Let us, then, engrave deep in our hearts this as the first and most sacred of commandments, to acknowledge and honour one God who is above all, and let the idea that gods are many never reach the ears of the man whose rule of life is to seek for truth in purity and goodness" (Philo, *Decal.* 65). See also in particular 2 Macc 1:24-25; *Ep. Arist.*132; Josephus, *Ant.* 3:91; 5:112; *Sib. Or.* 3:629; *Ps-Phoc.* 54. "The belief common to all Jews at the beginning of the first century was that their God was the only God..." (E. E. Urbach, "Self-Isolation or Self-Affirmation in Judaism in the First Three Centuries: Theory and Practice" in E. P. Sanders, et al., eds., *Aspects of Judaism in the Graeco-Roman Period* [London: SCM, 1981], 273). See further Urbach's *The Sages: Their Concepts and Beliefs* (Jerusalem: Magnes Press, 1979), chapter 2.

32. "The monotheism of the Old Testament is everywhere assumed" (Childs, *Biblical Theology*, 362).

33. Matt 4:10/Luke 4:8; Deut 6:13; 10:10.

34. Hahn, *Theologie*, 2.172 ("The theocentric character of the message of Jesus").

35. 1 Cor 8:4, 6; Gal 3:20; Eph 4:6. First Timothy, one of the latest members of the Pauline corpus, is most insistent on the point—1:17; 2:5; 6:15-16; similarly with the doxology added to Romans (Rom 16:25).

36. A similarly strong conviction in Israel's understanding of God (for example Exod 33:20; Deut 4:12; Sir 43:31; Philo, *Post.* 168-169; Josephus, *War* 7:346).

37. "No materials, however costly, are fit to make an image of him; no art has skill to conceive and represent it. The like of him we have never seen, we do not imagine, and it is impious to conjecture" (Josephus, *Ap.* 2:190-91). These characteristic and distinctive features of Judaism were widely recognized (for example Tacitus, *Hist.* 5.5.4; Juvenal, *Sat.* 14:97 characterized Jews as worshiping "nothing but the clouds") and provoked the charge that Jews were atheists, that is, because they did not recognize other gods (for example Josephus, *Ap.* 2:148).

38. See also 1 Cor 5:10-11; 6:9; 10:7; Gal 5:20; cf. Col 3:5; Eph 5:5.

39. Rom 1:20; Col 1:15; also 1 Tim 1:17.

40. See above note 37.

41. See particularly the essays by N. MacDonald, "The Origin of 'Monotheism,'" and R. W. L. Moberly, "How Appropriate Is 'Monotheism' as a Category for Biblical Interpretation?" in L. T. Stuckenbruck and W. E. S. North, eds., *Early Jewish and Christian Monotheism*, JSNTS 263 (London: T & T Clark International, 2004), 204–15 and 216–34 respectively; Childs regarded the term as "theologically inert" (*Biblical Theology*, 335). But see also Bauckham, "Biblical Theology," 188–96.

42. Bauckham proposes as a more satisfactory alternative to "monotheism," YHWH's "transcendent uniqueness" ("Biblical Theology," 210).

43. Hübner poses the issue sharply: "in no way is monotheism the clamp which holds together both Testaments on the question of God"; the decisive question for him is "What is the common link between the original Old Testament monolatry and the Pauline or generally New Testament monotheism?" (*Biblische Theologie*, 1.250, 254).

44. See below #3.2e.

45. Religion could serve imperial interests by recognizing not only Zeus and Jupiter to be the same god, but also that the local gods of nations and regions were manifestation of the same deity; hence the regular merging of Zeus with other gods—Zeus-Sarapis, Zeus-Dionysis, Zeus-Ammon, Zeus-Baal, even Zeus-Ahuramazda and Zeus-Helios-Sarapis (LSJ, *Zeus* II; Kleinknecht, *TDNT*, 3.76; R. MacMullen, *Paganism in the Roman Empire* [New Haven, Conn.: Yale, 1981], 83–84, 90).

46. As Marshall notes, "Romans might be seen as a theodicy" (*Theology*, 306; see also 330–36).

47. See above #2.4.

48. Unlike the all too human passions and conduct of the classic gods and goddesses of Greece and Rome.

49. O. Procksch, *TDNT*, 1.91; see for example Lev 20:3; 1 Chr 16:35; Pss 33:21; 103:1; Ezek 36:20-23.

50. See further below #4.2d.

51. The classic examples are the revelation to Moses in Exodus 3, the stern warnings of Exod 19:12-13, 21-24, and the salutary examples of Nadab and Abihu in Lev 10:1-3, of Achan in Josh 7, and of Uzzah in 2 Sam 6:6-7. The writer who best caught this sense of the shuddering awe evoked by the holy (*mysterium tremendum et fascinans*) was Rudolf Otto, *The Idea of the Holy* (London: Oxford University, 1923).

52. See also Pss 51:11; 143:10; Hag 2:5; Zech 4:6.

53. Gen 1:2; Job 26:13; Ps 33:6.

54. Gen 6:3, 17; 7:15, 22; Ps 104:29-30; Eccl 3:19, 21.

55. Jer 10:14; 51:17.

56. See above chapter 2, page 35.

57. Jdg 6:34; 14:6, 19; 15:14-15; 1 Sam 11:6.

58. A *ruach* from God could be an evil or a lying spirit (Jdg 9:23; 1 Sam 16:14-16; 1 Kgs 22:19-23).

59. For example Neh 9:20, 30; Isa 59:21; 63:11-14; Ezek 2:2; 3:1-4; Amos 3:7-8; Zech 7:12.

60. "In Judaism . . . the holy spirit is specifically the spirit of prophecy" (G. F. Moore, *Judaism in the First Centuries of the Christian Era*, 3 vols. [Cambridge, Mass.: Harvard University, 1927, 1930], 1.421).

61. Mark 1:10-11 pars.; Matt 12:18; Luke 4:14, 18; John 3:34; Acts 10:38.

62. For example Acts 11:16-17; Rom 8:9; 1 Cor 12:13; Gal 3:2-5; Heb 6:4; 1 John 3:24.

63. For example John 7:37-39; 2 Cor 3:3-6; Heb 2:2-4; 1 Pet 1:11-12. See also chapter 2 note 64 above and further #4.3a below.

64. In the OT only in Ps 51:11; Isa 63:10-11; cf. Ps 143:10 ("your good spirit").

65. See above chapter 2 note 73.

66. Rom 8:9; Phil 1:19; 1 Pet 1:11.

67. John 14:25-28; 15:26; 16:5-15.

68. I refer particularly to the famous iconographic representation of Genesis 18.

69. Particularly M. Barker, *The Great Angel: A Study of Israel's Second God* (London: SPCK, 1992); but see also Bauckham, "Biblical Theology," 206–17.

70. For example Gen 16:7-12; Exod 3:2.

71. Dan 8:16; 9:21; 10:13; Tob 12:15; *1 Enoch* 9:1-2; 20:1-8; 40; *Jub.* 1:27, 29; 2:2; etc.

72. The angelic figures of Ezek 8:2 and Dan 10:5-6 are described in similar terms to the vision of God in Ezek 1:26. See further C. Rowland, *The Open Heaven: A Study of Apocalyptic in Judaism and Early Christianity* (London: SPCK, 1982).

73. See for example P. R. Carrell, *Jesus and the Angels: Angelology and the Christology of the Apocalypse of John*, SNTSMS 95 (Cambridge, England: Cambridge University, 1997).

74. A. M. Goldberg, *Untersuchungen über die Vorstellung von der Schekhinah in der frühen rabbinischen Literatur* (Berlin, 1969). Janowski focuses his discussion of "the one God of the two Testaments" on the Shekinah theology rooted in the OT ("The One God," 310–16).

75. H. Kleinknecht, *TDNT*, 4.80–86.

76. Prov 1:20ff.; 2:16-19; 3:13-17; 5:7-10; 7:4-5 etc. R. N. Whybray, *Wisdom in Proverbs* (London: SCM, 1965) refers particularly to G. Boström, *Proverbiastudien: Die Weisheit und das fremde Weib in Spr. 1-9* (Lund, 1935).

77. Via represents a substantial body of opinion in finding it "especially difficult... to deny that the divine wisdom in Sirach 24:3-4, 30-31 is a being who came forth from God and then dwelt in heaven with God as a relatively autonomous being" (*What Is New Testament Theology?* 56–57). The logic here seems to me simply to ignore the poetic character of the imagery (note 80 below).

78. The basic meaning of *hypostasis* prior to the Cappadocians' formulation of God as Trinity—one *ousia* (being, essence) in three *hypostaseis*, one God in three modes of substantive being—is "the essential or basic structure/nature of an entity, 'substantial nature, essence, actual being, reality'" (BDAG 1040). W. O. E. Oesterley and G. H. Box, *The Religion and Worship of the Synagogue* (London: Pitman, 1911), however, defined the "hypostasization" of divine attributes as occupying "an intermediate position between personalities and abstract beings," that is, halfway between a person and a personification (195). This sense for *hypostasis* as midway between "person" and "attribute," which has been invoked to find in the Jewish concept of divine Wisdom a precedent for Trinitarian *theo-logy*, G. L. Prestige regarded as "pure delusion" (*God in Patristic Thought* [London: SPCK, 1952, paperback 1964], xxviii).

79. Childs observes that "Israel developed a variety of hypostatic-like forms by which to bear witness both to God's transcendence and his immanence," but continues, "Nor does the Old Testament make the move to separate God's 'real being' from his historical revelation in action even when employing predicates which were adapted from pagan mythology (Hab. 3:3ff.)" (*Biblical Theology*, 356–57); though the issue is posed more sharply in Israel's post-biblical literature. Cf. for example K. M. O'Connor, "Wisdom Literature and Experience of the Divine," in Kraftchick et al. eds., *Biblical Theology* 183-95: "She [Wisdom] is God present to the world, a symbolic representation of God's being, a manifestation of the deity in the guise of Wisdom" (194); others in my *Christology in the Making* (London: SCM, 1989; Grand Rapids, Mich.: Eerdmans, 1996), 326n22.

80. In *The Partings of the Ways* ([London: SCM, 1991, 2006], 10.5c, 260) I refer for example to Ps 85:10-11 ("righteousness" and "peace" kiss each other), Isa 51:9 (calling on the arm of the Lord to waken up) and *Jos. Asen.* 15:7-8 ("Repentance" depicted as "the Most High's daughter... a virgin, very beautiful and pure and chaste and gentle").

81. See below chapter 4 note 12.

82. Ps 33:6—"By the word of YHWH the heavens were made, and all their host by the breath (*ruach*; LXX *pneuma*) of his mouth"; similarly Ps 147:18; Isa 55:10-11. Note also how Word, Wisdom, and Spirit function as near synonyms in Wis 9:1-2, 17.

83. See above note 31.

84. *Migr.* 70-85; *Abr.* 83. On the basis of Exod 4:16 and 7:1 Philo concludes that Moses represents mind (*logos endiathetos*) and Aaron speech (*logos prophorikos*) (*Det.* 39-40, 126-32; *Migr.* 76-84; *Mut.* 208).

85. See particularly *Sac.* 80-83; *Ebr.* 157; *Som.* 1:102-14.

86. *Som.* 1:65-69; similarly *Post.* 16-20.

87. Details in *Jesus Remembered*, 177nn22–23 and further #15.8.

88. That it was as himself a sage that Jesus was initially (and still should be) remembered is the message of the Jesus Seminar and those who work from its hypotheses; see *Jesus Remembered*, #4.7.

89. The influence of the memory of Jesus' teaching is evident again and again in early Christian paraenesis; see again *Jesus Remembered*, 182nn48–49; and above chapter 2 note 41.

90. See particularly R. Bauckham, *James: Wisdom of James, Disciple of Jesus the Sage* (London: Routledge, 1999).

91. The several contributions of Geza Vermes have been influential here, starting with *Jesus the Jew* (London: Collins, 1973).

92. Contrast "the Teacher of Righteousness" of the Dead Sea Scrolls.

93. Mark 6:15 par.; 8:28 pars.; Luke 24:19.

94. See particularly the first two volumes of J. P. Meier, *A Marginal Jew* (New York: Doubleday, 1991, 1994); also *Jesus Remembered*, 153n60.

95. *Jesus Remembered*, 664–66; Schnelle, *Theologie*, 129.

96. Isa 11:1-2; Jer 23:5; 33:15; Ezek 34:24; 37:25; Hag 2:23; Zech 3:8; 6:12.

97. 4QFlor (4Q174) 1.10-12. See further my *Jesus Remembered*, 619–22, with bibliography.

98. *Jesus Remembered*, 627–54.

99. See particularly the classic treatment of N. A. Dahl, "The Crucified Messiah" (1960), *Jesus the Christ*, 27–47; and further *Jesus Remembered*, 628–34.

100. Luke 24:25-27, 46; Acts 3:11; 8:32-35; 17:2-3, 11; 1 Cor 15:3.

101. In Paul's letters the titular force of *christos* is clearly evident in only a few passages (most notably Rom 9:3-5 and 15:3); see further my *Paul the Apostle*, #8.5.

102. John 9:22 ("the Jews had already agreed that anyone who confessed Jesus to be the Messiah would be put out of the synagogue") is usually regarded as reflecting more of the post-70 situation; see my *Partings*, #11.5.

103. 1 Cor 1:23; Gal 3:13.

104. See further *Jesus Remembered*, #15.6.

105. 1 Kgs 2:3, 5, 7, 15; 4:1, 38; 5:22; 6:1; 9:1; 20:35; Amos 7:14.

106. Qumran spoke often of "sons of light," also "sons of the covenant" (details and further in Jesus Remembered, 710n21)

107. I discuss the issue in detail in *Jesus Remembered*, ##16.3-5.

108. Noteworthy, for example, is the fact "the son of man" is rendered as "I" in some parallel passages—Matt 5:11/Luke 6:22; Matt 10:32-33/Luke 12:8-9; Mark 8:27/Matt 16:3; Mark 10:45/Luke 22:27.

109. The influence of Dan. 7:13-14 is most obvious in the talk of "coming on the clouds of heaven" (Mark 13:26 pars.; 14:62 pars).

110. See particularly J. J. Collins, "The Son of Man in First-Century Judaism," *NTS* 38 (1992), 448–66; the view is standard in German scholarship (for example Stuhlmacher, *Biblische Theologie*, 1 #9; Schnelle, *Theologie*, 130–31), though the argument hangs almost entirely on 1 Enoch 46:1-3 and 4 Ezra 13:1-3.

111. The *Similitudes of Enoch* (1 Enoch 37-71) are absent from the DSS and may not have been added to the Enoch corpus before mid- or even late first century; and 4 Ezra was self evidently written after 70 C.E.

112. The three other non-Gospel references simply reflect OT usage: Heb 2:6 = Ps 8:4; Rev 1:13 and 14:14 allude to Dan 7:13.

113. Matt 19:28; 25:31 (*Jesus Remembered*, 756–57).

114. Cf. also John 5:27 with 1 *Enoch* 69:27.

115. *Jesus Remembered*, #12.4g; 754, 757-58, 761. See further below #4.3e.

116. It was with Nicea that the previously dominant Logos-christology gave way to Son-christology as the dominant category.

117. Again I discuss the data fully in *Jesus Remembered*, #16.2.

118. Jesus refers to God as "Father"—Mark/Q 3 or 4; Matthew more than 30; John about 100.

119. The principal influence here has been J. Jeremias, *The Prayers of Jesus* (London: SCM, 1967); also *Theology*, 63–68; see also *Jesus Remembered*, #16.2b.

120. Rom 8:15-16; Gal 4:6-7.

121. Exod 4:22; Jer 31:9, 20; Hos 11:1.

122. 2 Sam 7:14; 1 Chr 17:13; 22:10; Pss 2:7; 89:26-27.

123. 1QSa (1Q28a) 2:11-12; 4Q174 (4QFlor) 1:10-12.

124. Wis 2:13, 16, 18; 5:5; Sir 4:10; 51:10.

125. Wis 14:3; Sir 23:1, 4; 51:10.

126. Vermes, *Jesus the Jew*, 206–7; the references are *b. Ta'an* 24b; *Ber.* 17b; *Hul.* 86a.

127. Rom 1:4—"Appointed Son of God in power as from the resurrection of the dead"; Acts 13:33—"You are my Son; today I have begotten you" (quoted in reference to Jesus' resurrection). Probably we should see such texts alongside Acts 2:36 as expressive more of the early enthusiasm and excitement engendered by Jesus' resurrection (that is, over who Jesus was and what had happened to him) than of a change of status of Jesus (other than from dead to resurrected, of course!).

128. Is there an echo of Wis 9:10, 17 in Gal 4:4, 6—the sending of Wisdom "from the holy heavens" (Wis 9:10; Gal 4:4) and the sending of the holy spirit from on high (Wis 9:17; Gal 4:6)? See discussion and bibliography in my *Christology*, 38–46 and 283n152.

129. Cf. Matt 11:27; 18:20; 28:18-20. Matt 18:20, "Where two or three are gathered in my name, I am there among them," is often compared with *m. Abot* 3:2: "If two sit together and words of the Law (are spoken) between them, the Divine Presence rests between them."

130. The variant reading has "the only-begotten Son," but "only-begotten God" is probably the more original text.

131. John 4:34; 5:24, 30, 37; 6:38-39, 44; etc.

132. Isa 6:1-3; John 12:41; cf. Titus 2:13.

133. John 8:24, 28, 58; 13:19; cf. Isa 41:4; 43:10, 13; 46:4; 48:12. See further Stuhlmacher, *Biblische Theologie*, 2.228-32.

134. See also Hahn, *Theologie*, 2.199–203; Wilckens, *Theologie*, 1.1.34–35. Though whether we can speak of Jesus' own consciousness of pre-existence—cf. particularly S. Gathercole, *The Preexistent Son* (Grand Rapids, Mich.: Eerdmans, 2006); A. H. I. Lee, *From Messiah to Preexistent Son: Jesus' Self-Consciousness and Early Christian Exegesis of Messianic Psalms*, WUNT 2.192 (Tübingen, Germany: Mohr Siebeck, 2005)—is much more questionable (see my review of Gathercole in *RBL* http://www.bookreviews. org/BookDetail.asp?TitleId=5607); but the issue should not be ignored by biblical theology, especially since the stimulus of passages like Psalms 2 and 110 are so central to the above theses.

135. This observation does not exclude the use of the polite form of address, *kyrie*, meaning "sir," and denoting respect owed to a teacher or higher status person (for example Luke 5:12; 7:6; 9:54, 59, 61; 10:40; 13:8, 23, 25; 14:22; 19:8, 16, 18, 20, 25)

136. For example Luke 7:13; 10:1, 41; 12:42a.

137. The point was first noted by C. F. D. Moule, "The Christology of Acts," in L. E. Keck and J. L. Martyn, eds., *Studies in Luke Acts* (Nashville: Abingdon Press, 1966), 159–85.

138. As argued particularly by O. Cullmann, *The Earliest Christian Confessions* (London: Lutterworth, 1949).

139. Mark 12:36 pars.; 14:62 pars.; Acts 2:34-35; Rom 8:34; 1 Cor 15:25; Eph 1:20; Col 3:1; Heb 1:3, 13; 8:1; 10:12; 12:2; 1 Pet 3:22.

140. Part of the value of Luke's account of Jesus' ascension in Acts 1:9-11 is that he made clear that resurrection and ascension were two distinct events, whereas other references in the NT tend to run them together.

141. See particularly D. B. Capes, *Old Testament Yahweh Texts in Paul's Christology*, WUNT 2.47 (Tübingen, Germany: Mohr Siebeck, 1992).

142. Rom 1:7; 1 Cor 1:3; 2 Cor 1:2; 13:14; Gal 1:3; Eph 1:2; Phil 1:2; 1 Thess 3:11-13; 2 Thess 1:2; 2:16; Philem 3.

143. Rom 15:6; 2 Cor 1:3; 11:31; Col 1:3; also Eph 1:3, 17 and 1 Pet 1:3.

144. Bauckham draws a bold but justifiable conclusion from 1 Cor 8:6: "The only possible way to understand Paul as maintaining monotheism is to understand him to be including Jesus in the unique identity of the one God affirmed in the Shema" ("Biblical Theology," 224; see 220–26); but he does not mention the influence of Ps 110:1 or discuss 1 Cor 15:24-28.

145. Schnelle prefers to speak of "an exclusive monotheism in binitarian form"; "This God is one, but not alone; he has a name, a history and a face: Jesus Christ" (*Theologie*, 172, 197, 671).

146. *T. Ab.* 11, 13; *1 Enoch* 90:31; cf. Melchizedek in 11QMelch 13–14.

147. Though note also that the first Christians did not hesitate to speak of the day of judgment as "the day of the Lord" (1 Cor 5:5; 1 Thess 5:2; 2 Thess 2:2; 2 Pet 3:10).

148. Paul always attributed the "giving" of the Spirit to God—Rom 5:5; 2 Cor 1:22; 5:5; 1 Thess 4:8; also 2 Tim 1:7.

149. Cf. Acts 1:5; 11:15-17.

150. Above ##3.3d-e.

151. "Few issues in recent NT theology have commanded such unanimity of agreement as the source of the language and imagery used in these two passages [1 Cor 8:6 and Col 1:15-20]. By common consent, it was drawn from earlier Jewish reflection on divine Wisdom" (*Theology of Paul*, 269; bibliography note 12).

152. G. D. Fee, *Pauline Christology: An Exegetical-Theological Study* (Peabody, Mass.: Hendrickson, 2007) resists the consensus (595–602) but is deaf to allusions which appear obvious to others.

153. Prov 8:22, 25; Sir 24:9; the Logos as "the firstborn mother of all things" (Philo, *Qu. Gen.* 4:97; cf. *Ebr.* 30-31).

154 For example Prov 3:19; Wis 8:4-6; Philo, *Det.* 54.

155. Sir 43.26; cf. Philo, *Heres* 188; *Fuga* 112; *Qu. Ex.* 2.118.

156. For example, *Plant.* 18; *Som.* 1:239. See further my *Christology*, 207, 226–27; and further the fuller treatment of Philo in 220–28.

157. Philo, *Opif.* 33; *Conf.* 60-63; *Som.* 1:75.

158. See what appears to be Matthew's redaction of Q material in which Jesus is presented more as the emissary of Wisdom—Matt 11:19/Luke 7:35; Matt 11:25-30/Luke 10:21-22; Matt 23:34/Luke 11:49-51; Matt 23:37-39/Luke 13:34-35 (see my *Christology*, #25.1).

159. This included the thought of pre-existence—that Jesus was identified with the self-revelation of God in creation and in former times; most notably in texts like John 1:1-18; Phil 2:6-11; Col 1:15-20. See for example Hahn, *Theologie*, 2.215-25.

160. For the current train of thought that Paul applies to the gospel and Christ here see my *Romans*, 603–5.

161. See index in the Loeb edition of *Philo* vol. 10, 413.

162. John 1:1, 18; 20:28; Rom 9:5; Titus 2:13; Heb 1:8-9; 1 John 5:20.

163. Note also the still earlier rebuke of Jesus to "the Jews" that "you do not seek the glory that comes from the one who alone is God" (5:44).

164. See further particularly L. T. Stuckenbruck, *Angel Veneration and Christology: A Study in Early Judaism and in the Christology of the Apocalypse of John*, WUNT 2.70 (Tübingen, Germany: Mohr Siebeck, 1995).

165. I refer to the Greek verb *proskyneō* (for broader usage of the time see LSJ, 1518); the NT does not use the noun (*proskynēsis*).

166. Most obviously Matt 18:26; Acts 10:25; Rev 3:9.

167. Christian tradition has become quite familiar with a graduation of terms, from the veneration due to saints and the Virgin, to the full adoration proper only to God and Christ.

168. See particularly J. L. North, "Jesus and Worship, God and Sacrifice," in Stuckenbruck and North, eds., *Early Jewish and Christian Monotheism*, 186–202.

169. "No worship is offered to Wisdom; Wisdom has no priests in Israel" (*Christology*, 170); L. W. Hurtado, *Lord Jesus Christ: Devotion to Jesus in Earliest Christianity* (Grand Rapids, Mich.: Eerdmans, 2003), 33–37.

170. Cf. Childs: "Christians continued their worship completely within the idiom of the Jewish scriptures. There was no tension felt, nor was there ever a need expressed to reformulate the doctrine of God over against the synagogue" (*Biblical Theology*, 366–67). A key phrase here is "over against the synagogue."

171. Hurtado, *Lord Jesus Christ*, chapters 2-3.

172. See above note 142.

173. I had already made the following points in *Theology of Paul*, #10.5.

174. Rom 1:8; 7:25; Col 3:17.

175. I may refer simply to *Beginning from Jerusalem*, #21.3; for an example see chapter 4 note 122 below.

176. Frances Young sums up the position well in "The Trinity and the New Testament," in Rowland and Tuckett, eds., *The Nature of New Testament Theology*, 286–305: "the New Testament consistently presents the activity of Christ and the Spirit as the work of the one true God of the Law, the Prophets, Psalms and Wisdom. Under pressure that relationship had to be articulated in ways that the New Testament writers themselves had not envisaged" (299). Cf. Hahn, *Theologie*, 2.289–308.

4. The Theology of Salvation

1. BDAG gives the following range of meanings for the verb *sōzō*—"save, keep from harm, preserve, rescue; save from death, save/free from disease; keep, preserve, thrive, prosper, get on well; save/preserve from eternal death, bring (to) salvation, attain salvation" (982–83); *sōtēria*—"deliverance, preservation, salvation" (985–86).

2. Caird, *New Testament Theology*, chs. 3–8 and Marshall, *New Testament Theology*, 717–18 (see also 432–42, 474–78, 518–22) find "salvation" to be the main connecting theme in their theologies. For the major witnesses of New Testament theology (Jesus, Paul, John) "the combination of the belief in the presence of divine salvation through the

sending of Jesus and the expectation of the consummation of salvation through the coming of Jesus Christ in glory is constitutive" (Kümmel, *Theology* 329). As a further sample of his projected "Wredean" history of early Christian religion, Räisänen offers "Towards an Alternative to New Testament Theology: Different 'paths to salvation'," in Breytenbach and Frey, hrsg., *Aufgabe*, 175–203.

3. For example Jdg 2:16, 18; 3:9, 15, 31; 8:22; 9:17; 13:5; 1 Sam 9:16; 11:9; 23:5; 2 Sam 3:18; 9:19.

4. 2 Sam 14:4; 2 Kgs 6:26; 16:7; Ps 72:4; Hos 13:10.

5. Isa 45:20; 46:7; Jer 2:27-28; 3:23; 11:12; Hos 14:3.

6. For example Mark 3:4; 5:28, 34; 6:56; 10:52.

7. Rom 11:14; 1 Cor 7:16; 9:22; 1 Tim 4:16; Jas 5:20.

8. 1 Tim 1:1; 2:3; 4:10; Titus 1:3; 2:10; 3:4.

9. 2 Tim 1:10; Titus 1:4; 2:13; 3:6.

10. Paul would no doubt know of the centuries-old sanctuaries of Asclepius at Epidauros and Cos.

11. W. Foerster, *TDNT*, 7.1004–12.

12. Gen 1:3, 6, 9, 11, 14, 20, 24, 26; see also above chapter 3 note 81.

13. Gen 12:1-3; 13:14-17; 15:5-6, 12-20; 17:1-8; 18:17-19; 22:15-18; 26:2-5; 28:3-4, 13-15.

14. Deut 4:37; 6:10, 23; 7:7-8; 8:1, 17-18; 9:4-7, 26-29; 10:14-15; etc. A particularly fine expression of Israel's confidence in their covenant status is Ps 105:7-15 = 1 Chr 16:14-22.

15. See for example K. A. Kitchen, "Exodus, The," *ABD* 2.701—"Within the biblical tradition, few other events enjoyed anything like the prominence accorded so pervasively in the work of so many writers, or were deemed of such basic importance for Israel's history"; W. Brueggemann, "A Shattered Transcendence? Exile and Restoration," in Kraftchick et el., eds., *Biblical Theology*, 169–82.

16. N. H. Snaith, *The Distinctive Ideas of the Old Testament* (London: Epworth, 1944), 102—a book which first introduced me to a deeper study of the Old Testament.

17. Pss 5:7; 6:4; 13:5; 17:7; 21:7; etc.

18. Pss 106:1; 107:1; 117:2; Isa 54:8.

19. Ps 25:6; Isa 63:7; Jer 16:5; Lam 3:22; see also Ps 106:45; Isa 54:8, 10; Lam 3:32.

20. Num 14:18; Neh 9:17; Pss 86:15; 103:8; 145:8; Joel 2:13; Jon 4:2; Nah 1:3; see also Deut 7:9-10; 2 Kgs 13:23; 2 Chro: 30:9; Neh 9:31; Pss 111:4; 112:4; Isa 30:18; Jer 32:18; Sir 2:11; Wis 3:9; 4:15; 15:1; Pr. Man. 7; *Pss. Sol.* 9.8-11; *T. Jud.* 19.3; *T. Zeb.* 9.7; *Jos. Asen.* 11.10; Ps. Philo 13.10; 35.3; *4 Ezra* 7.33.

21. The protest against a general disparagement of Jewish soteriology as self-achieved, "works righteousness," was most effectively made by E. P. Sanders, *Paul and Palestinian Judaism* (London: SCM, 1977), to whom should be attributed the overdue correction of the imbalance of earlier treatments of Second Temple Judaism.

22. The point is disputed by C. VanLandingham, *Judgment and Justification in Early Judaism and the Apostle Paul* (Peabody, Mass.: Hendrickson, 2006); but see my *The New Perspective on Paul*, rev. ed. (Grand Rapids, Mich.: Eerdmans, 2008), 66–69.

23. Classically in the Westminster Confession, #7.5-6.

24. See further my *Theology of Paul*, #13.2.

25. See further "Faith, Faithfulness," *NIDB* 2 (2007): 407–23. "Steadfast love" and "faithfulness" are frequently linked—Gen 24:27; 32:10; Exod 34:6; 2 Sam 2:6; 15:20; Pss 25:10; 40:10, 11; 57:3; 61:7; 85:10; 86:15; 89:14; 98:3; 115:1; 138:2.

26. The psalmist relies on and rejoices in God's faithfulness regularly (for example Pss 25:10; 33:4; 40:10-11; 57:10; 71:22; 89:1-5; 108:4; 119:90).

27. See again #3.2a above.

28. See further my *Theology of Paul*, 341–42, with further bibliography in note 27.

29. "God's righteousness" is sometimes taken to be synonymous with "covenant faithfulness," but though the concepts overlap to a considerable extent their differing ranges of reference should be respected; see the discussion by M. Seifrid, "Righteousness Language in the Hebrew Scriptures and Early Judaism," in D. A. Carson, et al., *Justification and Variegated Nomism* Vol.1, WUNT 2.140 (Tübingen, Germany: Mohr Siebeck, 2001), 415–42; idem, "Paul's Use of Righteousness Language Against its Hellenistic Background," in D. A. Carson, et al., *Justification and Variegated Nomism* Vol. 2, WUNT 2.181 (Tübingen, Germany: Mohr Siebeck, 2004), 39–74; with my qualification in *The New Perspective on Paul*, 63–65.

30. Isa 45:8, 21; 46:13; 51:5, 6, 8; 62:1-2; 63:1.

31. Pss 51:14; 65:5; 71:15; 98:2; Isa 46:13; 51:5-8; 62:1-2. Stuhlmacher can even conclude that "when applied to God and his rule, 'righteousness' is always an expression of salvation.... God's righteousness appears surprisingly rarely in the Old Testament as a behavior that releases judgment (cf. Isa 1:27-28; 5:16; 10:22)" (*Biblische Theologie*, 1.327–29, 330–31).

32. For details see my *Romans*, 40–42, 132–36, 846–48.

33. On the importance of "holiness" see above #3.2d.

34. The purity laws were essentially to enable Israelites to enter the temple and partake in the temple cult.

35. This includes virtually ignoring of the Samaritan schism, and the Samaritans' claim that Mt Gerizim, rather than Jerusalem, was the historically validated temple; John 4:20-24 alludes to the dispute even while attempting to transcend it. In the biblical data there is no mention of the other temples that might have been seen as competitors to Jerusalem, notably at Leontopolis in Egypt (Josephus, *War*, 7:426-32; *Ant.* 13:65-73).

36. For more detail and discussion see E. P. Sanders, *Judaism: Practice and Belief 63 B.C.E.–66 C.E.* (London: SCM, 1992), 104–7, 110–12, 146–55.

37. See for example J. Milgrom, "Atonement," "Day of Atonement," *IDBS*, 78–83.

38. Lev 8:15; 16:16, 18-20.

39. Lev 4:10, 26, 31, 35; 5:6, 10, 13, 16, 18.

40. See particularly Gese, "Atonement," *Essays on Biblical Theology*, 93–116; B. Janowski, *Sühne als Heilsgeschehen* (Neukirchener-Vluyn, Germany: Neukirchener, 1982), 199–221; H. Merklein, *Studien zu Jesus und Paulus*, WUNT 43 (Tübingen, Germany: Mohr Siebeck, 1987), 15–39.

41. "The animal becomes sin in the literal sense, i.e., the sphere of *chatta'th* becomes concentrated in the animal.... Through the imposition of hands...the act of transfer is made manifest" (K. Koch, *TDOT*, 4.317).

42. As I have argued in *Theology of Paul*, 218–25.

43. 1 Kgs 8:30, 34, 36, 39, 50; 2 Chr 6:21, 25, 27, 30, 39.

44. Pss 25:11, 18; 32:1, 5; 65:3; 79:9; 85:2; 86:5; 99:8; 103:3; 130:4.

45. See further #6.2b.

46. Lev 18:5; Deut 30:19-20.

47. Deut 10:16; Jer 4:4; 9:25-26; Ezek 44:9; 1QpHab 11:13; 1QS 5:5; 1QH 10[=2]:18; 21:5[=18.20]; Philo, *Spec. Leg.* 1:305.

48. Particularly a feature of the Isaianic writings—Isa 11:6-8; 25:7-8; 29:18; 32:14-20; 35:1-2, 5-6; 42:7, 18; 44:3; 49:5-6, 22-26; 51:3; 56:8; 60:4, 9; 66:20.

49. Isa 32:15; 44:3; Ezek 39:29; Joel 2:28–3:1.

50. Isa 4:4; 27:9; Jer 31:34; see also *Jub.* 22:14-15; *Pss. Sol.* 18:5.

51. Isa 2:2/Mic 4:1; Ezek 38:16; Dan 2:28; 10:14; Hos 3:5; and regularly in the DSS.

52. Dan 8:17; 11:35, 40; 12:4, 9.

53. 1QpHab 7:7, 12; 1QS 4:16-17; 4QMMT C14; 5Q16; *1 Enoch* 10:12; 16:1; 22:4; *T. Levi* 10.2; *T. Zeb.* 9:9; *T. Ben.* 11:3; *T. Mos.* 12:4.

54. See for example T. J. Lewis, "Dead, Abode of," *ABD*, 2.101–5.

55. Dan 12:2; 2 Macc 7:9-14, 23, 29.

56. Luke 4:18-21, quoting Isa 61:1-2.

57. Matt 6:10/ Luke 11:2.

58. Matt 12:41-42/Luke 11:31-32; Matt 13:16-17/Luke 10:23-24; Mark 2:18-22 pars.; Matt 13:44-46. See further *Jesus Remembered*, #12.5; Wilckens, *Theologie*, 1.1.136–84; Schnelle, *Theologie*, 71–94.

59. Matt 11:2-6/Luke 7:18-23, with allusion to the Isaiah passages—Isa 26:19; 29:18; 35:5-6; 42:7, 18; 61:1. The DSS have provided the remarkable parallel in Qumran's messianic hope (4Q521). See also Matt 11:7-19/Luke 7:24-35; 16:16.

60. Mark 3:22-27 pars.; Matt 12:27-28/Luke 11:19-20. That there were two overlapping but different collections of Jesus' sayings on the subject (Mark 3:22-29 and Q = Luke 11:15-26) indicates that the material played an important role in shaping the earliest Christian understanding of Jesus' mission.

61. Mark 2:15-16; Matt 11:19/Luke 7:34; Luke 15:1-2; 19:10; see *Jesus Remembered*, ##13.5, 14.8.

62. Mark 2:5, 9 pars.; Luke 7:48-49.

63. See chapter 2 note 31 above.

64. Classically in 1 Cor 15:1-19.

65. CD 6:19; 8:21; 19:33-34; 20:12; 1QpHab 2:3-6; cf. 1QSb (1Q28b) 3:26; 5:21-23.

66. Mark 14:24 pars; 1 Cor 11:25.

67. 2 Cor 3:6 very probably alludes to the promise of a new covenant in Jer 31:31; see those cited in *Theology of Paul*, 147n103.

68. Rom 4:3-12; Gal 3:6-9.

69. Note particularly 1 Macc 2:52; Jas 2:23; see further my *Romans*, 200–202; *Theology of Paul*, 225n95, 375n167; *New Perspective on Paul* (2005), 43n179; (2008) 47n185. See further below chapter 6 at note 72.

70. Notably in the Gospels; see *Jesus Remembered*, 500–503, 549–53.

71. See particularly CD 3:12–4:12; 4QFlor. 1:1-7; B. Gärtner, *The Temple and the Community in Qumran and the New Testament*, SNTSMS 1 (Cambridge, England: Cambridge University, 1965), chs. 2 and 3.

72. See again *Jesus Remembered*, 514–15, 631–33.

73. Particularly Matt 5:23-24; 17:24-27; Acts 3:1; 21:20; see *Beginning from Jerusalem*, #23.5, and below note 92.

74. Mark 13:26-30; Acts 3:19-21; 1 Cor 16:22; 1 Thess 1:10; 4:13-18; see further below #4.3d.

75. Acts 7:44, 48; Gal 4:25-26; Heb 8–10; Rev 7:15; 11:1-2, 19; 15:5-8; 21:22.

76. 1 Cor 3:16-17; 6:19.

77. It has always remained a puzzle to me how it could be that Catholic tradition,

exemplified in Vatican II's *Lumen Gentium* #28, could use Hebrews of all documents to validate a continuing order of priesthood with the character of the defunct Aaronic priesthood; see my *Partings of the Ways*, 115–19, 127–28.

78. 1 Pet 2:5; Rev 1:5.

79. Rom 15:16; Phil 2:25.

80. Rom 14:14, 20; 1 Cor 6:11; 10:25-26; see also 1 Tim 1:5; 3:9; Jas 1:27; 1 Pet 1:22.

81. For detail see my *Partings of the Ways*, 333–37.

82. In Christian tradition it became the established dogma that the Spirit is given through baptism, though that is less clear in the NT documents themselves.

83. See also for example C. M. Tuckett, "Atonement in the NT," *ABD*, 1.518–22.

84. Mark 12:1-9; Luke 11:49-51; Acts 7:52; 1 Thess 2:15.

85. Räisänen thinks "the vicarious effects ascribed to deaths of Maccabean martyrs" were the "more likely source for the notion of the offering of a human life for others" ("Towards an Alternative to New Testament Theology," 187, citing other bibliography in note 46), though it should be noted that the Maccabean martyrs' death could be so thought of by the application of sacrificial categories to them (4 Macc 17:21-22). In observing the variety of images and models used by the early Christians, Räisänen also notes that "what was primary was the experience of new life which the people claimed to enjoy" (190).

86. Insofar as the Acts sermons have a theology of the cross, it is of suffering followed by vindication—Acts 3:13, 26; 4:27, 30; 5:30; 8:30-35 (including the exposition of Isa 53); 10:39.

87. 1 Cor 6:19-20; 7:23; cf. Mark 10:45; 1 Tim 2:6; Titus 2:14; 1 Pet 1:18; 2 Pet 2:1; Rev 5:9.

88. Rom 5:10; 11:15; 2 Cor 5:18-21; Eph 2:14-16; Col 1:20.

89. Col 2:15; implied also in Rom 8:35-38; 1 Cor 15:24-25; Phil 2:10; John 12:32; Rev 12:7-12.

90. Rom 6:9; 1 Cor 15:54-57; Heb 2:14-15; 1 John 3:8.

91. John 1:29; Rom 3:25; 4:25; 8:3; 1 Cor 15:3; 2 Cor 5:21; Heb 9:11-14; 10:11-18; 1 Pet 1:18-19; 2:24; 1 John 2:2; 4:10; Rev 1:5; 5:9. That God made this provision, and thus manifested his love, is a repeated theme—particularly John 3:16; Rom 3:25; 8:32; 2 Cor 5:21; 1 John 4:10. On the question of the influence of Isaiah 53, not least on Jesus, see particularly B. Janowski and P. Stuhlmacher, eds., *The Suffering Servant: Isaiah 53 in Jewish and Christian Sources* (Grand Rapids, Mich.: Eerdmans, 2004), and S. McKnight, *Jesus and His Death: Historiography, the Historical Jesus, and Atonement Theory* (Waco, Tex.: Baylor University, 2005). The Gospel data leave me uncertain (*Jesus Remembered*, 809–18).

92. The circumstances envisaged in Acts 21:20-26 are presumably those covered by the legislation in Num 6:9-12, where a Nazirite's "separation" has been defiled by contact with a corpse; the defilement required a seven-day purification and the shaving of the previously uncut hair; and on the eighth day the offering of two turtle doves or young pigeons, the one as a sin offering, the other as a burnt offering in atonement for his sin.

93. See *Unity and Diversity*, #54.

94. For the issues and bibliography see *Theology of Paul*, ##9.2–3.

95. Rom 8:3; Gal 4:4-5; Phil 2:6-8; Heb 2:14-17; 1 Pet 1:18-20; 1 John 4:10. The "glory" of John 1:14 includes the glory of the cross (John 12:23; 13:31). Cf. Hahn, *Theologie*, 1.623–24; 2.399–402, 405, 408–9.

96. For example Deut 7:28; 9:26; 15:15; Pss 25:22; 31:5; Isa 43:1, 14; 44:22-24; 51:11; 52:3; Luke 2:38; Rom 3:24; Eph 1:7, 14; Heb 9:12. Marshall draws attention to A. J.

Hultgren, *Christ and His Benefits: Christology and Redemption in the New Testament* (Philadelphia: Fortress Press, 1988), who distinguishes four categories in the NT for the understanding of Jesus' work of redemption: redemption accomplished in Christ; redemption confirmed through Christ; redemption won by Christ; and redemption mediated by Christ (*Theology*, 727–30).

97. As for example in Acts 20:32; Gal 3:18; Eph 1:11, 14, 18; Col 1:12; Heb 9:15; 1 Pet 1:4.

98. The passage is both reflected in Jesus' proclamation of the good news (Matt 11:5/Luke 7:22) and cited in Rom 10:15.

99. *Jesus Remembered*, #13.2a.

100. "Repent/repentance" appear in Paul only in Rom 2:4; 2 Cor 7:9-10; 12:21; also 2 Tim 2:25; and never in the Johannine Gospel or Epistles. "Forgive/forgiveness of sins" appears only in Col 1:14; Eph 1:7; John 20:23; 1 John 1:9; 2:12.

101. 2 Cor 1:22; Eph 1:13; 4:30.

102. John 3:3, 5; 1 Cor 4:15; Jas 1:18; 1 Pet 1:3.

103. Rom 8:15; Gal 4:5; Eph 1:5.

104. 2 Cor 11:2; Eph 5:25-26.

105. Rom 6:3-6; 7:4, 6; Gal 2:19; Col 2:20; 3:3.

106. See above #4.2c.

107. A repeated canon of Jewish justice (Exod 23:7; Prov 17:15; 24:24; Isa 5:23; Sir 42:2; CD 1:19).

108. "In Christ" occurs eighty-three times in the Pauline corpus, and "in the Lord (Jesus)" a further forty-seven times; for more detail see my *Theology of Paul*, #15.2.

109. John 6:56; 14:17; 15:4-7; 1 John 2:6, 24, 27, 28; 3:6, 9, 24; 4:12, 13, 15, 16.

110. C. F. D. Moule faced up to this feature in chapter 2 of his *The Origin of Christology* (Cambridge, England: Cambridge University, 1977).

111. In *Theology of Paul* I note that of the three major modes by which Paul expressed his soteriology, justification by faith (#14), participation in Christ (#15), and the gift of the Spirit (#16), the last has not been given the attention it deserves. Typically it has been deduced from one or two passages (notably 1 Cor 12:13) that the Spirit was given in or through baptism, though no NT writer takes any pains to make this explicit.

112. Particularly Rom 8:4; 12:1-2; 2 Cor 3:18; 4:16–5.5; Phil 1:9-11; cf. Heb 6:4-5.

113. Rom 8:15-16; Gal 4:6-7.

114. A. Schweitzer, *The Mysticism of Paul the Apostle* (London: A & C Black, 1931) famously described "the doctrine of righteousness by faith" as "a subsidiary crater, which has formed within the rim of the main crater—the mystical doctrine of redemption through being-in-Christ" (225). The dispute was revived by Sanders, *Paul and Palestinian Judaism*, 502–8; and see now D. A. Campbell, *The Quest for Paul's Gospel: A Suggested Strategy* (London: T & T Clark International, 2005).

115. So for example F. W. Horn, *Das Angeld des Geistes: Studien zur paulinischen Pneumatologie*, FRLANT 154 (Göttingen, Germany: Vandenhoeck & Ruprecht, 1992), 175; but see V. Rabens, *The Holy Spirit and Ethics in Paul: Transformation and Empowering for Religious-Ethical Life*, WUNT II (Tübingen, Germany: Mohr Siebeck, 2009), chs. 2-3.

116. The imagery, drawing on Gen 2:7, is most effectively played on in Ezek 37:9-10. See further above #2.4b.

117. "Salvation is a threefold act of God: an accomplished fact, an experience continuing in the present, and a consummation still to come" (Caird, *Theology*, 118; also 179).

118. Particularly Mark 13:5-37 pars.

119. Mark 8:38 pars.; 14:62 par.

120. For example Mark 13:7-8; Luke 19:11.

121. Two famous examples are C. H. Dodd, *The Parables of the Kingdom* (London: Religious Book Club, 1935), who argued that the kingdom of God was "a matter of present experience" (46); and R. Bultmann, *The Gospel of John* (Oxford: Blackwell, 1971), who attributed the future references in John's Gospel (as in John 5:28-29) to an ecclesiastical redactor.

122. J. A. T. Robinson, "The Most Primitive Christology of All?" *Twelve New Testament Studies* (London: SCM, 1962), 139–53.

123. See for example the review of the data in C. Rowland, "Parousia," *ABD*, 5.166–70.

124. H. Reimarus, *Fragments*, (London: SCM, 1971) does not hesitate to echo 1 Cor 15:17: "if Christ neither has nor does come again to reward the faithful in his kingdom, then our belief is as useless as it is false" (228)

125. See further C. D. Myers, "The Persistence of Apocalyptic Thought in New Testament Theology," in Kraftchick et al., eds., *Biblical Theology*, 209–21, especially 211–16. Myers concludes: "the pervasiveness and persistence of apocalyptic thought in the NT can only be explained by realizing that apocalyptic is essential to early Christian belief" (221).

126. As in Rom 5:1, 5 and 1 Thess 1:6.

127. For example Pss 33:18, 22; 42:5, 11; 69:6; 130:5, 7.

128. Echoing Isa 11:10, as also Paul in Rom 15:12.

129. 1 Cor 13:13; Col: 1:4-5; 1 Thess 1:3.

130. 2 Cor 1:10; Phil 1:20; Col 1:23, 27; 1 Tim 1:1; 4:10; 5:5.

131. 1 Cor 1:18; 15:2; 2 Cor 2:15.

132. Rom 3:24; 1 Cor 1:30; Eph 1:7; Col 1:14; also Heb 9:15.

133. Rom 8:23; Eph 1:14; 4:30; also Luke 21:28.

134. Rom 8:23; 2 Cor 5:5; Eph 1:13-14.

135. It remains a puzzle to me that intense focus on the forensic aspect of Paul's soteriology has tended to overshadow the aspect of transformation in so much Lutheran and Reformed NT theology, when Paul himself was evidently so comfortable with both; see *The New Perspective on Paul* (2005), 63–86, (2008) 71–95.

136. Rom 8:29; Eph 4:24; Col 3:10.

137. Rom 8:10-11, 17-23; 2 Cor 4:10-11, 16–5:5; Phil 3:10-11, 21.

138. The passion narratives of the Gospels; Heb 2:10-18; 5:7-10; 1 Pet 3:17-22; Rev 7:4-14.

139. Michael Wolter, "The Theology of the Cross and the Quest for a Doctrinal Norm" in Rowland & Tuckett, ed., *The Nature of New Testament Theology*, 263–85, critiques British NT scholarship for failing to grasp the critical and polemical function of Paul's *theologia crucis* as grasped by German theology (272–73).

140. Heikki Räisänen focuses on this subject in what he describes as a draft of the second chapter of his projected "Wredean" account of early Christian ideas; see above #2 note 32.

141. For example Matt 5:29-30; 13:42, 50; 25:41; Mark 9:43-47; Luke 12:5; 16:22-26; Rev 19:20; 20:7-15.

142. See below #5.3a.

143. Rom 8:18, 21, 30; 1 Cor 2:7; 2 Cor 4:17; 1 Thess 2:12; 2 Thess 2:14; 2 Tim 2:10; Heb 2:10; 1 Pet 1:7; 5:1, 4. The implication that the glory is the glory of the original creation, restored or enhanced, is given by the Adam echoes in Rom 3:23, 8:21, and Heb 2:5-8.

144. Those who know William Blake's great poem "The New Jerusalem," and of the emotion with which it is sung on the last night of the Proms (Promenade Concerts) each year in London's Albert Hall, will take the point.

Bring me my bow of burning gold! Bring me my arrows of desire!
Bring me my spear! O clouds, unfold! Bring me my chariot of fire!
I will not cease from mental fight, Nor shall my sword sleep in my hand
Till we have built Jerusalem In England's green and pleasant land.

5. The Church of God

1. In what follows cf. particularly Scobie, *Ways of Our God*, ch. 11.

2. This point has been regularly made in recent years. See particularly B. F. Meyer, *The Aims of Jesus* (London: SCM, 1979), 133–37, 153–54, 161, 223–41; E. P. Sanders, *Jesus and Judaism* (London: SCM, 1985), 61–119; N. T. Wright, *Jesus and the Victory of God* (London: SPCK, 1996), 126–31 and passim. See further below #5.3a.

3. Details in *Theology of Paul*, 20.2.

4. See for example A. L. Williams, *Adversus Judaeos* (Cambridge, England: Cambridge University, 1935); other bibliography in *The Partings of the Ways*, 342n11.

5. See above chapter 4 note 13.

6. Rom 9:6-13; Gal 4:21-31.

7. For the thought of Israel as God's inheritance, see for example 1 Kgs 8:51, 53; Pss 22:12; 74:2; Isa 6:17; Jer 10:16; Mic 7:18; Sir 24:8.

8. 1 Chr 16:13; Pss 89:3; 105:6; Isa 42:1 (LXX); 43:20; 45:4; 65:9, 15, 22; Sir 46:1; 47:22; Wis 3:9; 4:15; *Jub.* 1:29; *1 Enoch* 1:3, 8; 5:7-8; 25:5; 93:2; 1 QS 8:6; CD 4:3-4; 1QM 12:1, 1QH 10 [=2]:13; 1QpHab 10:13; *Sib. Or.* 3:69. See also G. Schrenk, *TDNT*, 4.182-84.

9. Mark 13:20, 22, 27 pars.

10. Col 3:12; Titus 1:1; 1 Pet 1:1.

11. "In spite of the fact that the primary direction of New Testament tradition arose from the impact on the early church of Jesus as God's new redemptive intervention, it is equally astonishing that this new revelation of God's will has been made consistently and immediately in terms of its relation to God's prior commitment to Israel" (Childs, *Biblical Theology*, 212).

12. Gen 14:16; 15:5; 22;17.

13. Gen 14:14-15; 15:17-21; 17:8.

14. Galatians 3; Romans 4.

15. See also L. H. Schiffman, *Who Was a Jew? Rabbinic and Halakhic Perspectives on the Jewish-Christian Schism* (Hoboken, N.J.: Ktav, 1985).

16. See further W. D. Davies, *The Gospel and the Land: Early Christianity and Jewish Territorial Doctrine* (Berkeley: University of California, 1974); B. W. Anderson, "Standing on God's Promises: Covenant and Continuity in Biblical Theology" in Kraftchick et al., eds., *Biblical Theology*, 145–54.

17. Sir 44:21; *Jub.* 17:3; 22:14; 32:19; *1 Enoch* 5:7; Philo, *Som.* 1:175; *Mos.* 1:155; rabbinic references in Str-B 3:209.

18. Israeli settlers in the West Bank of the Jordan are well aware that in some versions of the promise the land promised is from the Nile to the Euphrates (Gen 15:18; Deut 1:7-8; cf. Deut 11:24; Josh 1:4)—a fact of explosive political significance too little appreciated by Christians who support the settlers on the basis of the promise to Abraham.

19. This contrast was a leading motif in F. C. Baur, *The Church History of the First Three Centuries*, 2 vols. (London: Williams & Norgate, 1878–79), 5–6, 33, 43, 47, and has been a blight on Jewish-Christian dialogue and on mutual understanding more or less ever since.

20. See further A. F. Segal, "Universalism in Judaism and Christianity" in T. Engberg-Pedersen, ed., *Paul In his Hellenistic Context* (Minneapolis: Fortress Press, 1995), 1–29; J. D. Levenson, "The Universal Horizon of Biblical Particularism" in M. G. Brett, ed., *Ethnicity and the Bible* (Leiden, Netherlands: Brill, 1996), 143–69; J. D. G. Dunn, "Was Judaism Particularist or Universalist?" in J. Neusner and A. J. Avery-Peck, eds., *Judaism in Late Antiquity*. Part 3 Volume 2: *Where We Stand: Issues and Debates in Ancient Judaism* (Leiden, Netherlands: Brill, 1999), 57–73.

21. 2 Macc 2:21; 8:1; 14:38.

22. Exod 20:5; 34:12-16; Num 25:11-13; Deut 4:23-24; 5:9; etc.

23. Gen 34; Jdg 9:2-4; *Jub.* 30.

24. Num 25:1-13; Sir 45:23-24; 1 Macc 2:54.

25. 1 Kgs 18:36-40; Sir 48:2-3; 1 Macc 2:58.

26. 1 Macc 2:23-27; Josephus, *Ant.* 12:271.

27. Acts 22:3-4; Gal 1:13-14; Phil 3:5-6.

28. See my "Paul's Conversion—A Light to Twentieth Century Disputes" in J. Ådna et al., eds., *Evangelium—Schriftauslegung—Kirche*, P. Stuhlmacher FS (Göttingen, Germany: Vandenhoeck & Ruprecht, 1997), 77–93, reprinted in *The New Perspective on Paul*, ch. 15; also *Theology of Paul*, #14.3

29. Notably Lev 17:8-9, 10-14; 18:26.

30. See for example E. Schürer, *The History of the Jewish People in the Age of Jesus Christ*, revised and edited by G. Vermes and F. Millar, 4 vols. (Edinburgh, Scotland: T & T Clark, 1973–87), 3.165–68; J. M. Lieu, "The Race of the God-fearers," *JTS* 46 (1995): 483–501; I. Levinskaya, *The Book of Acts in its Diaspora Setting* (Grand Rapids, Mich.: Eerdmans, 1996), chs. 4–7; B. Wander, *Gottesfürchtige und Sympathisanten: Studien zum heidnischen Umfeld von Diasporasynagogen*, WUNT 104 (Tübingen, Germany: Mohr Siebeck, 1998).

31. Gen 12:3; 18:18; 22:17-18; 26:4; 28:14.

32. See R. W. L. Moberly, *The Bible, Theology, and Faith: A Study of Abraham and Jesus* (Cambridge, England: Cambridge University, 2000), 120–26.

33. Sir 44:19-21; Jdt 8:26; 1 Macc 2:52; *Jub.* 17:15-18; 18:16; 19:8; *m.* '*Abot* 5:3.

34. Amos 3:12; 5:3, 14-15; 9:1-4.

35. Mic 2:12-13; 4:6-7; 5:7-8; 7:18-20.

36. Isa 6:11-13; 7:3.

37. Hag 1:12, 14; 2:2; Zech 8:6, 11, 12.

38. *Perushim*, from *parash*, "to separate"; see for example Schürer, *History*, 2.396–97; A. J. Saldarini, *Pharisees, Scribes and Sadducees in Palestinian Society* (Edinburgh, Scotland: T & T Clark, 1988), 220–25.

39. Josephus, *War* 1:110; 2:162; *Ant.* 17:41; *Life* 191; Acts 22:3; 26:5; see particularly A. J. Baumgarten, "The Name of the Pharisees," *JBL* 102 (1983): 413–17.

40. Gal 1:13-14; Phil 3:5-6.

41. 1QS 2:9; 3:25; 8:9; 11:7.

42. For example 1QS 2:4-10; CD 1:11-21; 1QH 10[=2]:8-19; 1QpHab 5:3-8; 4Q174 [= 4QFlor] 1:7-9.

43. 1QH 10[=2]:14-16, 31-32; 12[=4]:9-11; 4QpNah. 1:2, 7; 2:2, 8; 3:3-7.

44. As I argue in my *The Epistles to the Colossians and to Philemon*, NIGTC (Grand Rapids, Mich.: Eerdmans, 1996), 29–35.

45. *Pss. Sol.* 1:8; 2:3; 4:1-8; 7:2; 8:12-13; 17:5-8, 23.

46. Isa 49:5-6, 22-26; 56:8; 60:4, 9; 66:20.

47. Jer 3:18; 31:10; Ezek 34:12-16; 36:24-28; 37:21-23; 39:27; Zeph 3:20; Zech 8:7-8; Tob 14:5-6; Sir 36:13-16; Bar 4:37; 2 Macc 1:27; *1 Enoch* 90:33; *Jub.* 1:15-18; *Pss. Sol.* 11:1-9; 17:31, 44; 11Q19 [Temple] 55:9-13.

48. *T. Levi* 14-16; *T. Jud.* 23; *T. Iss.* 6; *T. Zeb.* 9:5-9; *T. Dan* 5:4-9; *T. Naph.* 4; *T. Ash.* 7; *T. Ben.* 9:1-2; see H. W. Hollander and M. de Jonge, *The Testaments of the Twelve Patriarchs* (Leiden, Netherlands: Brill, 1985), 39–40, 53–56.

49. See above #3.3b.

50. Ps 2:8-9; Zeph 2:9-11; Sir 36:1-9; Bar 4:25, 31-35; *Jub.* 15:26; *1 Enoch* 90:19; 1QM; *4 Ezra* 12:33; 13:38; *2 Bar.* 40:1.

51. Again notably Isa 18:7; 45;14; 60:3-16; 61:5-6; but also Hag. 2:7-9; 1QM 12:14; 4Q504 4:9-12; *Pss. Sol.* 17:30-31; *Sib. Or.* 3:772-776.

52. Pss 22:27-28; 86:9; Isa 22:2-4 = Mic 4:1-3; Isa 45:20-23; 56:6-8; 66:19-20, 23; Jer 3:17; Zeph 3:9-10; Zech 2:11-12; 8:20-23; 14:16-19; Tob 13:11; 14:6-7; *1 Enoch* 10:21; 90:30-36; *Sib. Or.* 3:715-719. See further T. L. Donaldson, "Proselytes or 'Righteous Gentiles'? The Status of Gentiles in Eschatological Pilgrimage Patterns," *JSP* 7 (1990): 3–27; Scobie, *Ways of Our God*, 514–22..

53. See notes 46–48 above.

54. As infamously argued by W. Grundmann, *Jesus der Galiläer und das Judentum* (Leipzig, Germany: Wigand, 1941), with the twin theses: "Galilee was Gentile" and "Jesus was no Jew" (166–75). There are disturbing, if unintended, echoes in J. D. Crossan, *The Historical Jesus: The Life of a Mediterranean Jewish Peasant* (San Francisco: Harper, 1991).

55. *Ioudaios* of course means initially "Judean," but it is clear that by the time of Jesus it had become a religious identifier ("Jew") as much as if not more than a territorial iden-tifier ("Judean"); see S. J. D. Cohen, *The Beginnings of Jewishness: Boundaries, Varieties, Uncertainties* (Berkeley: University of California, 1999), ch. 3 ("*Ioudaios, Iudaeus*, Judean, Jew"). So "Galilean Jew" is not an oxymoron; see further my *Jesus Remembered*, #9.6.

56. See again my *Jesus Remembered*, 315–17; though G. Vermes, *The Religion of Jesus the Jew* (London: SCM, 1993) overemphasizes the traditional character of Jesus' Jewishness.

57. See above note 2.

58. See also Isa 44:22; 55:7; Ezek 18:30; Hos 3:5; 6:1; 14:2; Joel 2:12-13; Zech 1:3; Mal 3:7.

59. The symbolism is clearest in Matt 19:28/Luke 22:30.

60. Matt 18:12/Luke 15:4; Mark 14:27/Matt 26:31; Matt 10:6; 15:24; Luke 12:32.

61. For example Gen 49:24; Ps 28:9; Isa 40:11; Jer 13:17, 20; Ezek 34; other references in *Jesus Remembered*, 511n107.

62. See above #4.3c.

63. Particularly Matt 5:3/Luke 6:20; Matt 11:5/Luke 7:22.

64. Particularly Deut 15:7-11 and 24:10-15, 19-22. The prominence of the concern for the poor within Israel is obvious from the many references in the Psalms and the prophets; for details see *Jesus Remembered*, 518–19nn140–143. See also #6.2b below.

65. See particularly R. A. Horsley, ed., *Paul and Empire: Religion and Power in Roman Imperial Society* (Harrisburg, Pa.: Trinity Press International, 1997); N. T. Wright, "A Fresh Perspective on Paul," *BJRL* 83 (2001): 21–39; also *Paul: Fresh Perspectives* (London: SPCK, 2005), ch. 4.

66. Outside the Gospels, Jesus' descent from David as such is referred to only in Rom 1:3 ("according to the flesh") and 2 Tim 2:8; and the Greek translation of "Messiah" (*Christos*) has already lost most of its titular connotation in Paul's letters.

67. Matt 8:5-13/Luke 7:1-10; Mark 7:24-30/Matt 15:21-28.

68. See further J. Jeremias, *Jesus' Promise to the Nations* (London: SCM, 1958).

69. Matt 11:22/Luke 10:14; Matt 12:41/Luke 11:32.

70. Matt 28:19-20; Mark 13:10; Luke 24:47.

71. Pss 1:1, 5; 10:3; 28:3; 37:32; 50:16-18; 71:4; 82:4; 119:53, 155.

72. Ps 9:17; Tob 13:6; *Jub.* 23:23-24; *Pss. Sol.* 1:1; 2:1-2; Luke 6:33 (*hoi hamartōloi*) = Matt 5:47 (*hoi ethnikoi*); Mark 14:41 pars.; cf. K. H. Rengstorf, *TDNT*, 1.325-26, 328.

73. For the following see further *Jesus Remembered*, #13.5a.

74. 1 Macc 1:34; 2:44, 48.

75. *1 Enoch* 1:7-9; 5:4, 6-7; 22:9-13; 94-104; see also above #5.2c.

76. 1QpHab 5:1-12; 1QH 10[= 2]:10-12; 12[=4]:34; CD 2:3; 11:18-21; 19:20-21; 4Q174 [4QFlor] 1:14.

77. For example 1QS 5:7-13; 1QH 15[= 7]:12; CD 4:6-8.

78. See again above #5.2c.

79. See particularly S. McKnight, *A Light among the Gentiles: Jewish Missionary Activity in the Second Temple Period* (Minneapolis: Fortress Press, 1991); M. Goodman, *Mission and Conversion: Proselytizing in the Religious History of the Roman Empire* (Oxford, England: Clarendon, 1994). The readiness of "scribes and Pharisees" to "cross sea and land to make a single proselyte" (Matt 23:15) probably refers to the zeal of an Eleazar to ensure that would-be converts to Judaism, like king Izates of Adiabene, were converted all the way (Josephus, *Ant.* 20.38-46). Matt 23:15 may reflect the experience of churches like those in Galatia and Philippi when traditionalist Jewish believers attempted to persuade the Gentile converts to be circumcised (become, in the traditionalists' view, full/genuine proselytes).

80. I may refer simply to my *Beginning from Jerusalem*, #27.

81. *Koinos* in ordinary Greek means simply "common, ordinary." The sense of "profane, unclean" derives from the use of *koinos* as equivalent to the biblical *tame'* (for example, Lev 11:4-8; Deut 14:7-10; Judg 13:4; Hos 9:3) or *chol* (Lev 10:10; Ezek 22:26; 44:23), a step taken subsequent to the LXX rendering of the OT, but reflecting the increasing purity concerns of the Maccabean and post-Maccabean period (1 Macc 1:47, 62). In Mark 7:2, 5, Mark has to explain the unusual use of *koinos* = "defiled" to his Greek audience.

82. Cf. for example Gal 3:1-5; 1 Cor 1:4-7; Heb 2:4.

83. Even so, that the development of the Gentile mission did not prove acceptable to a substantial proportion of the Jewish believers is the testimony of Acts 21:20-21 and subsequently of the Jewish Christian sects.

84. Rom 15:20-21 (= Isa 52:15); 2 Cor 6:1-2 (= Isa 49:8); Phil 2:16 (cf. Isa 49:4).

85. Acts 13:47 (= Isa 49:6); 26:16-18 (cf. Isa 42:7); also 18:9-10 (cf. Isa 41:10; 43:5).

86. Here and in the following paragraph I draw on my "Paul: Apostate or Apostle of Israel?" *ZNW* 89 (1998): 256–71; also "The Jew Paul and His Meaning for Israel" in U. Schnelle and T. Söding, eds., *Paulinische Christologie: Exegetische Beiträge*, H. Hübner FS (Göttingen, Germany: Vandenhoeck & Ruprecht, 2000), 32–46; see also #1 note 18 above. Note Childs's more general observation: "it is equally astonishing that this new revelation of God's will has been made consistently and immediately in terms of its relation to God's prior commitment to Israel" (*Biblical Theology*, 212).

87. See further my *New Perspective on Paul* (2005), 26–33; (2008), 29–36.

88. Rom 14:1–15:6; 1 Cor 8–10.

89. The actual terms of "the apostolic decree" are a matter of some confusion in the textual tradition (see for example the discussion in B. M. Metzger, *A Textual Commentary on the Greek Testament* [London: UBS, 1975], 429–34), though that very confusion is a reminder that the terms of association continued to be debated and revised during the period when, as we may infer, "the apostolic decree" played a vital role as the basis of mixed churches.

90. Lev 17:8-9, 10-14; 18:26. See particularly R. J. Bauckham, "James and the Jerusalem Church" in R. Bauckham, ed., *The Book of Acts in its First Century Setting*. Vol. 4: *Palestinian Setting*, 452–62.

91. 1 Cor 16:1-4; 2 Cor 8:1-7; Rom 15:25-32.

92. See above chapter 4 note 110.

93. For example Rom 8:1; 1 Cor 15:18; 2 Cor 5:17; Gal 1:22; Phil 1:1; 1 Thess 2:14.

94. Gal 3:6-9, 14, 27-29. To similar effect but less vulnerable to counter exegesis, Romans 4.

95. Particularly Rom 12:4-5; 1 Cor 12.

96. I made this suggestion in my *Romans*, 704–5.

97. 1 Cor 10:16; 12:27.

98. 1 Cor 10:16-22; 12:14-26.

99. See above chapter 4 note 109.

100. Matt 2:15; 12:17-21; 21:42; 26:31.

101. Matthew's five sermons as compared with Moses' five books; John 1:17; 5:39-47; Heb 1:1-2; 3:1-6.

102. Acts 2:23; 3:14-15; 10:39.

103. See also Hübner, *Biblische Theologie*, 1.90–100. Childs notes that despite the writer of Hebrews seeing "the old Israel as provisionary, obsolete, and imperfect, he does not relegate Israel's scriptures to the past, but continues to view the biblical text as God's living voice addressing a pilgrim people who await the heavenly city (13.14)" (*Biblical Theology*, 439). But Lincoln presses the point: "The issue . . . with which biblical theology in particular must continue to wrestle, is whether, and if so how, it is possible to respect the continuing religious validity of the synagogue . . . while still holding to the claim at the heart of Hebrews and the New Testament as a whole—namely, that Jesus Christ is the decisive revelation of God for all human beings" ("Hebrews and Biblical Theology," 335–56).

104. L. T. Johnson, "The New Testament's Anti-Jewish Slander and the Conventions of Ancient Polemic," *JBL* 108 (1989): 419–41: "by the measure of contemporary Jewish polemic, the NT's slander against fellow Jews is remarkably mild" (441).

105. For example this is the heading under which Strecker (*Theology*, 203–8) and Childs (*Biblical Theology*, 248) discuss Romans 9–11.

106. "Jew/Greek, Jew/Gentile"—1:16; 2:9-10, 17-24; 3:9, 29; 9:24; 10:12; "Israel"—9:6, 27, 31; 10:19, 21; 11:2, 7, 11, 23, 25, 26.

107. Gal 6:16 ("Peace and mercy be also upon the Israel of God") poses the same question ("Who is [this] Israel?") but does not provide as clear an answer as does Romans 9.

108. This is regularly referred to as a *Sonderweg*, a special way for Israel to be saved (other than through the gospel). See for example J. G. Gager, *Reinventing Paul* (New York: Oxford University, 2000), 59–61 (drawing especially on F. Mussner, L. Gaston, and S. Stowers).

109. See particularly R. Hvalvik, "A 'Sonderweg' for Israel: A Critical Examination of a Current Interpretation of Romans 11:25-27," *JSNT* 38 (1990): 87–107; T. L. Donaldson, "Jewish Christianity, Israel's Stumbling and the *Sonderweg* Reading of Paul," *JSNT* 29 (2006): 27–54; B. W. Longenecker, "On Israel's God and God's Israel: Assessing Supersessionism in Paul," *JTS* 58 (2007): 26–44.

110. Rom 1:16; 2:9-10; 3:9; 4:11, 16; 9:7; 10:4, 12-13; 15:11.

111. Cf. Hahn, *Theologie*, 2.656–58.

112. But I can at least refer to my *Unity and Diversity*, chs. 6–9.

6. The Ethical Outworkings

1. See for example H. M. Müller, " 'Evangelium latuit in lege': Luthers Kreuzespredigt als Schlüssel seiner Bibelhermeneutik" in *Jesus Christus als die Mitte der Schrift*, O. Hofius FS, ed. C. Landmesser, et al., BZNW 86 (Berlin: de Gruyter, 1997), 101–26: "the distinction between law and gospel grew out of Luther's exegetical work in his conversation with the apostle . . . the distinction between law and gospel as basis for the teaching of justification by faith." "Only he who takes up this distinction and lets his thinking be led by it is, according to Luther, a good theologian" (101–2; also 107–9). And further R. Bergmeier, "Das Gesetz im Römerbrief," *Das Gesetz im Römerbrief und andere Studien zum Neuen Testament*, WUNT 121 (Tübingen, Germany: Mohr Siebeck, 2000), 31–35, who notes, inter alia, Harnack's observation that "the whole sphere of the law belongs religiously according to Luther 'to an outdated stage; whoever does not recognize this must remain a Jew'" (34). See further my *New Perspective on Paul*, chapter 1 notes 88, 89.

2. Typically in Deut 4:45; also 4:1, 5, 8, 14, 40; 5:1, 31; 6:1, 2, 17, 20; 7:11; 8:11; 11:1, 32; etc.

3. See #4.2b-c; #5.2a.

4. See above chapter 4 note 21.

5. Sanders summarized the phrase as follows: "covenantal nomism is the view that one's place in God's plan is established on the basis of the covenant and that the covenant requires as the proper response of man his obedience to its commandments, while providing means of atonement for transgression" (*Paul and Palestinian Judaism*, 75; see also 236, 420, 544).

6. Particularly D. A. Carson, et al. eds., *Justification and Variegated Nomism. Vol. 1: The Complexities of Second Temple Judaism*, WUNT 2.140 (Tübingen, Germany: Mohr Siebeck, 2001). F. Avemarie, *Tora und Leben: Untersuchungen zur Heilsbedeutung der Tora in der frühen rabbinischen Literatur* (Tübingen, Germany: Mohr Siebeck, 1996), is generally thought to have provided a crushing response to Sanders, and his monograph does necessitate a more careful statement of rabbinic Judaism's variegated views on the subject (see

also his "Erwählung und Vergeltung. Zur optionalen Struktur rabbinischer Soteriologie," *NTS* 45 [1999]: 108–26). But note also Avemarie's "Bund als Gabe und Recht: Semantische Überlegeungen zu berît in der rabbinischen Literatur" in F. Avemarie and H. Lichtenberger, eds., *Bund und Tora: Zur theologischen Begriffsgeschichte in alttestamentlicher, frühjüdischer und urchristlicher Tradition* (Tübingen, Germany: Mohr Siebeck, 1996), 163–216, whose conclusion is far more sympathetic to Sanders's notion of "covenantal nomism" (213–15). Stuhlmacher's critique, that "'covenantal nomism' is a tautology since *berît* and *diathēke* mean primarily 'regulation' or 'obligation'" (*Biblische Theologie*, 1.255), ignores both the "essential characteristic [of the biblical *diathēke*]...that it is the declaration of one person's initiative" (BDAG, 228) and the predominantly promise/grace character of the covenants given by God (Gen 9:9-17; 15:18; 17:2-8; Exod 2:24; 6:4-5). Scobie quotes W. Brueggemann's definition: "By 'covenant' the OT means 'an enduring commitment by God and his people based on mutual vows of loyalty and mutual obligation through which both parties have their lives radically affected and empowered'" (*Ways of Our God*, 475).

7. I mount a fuller defense of the phrase in *The New Perspective on Paul* (2005), 55–63; (2008), 60–71.

8. Classically in Tertullian, *De Pudicitia*, 6.3–5, and the Westminster Confession, #19.3.

9. *ABD*, 4.242–52. Greengus notes the degree of overlap with Ancient Near East law codes, and observes the absence of biblical laws regulating the activities of merchants, professions, traders, and craftsmen.

10. *Lex talionis* = the law of retaliation, whereby punishment resembles the offense committed in kind and degree.

11. The strong protests against the abuse of the law in regard to the poor are especially prominent in Amos, Micah, and Isaiah; see particularly Amos 5:21-24; Micah 3; Isa 58:3-7.

12. Luke 6:22; Matt 11:5. See *Jesus Remembered*, #13.4.

13. Dan 4:27; Sir 3:30; 29:12; 40:24; Tob 4:10; 12:9; 14:11; see also G. Schrenk, *TDNT*, 2.196.

14. See for example *Jesus Remembered*, 269 and 295; more detail in E. P. Sanders, *Jewish Law from Jesus to the Mishnah* (London: SCM, 1990), 214–27.

15. See above chapter 5 note 45.

16. Lev 11:44-45; 19:2; 20:26; 21:8.

17. Sanders, *Judaism*, 70–72, 218.

18. J. Milgrom, *Leviticus*, AB 3, 2 vols. (New York: Doubleday, 1991) observes that "the priestly legislators are very much concerned with the need to eliminate, or, at least, control the occurrence of impurity anywhere in the land—whether in the home, on the table, or in the bed" (1.1007).

19. A point which Sanders has repeatedly and rightly stressed—*Jewish Law*, 33–34; also *Judaism*, 71, 218.

20. I have drawn attention to this function of the law in several publications, beginning in *Romans*, lxix–lxxi. In view of some misunderstanding on the point, I should emphasize here that this function, already referred to by allusion to Eph 2:14 ("the dividing wall"), does not replace the others, nor was it the sole or primary function of Israel's law.

21. The phrase was used by H. Lichtenberger, "The Understanding of the Torah in the

Judaism of Paul's Day: A Sketch" in J. D. G. Dunn ed., *Paul and the Mosaic Law*, WUNT 89 (Tübingen, Germany: Mohr Siebeck, 1996; Grand Rapids, Mich.: Eerdmans, 2001), 22–23, drawing on Avemarie's *Tora und Leben*, 376–99, 582.

22. Israel's failure to obey would cause the Lord's name to be profaned in the sight of the nations (for example Ezek 20:14, 22; 36:17-23; Isa 52:5).

23. Deut 2:24–3:18; 4:3, 25-31, 37-38, 40; 5:32-33; 6:24; 7:1-2, 12-24; 8:1, 19-20.

24. Rom 10:5; Gal 3:12.

25. This is the most straightforward way to translate the Hebrew—*yachai bahem*.

26. B. A. Levine, *The JPS Torah Commentary on Leviticus* (Skokie, Ill.: Varda Books, 2004), 91. "The Torah is given to Israel so that it can *stay alive before God* and not lose itself in godlessness" (Stuhlmacher, *Biblische Thelogie*, 1.260).

27. Neh 9:29; Prov 3:1-2; 6:23; Sir 17:11; Bar 3:9; 4:1; *Ep. Arist.* 127; *T. Mos.* 12:10; Philo, *Cong.* 86-87; ps-Philo, *LAB* 23:10; *4 Ezra* 7:21.

28. See further my *Galatians*, BNTC (London: Black, 1993), 192–94.

29. See also *Pss. Sol.* 3:11-12; 9:5.

30. S. J. Gathercole, *Where Is Boasting? Early Jewish Soteriology and Paul's Response in Romans 1–5* (Grand Rapids, Mich.: Eerdmans, 2002) Part One (quotations from 90).

31. See above note 5.

32. See further my defence of "covenantal nomism" as a still useful summary of the double aspect of Israel's soteriology (above note 7).

33. On the Mishnah see particularly J. Neusner, *Judaism: The Evidence of the Mishnah* (Chicago: University of Chicago, 1981).

34. See further above #5.2c.

35. For example, E. Stauffer depicted Jesus as "the one who announces a morality without legalism, which in principle is free of any tie to the Mosaic Torah and Jewish obedience to the Torah" (cited by G. Theissen and A. Merz, *The Historical Jesus: A Comprehensive Guide* (London: SCM, 1998), 347. Is it quite fair to see in the antitheses of Matt 5:31-48 an "explicit criticism of the Torah" (Stuhlmacher, *Biblische Theologie*, 1.104)? See further *Partings of the Ways*, chapter 6 at note 2, and *Jesus Remembered*, 564. Schnelle prefers to speak of Jesus "de-centring" the Torah (*Theologie*, 124).

36. Mark 2:23–3:5; 7:1-23.

37. See further *Jesus Remembered*, #14.4, and in what follows ##14.5 and 14.8.

38. 1Q28a = 1QSa 2.3-10; further detail in *Jesus Remembered*, 604.

39. This I take to be Matthew's message in the famous paragraph about Jesus fulfilling the law and urging his disciples to a righteousness which exceeds that of the scribes and Pharisees (Matt 5:17-20).

40. Two generations later, Rabbi Akiba is recalled referring to Lev 19:18 as "the greatest general principle in the Torah" (*Sipra on Lev* 19:18).

41. Rom 13:8-10; Gal 5:14; Jas 2:8; Did 1:2; 2:7; Barn 19:5. Note how in both Romans and Galatians Paul links the love command with allusion to how Jesus himself acted (Rom 15:2-3; Gal 6:2); apart from Rom 13:9 and Gal 5:14, Rom 15:2 is the only reference to the "neighbor" in the undisputed Paulines. Note also the strong emphasis on love in 1 John—particularly 3:16-18; 4:7-12, 16-21. See also Hahn, *Theologie*, 2.670–72, 694–95.

42. A. Schweitzer, *The Quest of the Historical Jesus* (London: SCM, 2000), 454–56.

43. *Jesus Remembered*, #14.9. See also Wilckens, *Theologie*, 1.1.238–81; Schnelle, *Theologie*, 94–104.

44. Luke 4:16-21; as implied also in Luke 6:20 and Matt 11:5/Luke 7:22.

45. Cf. Mark 2:15-19 pars.; Luke 14:1-24; 15:1-2, 23, 32; Matt 8:11-12/Luke 13:28-29.

46. Matt 26:28/Mark 14:24; Luke 22:20/1 Cor 11:25.

47. See again *Jesus Remembered*, 181–84 for the detail; also chapter 3 at note 89.

48. Cf. for example James 2 with Galatians 5.

49. We explored some of the tensions in #5.3 above.

50. Note the sub-title of Alan Segal's eirenic treatment—*Paul the Convert: the Apostolate and Apostasy of Saul the Pharisee* (New Haven, Conn.: Yale University, 1990).

51. When "the apostolic decree" (Acts 15:20, 29; 21:25; see above chapter 5 at note 90) came into operation and whether it had any force in the Pauline churches are disputed issues; Paul's own counsel on the subject (Rom 14:1–15:6; 1 Cor 8-10) does not seem to take it into account.

52. Note particularly Rev 2:6, 14-15, 20.

53. "Without doubt Paul introduces a polarity between law and gospel unknown to the Old Testament" (Childs, *Biblical Theology*, 553).

54. Gal 4:1-2; also 4:22-25.

55. See above #4.3e.

56. As Stuhlmacher notes: "Not a single one of the Old Testament, early Jewish, or New Testament parallels to Gal 3:19 sees the gift of the Torah through the angels (and Moses) as something negative (cf. Deut 33:2 LXX; *Jub.* 1:29; Philo, *Som.* 1:140-43; Josephus, *Ant.* 15:136; Acts 7:53; Heb 2:2). Neither does Paul do so. In Gal 3:20 he does not deprecate the law, but he does subordinate Moses to God's one true mediator, Christ" (*Biblische Theologie*, 1.265).

57. The verb used is *phroureō*, which has the range: (1) "to maintain a watch, guard"; (2) "to hold in custody, detain, confine"; (3) "to provide security, guard, protect, keep" (BDAG, 1066–67).

58. For more detail and bibliography see my *Galatians*, 198–99.

59. See #6.2c above.

60. See further above #5.3c and below #6.3c.

61. For clarification of my understanding of "works of the law" (some of my earlier formulations proved misleading), see *The New Perspective on Paul* (2005), 22–26; (2008), 23–28.

62. As noted above (chapter 5 note 39), *akribeia*, "exactness, precision," was a term which characterized a Pharisaic (and previously Pauline) priority (Acts 22:3; 26:5).

63. See #4.3b above and chapter 4 note 67.

64. Jer 31:34; Ezek 11:20; 36:27. Following H. Gese and K. Koch, Stuhlmacher speaks of these as the "Zion Torah" and notes that "according to its contents, then, the 'Zion Torah' corresponds to the law of Sinai" (*Biblische Theologie*, 1.257).

65. The contrast of Rom 12:2 (discernment of God's will made possible by the renewing of the mind) with what Paul had already characterized as the boasting of the Jewish interlocutor in 2:18 (knowledge of God's will and ability to discern what really mattered by reference to the law) should not be missed.

66. So for example Hahn, *Theologie*, 1.238–41.

67. In this passage Paul speaks of "sin" both as a power experienced in human lives which operates by provoking human appetites to excess, desire into lust, and as the sinful thought and act which breaches the law (trespass).

68. Rom 7:14-25; note 8.3a.

69. Rom 7:23, 25; 8:2.

70. I can understand why many commentators find it hard to see in "the *nomos* of the Spirit of life" (Rom 8:2) a reference to the law; but that "the law of sin and death" is a summary reference to what Paul has described in 7:7-13 seems to me obvious beyond reasonable dispute. See *Theology of Paul*, 642–49; also J. L. Martyn, "*Nomos* plus Genitive Noun in Paul: The History of God's Law" in J. T. Fitzgerald, et al., eds., *Early Christianiy and Classical Culture*, A. J. Malherbe FS, SuppNovT 110 (Leiden, Netherlands: Brill, 2003), 575–87; E. Lohse, *Römer*, KEK (Göttingen, Germany: Vandenhoeck & Ruprecht, 2003), 230; R. Jewett, *Romans*, Hermeneia (Minneapolis: Fortress Press, 2007)—"under the power of sin and flesh, the law was distorted and became an instrument concerning honor for oneself and one's group. But in Christ the law regains its proper spiritual function, which leads to genuine life (7:10-14; 8:4)" (481).

71. Stuhlmacher has referred repeatedly to Rom. 10:4 and argued that "from his Damascus experience, Paul learned to see in the crucified and risen Christ 'the end of the law' (as a way of salvation)" (here *Biblische Theologie*, 1.248, 299–300); cf. for example Hahn, *Theologie*, 2.348–49. But it should be noted that Rom 10:4 continues: "a means to righteousness (or way to salvation) for all who believe"—the "to all who believe" carrying forward Paul's principal concern that the gospel is for *all* who believe, "Jew first but also Greek" (1:16; 3:22; 4:11, 16; 10:11-13)

72. It is doubtful whether Paul ever used *pistis* in the sense of human "faithfulness"; he consistently understands *pistis* as "faith," as trust and reliance on God to know his will, as most clearly in Rom 14:22-23; see my *Romans*, 827–29; *Theology of Paul*, 635–36.

73. "The entire expression "the law of the Spirit of life in (through) Christ Jesus" takes up the language of the *nomos pneumatikos* from Rom 7:12 and recalls Jer 31:31-34 (cf. also *1 Enoch* 61:7, 11; *Jub.* 1:15, 23; *T. Levi* 18:11-14)" (Stuhlmacher, *Biblische Theologie*, 1.266).

74. Rom 5:5; Gal 5:22.

75. Rom 13:8-10; Gal 5:14.

76. For this understanding of "the law of faith," "the law of the Spirit," "the law of Christ" see further my discussion with other and counter bibliography in *Theology of Paul*, #23; also *The New Perspective on Paul*, chs. 11 and 21; cf. especially Hahn, *Theologie*, 1.234–42, 289–90.

77. The parallel stages in the arguments of Rom 3:27–4:22 and Jas 2:18-24 can best be explained if James was responding to what was understood to be Pauline teaching in traditional Jewish Christian circles.

78. "Paul's formula of 'faith active in love' (Gal 5:6) could be used as an epitome of James' ethics" (Räisänen, "Towards an Alternative to New Testament Theology," 183). "Living faith necessarily comes to concrete expression in the actions of love" (Hahn, *Theologie*, 1.289–90).

79. The ways in which 1 Cor 7:19 is interpreted by different commentators is very instructive; see the index references to the verse in *The New Perspective on Paul*.

80. T. R. Schreiner, *Romans* (Grand Rapids, Mich.: Baker, 1998), 404–7; idem, *The Law and its Fulfilment: A Pauline Theology of Law* (Grand Rapids, Mich.: Baker, 1993)—"the Spirit, not self-effort, produces obedience"; "the Spirit's work in a person produces obedience to the law (Rom 2:26-29).... The works that are necessary for salvation...are evidence of a salvation already given" (187–88, 203; further ch. 6).

81. Gathercole, *Where Is Boasting?* 132, 223, 264; see further *The New Perspective on Paul* (2005), 74–75; (2008), 82–83.

82. Rom 8:4, 14; Gal 5:16, 18, 25.

83. Rom 7:6; 8:5-8; Gal 5:16-23.

84. Rom 2:28-29; Phil 3:3.

85. 2 Cor 3:3, 6; Jer 31:34.

86. Rom 13:8-10; Gal 5:14.

87. See again chapter 2 note 41 above; on Col 2:6 see my *Colossians and Philemon*, 138–41. I believe Rom 6:17 should be understood similarly (*Romans*, 343–4).

88. 1 Cor 14:29; 1 Thess 5:21.

89. *Oikodomē* is the key term in 1 Cor 14—14:3-5, 12, 17, 26.

90. An intriguing early precedent for a "Don't ask, don't tell" strategy in dealing with a highly sensitive issue with controversial outworkings in practice.

91. See further my *New Perspective on Paul* (2005), 63–80; (2008) 71–89.

92. For example Rom 6:12-23; Col 3:5-17.

93. For a recent heartfelt statement see P. Stuhlmacher, "Christus Jesus ist hier, der gestorben ist, ja vielmehr, der auch auferweckt ist, der zur Rechten Gottes ist und uns vertritt" in F. Avemarie and H. Lichtenberger, hrsg., *Auferstehung—Resurrection*, WUNT 135 (Tübingen, Germany: Mohr Siebeck, 2001), 351–61.

94. As in Rom 4:5; 8:31-39.

95. The criticism made particularly by Avemarie and Carson (above note 6).

96. Rom 2:6-11; 1 Cor 3:8; 2 Cor 5:10; 11:15; Col 3:25; cf. Matt 16:27; John 5:28-29; Rev 20:11-15.

97. For example 1 Cor 3:14; 9:24-25; Phil 3:14; Col 3:24; 2 Tim 4:8; cf. Matt 5:12; 6:1-6; 10:41-42; 19:21; 25:34-40.

98. 1 Cor 3:17; 10:6-12; 11:27-29; 2 Cor 12:21; 13:5; Gal 5:4; 6:7-8; Col 1:22-23; note also Heb 2:1-3; 3:7–4:11; 6:4-6; 10:26-31; 12:14-17.

99. M. D. Hooker, "Paul and 'Covenantal Nomism'" (1982), *From Adam to Christ: Essays on Paul* (Cambridge, England: Cambridge University, 1990), 157.

100. 1 Cor 1:18; 15:2; 2 Cor 2:15.

101. Gal 3:3; Phil 1:6.

102. See further my *Theology of Paul*, #18. A fresh study is required of Paul's understanding of "perfection/maturity" in comparison with the same concept in Second Temple Judaism.

103. Rom 5:4; 2 Cor 2:9.

104. Rom 12:2; 2 Cor 3:18; Col 3:10.

105. 1 Cor 1:8; 2 Cor 11:2; Phil 1:6, 10; Col 1:22, 28; 1 Thess 3:13; 5:23.

106. "Paul's doctrine of justification by faith apart from the works of the law does not remove the sense of the Christian's continuing accountability before God much in line with the prophetic preaching and the paraenesis of Matthew" (Childs, *Biblical Theology*, 546).

107. Rom 8:13; 1 Cor 15:2; Gal 6:8; Col 1:23; note also Mark 13:13.

108. Rom 11:21-22; 1 Cor 9:24-27; note also 1 Cor 3:16-17; 10:9-12; 2 Cor 13:5; Gal 5:4; 6:7-8; Col 1:23; 1 John 2:19.

109. Rom 6:22-23; 1 Cor 15:10; Gal 2:20; Phil 2:13; 4:13.

110. Here I develop further the points already made in #4.3d above.

111. Particularly Rom 8:17-23 and Phil 3:10-11.

112. Consider, for example, 2 Cor 5:21 and Phil 3:7-11.

113. The issue classically posed by Schweitzer's characterization of justification as "a subsidiary crater" (chapter 4 note 114 above), which was itself an understandable reaction to the way in which Paul's forensic imagery had been allowed to swamp his other imagery.

114. Hübner justifiably points to the correspondence between Ezek 36–37 and Rom 8:1-17 (*Biblische Theologie*, 301–6).

115. The range of personal and social ethical responsibility which can be covered by "love your neighbour as yourself" is well illustrated by Scobie, *Ways of Our God*, ch. 19.

Conclusion

1. I have, for example, been unable to go in any detail into the profundities of John's Gospel, or the ecclesiology of the Pastoral Epistles, or the very distinctive character of the letter to the Hebrews, or the apocalypse of John the seer.

2. I draw these final reflections from my "New Testament Theologizing" essay in Breytenbach and Frey, hrsg., *Aufgabe*, 245–46.

3. We might think, for example of Isa 7:14 as rendered in Matt 1:23 (LXX), or of Micah 5:2 in Matt 2:6, or of Zech 11:13 in Matt 27:9-10, or Hab 2:4 in Rom 1:17, not to mention the puzzles of texts such as Matt 2:23, 1 Cor 2:9, and James 4:5 (see for example my *Unity and Diversity*, #23).

4. D. Brown, *Tradition and Imagination: Revelation and Change* (Oxford, England: University Press, 1999); *Discipleship and Imagination: Christian Tradition and Truth* (Oxford, England: University Press, 2000).

INDEX OF SCRIPTURES AND OTHER ANCIENT WRITINGS

Old Testament

Joshua

Judges

1 Samuel

2 Samuel

1 Kings

Proverbs

Ecclesiastes

Isaiah

New Testament

Mark

John

Dead Sea Scrolls

Philo

Old Testament Pseudepigrapha

Rabbinic Traditions

Early Christian Literature

Greek and Roman Literature